the **god** conspiracy

OSHO

OSHO is a registered trademark of OSHO International Foundation,
www.osho.com/trademarks

All chapters of this book except the Preface are taken from a series of tlaks given by Osho to an audience of friends and seekers in Pune, India. These talks were originally given and published under the title, 'God is Dead – Now Zen is the only Living Truth'. The Preface is taken from other talks given by Osho at earlier points in time and is intended to provide a wider context for the reader. The original text of this series as well as an audio recording are available at the OSHO Library at www.osho.com

Osho comments in this work on excerpts from:
Sutras (chapters 1-6): From *Collection of Zen* stories by Seizan Yanagida (5-6 books). Tokyo (Japan): Chuokoronsha, © 1978. Used by permission of Sekai no meicho 18-zengoroku, Chuokoron-Sha, Inc., Japan.
Haikus: Chapter 1: Unknown Source.
Chapter 2: From *Monkey's raincoat* by Basho Matsuo, Leonore Mayhew. Tuttle Co. © 1985. Used by permission of Ms. Leonore Mayhew.
Chapter 3: From *Autumn Wind Haiku: Selected poems by Kobayashi Issa* by Lewis Mackenzie. Published by Kodansha International Ltd. Copyright © 1999 by Kodansha International Ltd.
Chapter 4: From *The grace of zen* by Chuya Ito. Seabury Press © 1976.
Chapter 5: Unknown Source.
Chapter 6: From *Snow falling from a bamboo leaf* by Hiag Akmakjian. Capra Press © 1979.`
Chapter 7: Unknown Source.

OSHO MEDIA INTERNATIONAL

New York • London • Mumbai
an imprint of
OSHO INTERNATIONAL
www.osho.com/oshointernational

Distributed by Publishers Group Worldwide
www.pgw.com

Library of Congress Cataloging-in-Publication Data is available

ISBN 13: 978-0-9818341-0-8
ISBN 10: 0-9818341-0-8

Printed in China

10 9 8 7 6 5 4 3 2 1

Design by Terry Jeavons
Copyright cover image © OSHO International Foundation, Switzerland

the **god** conspiracy

the path from superstition
to superconsciousness

OSHO

CONTENTS

Preface

The skeptical mind is one of the most beautiful things in the world.

It has been condemned by the religions because they were not capable of answering skeptical questions; they wanted only believers.

And the skeptical mind is just the opposite of the believer.

I am all in favor of the skeptical mind. Do not believe anything unless you have experienced it. Do not believe anything — go on questioning, however long it takes.

Truth is not cheap. It is not available to the believer; it is available only to the skeptical.

Just remember one thing: don't be skeptical halfheartedly. Be a total skeptic. When I say be a total skeptic, I mean that your skeptical ideas should also be put to the same test as anybody else's beliefs. Skepticism, when it is total, burns itself out because you have to question and doubt your skepticism too. You cannot leave your skepticism without doubt; otherwise that is the standpoint of the believer.

If you can doubt the skeptic in you, then the mystic is not far away.

What is a mystic? — one who knows no answer, one who has asked every possible question and found that no question is answerable. Finding this, he has dropped questioning. Not that he has found the answer — Life is a mystery, not a question. Not a puzzle to be solved, not a question to be answered but a mystery to be lived, a mystery to be loved, a mystery to be danced.

A totally skeptical mind is bound to finally become a mystic; hence, my doors are open for all. I accept the skeptic because I know how to turn him into a mystic. I invite the theist because I know how to destroy his theism. I invite the atheist because I know how to take away his atheism. My doors prevent nobody, because I am not giving you any belief. I am giving you only a methodology, a meditation to discover for yourself what in reality is the case.

I have found that there is no answer. All questions are futile, and all answers are more futile. Questions have been asked by foolish people, and great philosophies have arisen because of their questions. These philosophies are created by the cunning and the shrewd.

But if you want to have a rapport with reality, you have to be neither a fool nor shrewd. You have to be innocent.

So whatever you bring — skepticism, atheism, theism, communism, fascism, any type of nonsense you can bring here — my medicine is the same.

It does not matter what kind of nonsense is filled in your head when you come here. I will chop your head without any distinction. Who is sitting on your head does not matter — my concern is chopping!

I am just a woodcutter.

? Can you say something about doubt and negativity? What is the difference?

The difference between doubt and negativity is great. They look alike; on the surface they have the same color, but deep down the difference is unbridgeable.

First, doubt is not negativity; neither is it positivity. Doubt is an open mind, without any prejudice. It is an inquiring approach. Doubt is not saying anything, it is simply raising a question. That question is to know, to find what the truth is.

Doubt is a pilgrimage. It is one of the most sacred values of human beings. Doubt does not mean no. It simply says, "I do not know, and I am prepared to know. I am ready to go as far as possible, but unless I myself come to know, how can I say yes?"

Negativity has already said no. It is not inquiry. It has come to a conclusion, the same way somebody has come to the conclusion to say yes. One man says God is; his statement is positive. The other says there is no God; his statement is negative. But both are sailing in the same boat, they are not different people. They have not inquired. Neither the theist has doubted nor the atheist has doubted; both have accepted borrowed knowledge. Doubt says, "I myself would like to know, and unless I know for myself, it is not knowledge. Only my experience is going to be decisive." He is not arrogant, he is not denying anything. He is just open for inquiry.

Doubt is not disbelief — that's how religions have been confusing people. They confuse doubt with disbelief. In fact disbelief and belief are exactly the same. Both accept knowledge from others, from books, from masters. And remember, anything that you do not know, yet you have started believing or disbelieving in it... you have missed a great opportunity for inquiry. You have closed the doors already, by yes or by no. You have not traveled. It is easier to say yes, it is easier to say no, because there is nothing you have to do. But to doubt needs guts.

To doubt needs courage to remain in the state of not-knowing, and go on questioning everything till the moment you yourself arrive at the reality. When you come to the reality there is no negativity, no positivity. You simply know — it is your experience. I will not say it is positivity because positivity always has the other pole of negativity. An experience goes beyond both; the whole world of polarities is transcended. That is true wisdom.

Doubt is the way to truth. No or yes are not ways to truth; they prevent you. It will look very strange to say that yes does the same thing as no. In dictionaries they are opposites, but in reality they are not. They look opposite only, but both have not asked the question. Both have not tried to find out what the case is.

The communist believes, exactly as the catholic believes. The communist believes that there is no God. You can call it disbelief, but it is his belief. He has not inquired, he has not meditated; he has done nothing to find out that there is no God. The theist says there is a God. He has also done nothing. Both have chosen without moving an inch towards truth. That's why a very strange thing happens: the person who is a theist, a believer, can become a disbeliever, an atheist, in a single moment; and vice versa.

Before the revolution in Russia, Russia was one of the most theistic, religious countries of the world. Millions of people in Russia could have sacrificed their life for God. After the revolution, when the authority changed, when the priest changed, when The Holy Bible was replaced by the holy *Das Kapital*, within ten years the whole country became atheist.

It was amazing! People who had believed their whole life that there is God started disbelieving. Even communists could not comprehend that these people were the same people who could have died for God — and now they are ready to die for no-God? Nobody has analyzed the situation up to now, what happened there. This is the analysis of the fact: negativity and positivity are both belief systems.

Doubt is against both. Doubt is the insistence of the individual that he wants to taste, to experience the truth. He is not ready to accept it from anybody else, this way or that.

They are very, very rare people who doubt. But let me say to you: Blessed are those who doubt, because they shall inherit the kingdom of truth. It is arduous to doubt, it is risky, it is dangerous. One is going into the unknown, with no preparation, with no prejudice. He is entering into the dark hole, not even believing that there will be the other end of the tunnel, and he will again come out of darkness. There is no belief; he simply takes the challenge. There is only a quest, a question. He himself becomes a question.

It is very consoling to have the answer, and if it is freely available, as it is.... Jesus says, "Just believe in me and you need not bother: I will take care. I will choose you at the Day of Judgment. I will recommend you to God: `These are my people — they should be allowed in paradise.' All you have to do is believe." A real shortcut — simple belief. That's why thousands of people around the world have believed, and thousands of others have disbelieved. Their sources are different but the basic approach is the same.

In India there was a very ancient philosophy, charvaka. That philosophy says there is no God, no heaven, no hell, no punishment for your bad actions and no reward for your good actions. Thousands believed in it. It is negative, absolutely negative, but very comfortable. You can steal, you can murder, you can do anything you like; after death nothing survives. In many ways the West has lagged behind the East, particularly as far as religion, philosophy and culture are concerned. Charvaka is a 5000-year-old ideology; Karl Marx just in the last stage of the previous century said there is no God. He was not aware of charvaka, he thought he had come to a great discovery. For five thousand years charvakas had already been saying that; but they had not inquired.

The man who created the philosophy was Brihaspati — must have been a man of charismatic personality. He convinced people that you can do anything you want to because the thief, the murderer, the saint, all fall: dust unto dust. And after death nothing is left; the saint disappears, the sinner disappears. So don't bother at all about afterlife, there is none. This is not inquiry, because charvakas and their master Brihaspati have never gone beyond death. According to their philosophy, if they had gone beyond death they would have not come back — so on what grounds do they say that there is nothing left? Nobody has visited the land of death. But it is very easy to believe.

His famous statement is worth quoting. Brihaspati says, *Rinam kritva ghritam pivet*: "Even if you have to borrow money, borrow it, but drink ghee as much as you can" — because after death you are not going to be questioned, punished. The person who had given you money cannot drag you into the court of God; there are no such things. His whole philosophy is simply, "Eat, drink and be merry." You can believe in it — the theists will call it *dis*belief.

That's what Karl Marx did for the communists. He said that there is no soul, no consciousness; it is a by-product of matter, so when the body falls apart, nothing is left. This became a very dangerous attitude, because communists could kill people without thinking twice. Their belief was that by killing you are not committing any sin. There is nobody inside a person; there is no inside. A man is chemistry, biology, physiology — but there is no soul. Joseph Stalin could kill almost one million people after the revolution without feeling even a slight doubt about what he was doing.

In Soviet Russia man was reduced to a mechanism. You can kill — nothing is killed, because there was nobody in the first place. It is just like a clock functioning. It moves, it shows you the time; that does not mean that there is somebody inside. You can take the clock apart and you will not find anything. That's what Karl Marx preached to the communists, that man is also just like a clock. And soon almost half the world believed in Karl Marx. Strange — these same people had believed in God. Russians, Chinese, Indians, Mohammedans — all kinds of people changed their yes to no. To change yes into no is so easy because they are not different. Basically they give you a consolation without the arduous journey to truth.

I asked many communists, very old communists.... In India, S.A. Dange was a member of the international communist party along with Lenin, Trotsky, and Stalin. He was an eyewitness to the Russian revolution. I asked him, "Have you ever meditated?"

He said, "Meditated — for what? Why should I meditate?"

I said, "If you have never meditated, then you don't have the authority to say that there is no soul, no God, no consciousness. Without going inside yourself, how can you say that there is nobody? And see the absurdity of it: who is saying that there is nobody? Even to deny, you will have to accept that there is somebody. Even to say that there is nobody, somebody has to be assumed."

The same is the situation of religions.

Nobody has encountered God — no Christian, no Hindu, no Mohammedan — but they have all said yes because the crowd in which they were born was the crowd of theists. To say no amongst that crowd would have created difficulties for them. Yes was simply the accepted rule of the game. They have worshipped, they have prayed, not knowing why they were doing it. But everybody else is doing it so it must be right.

When the crowd changed — for example in Russia, the same people who were so certain of God became uncertain. It took ten years to change from one certainty to another certainty... an interval of uncertainty, but uncertainty is not doubt.

Doubt is simply a question, and doubt says, "I want to *know*." It has no ideology. Doubt is absolutely pure quest.   .

You have asked, "What is the difference between doubt and negativity?"

Negativity and positivity are both the same. Doubt is different from both. It does not make you a theist, it does not make you an atheist. Positivity makes you a religious believer, a theist; negativity makes you an unbeliever, irreligious, an atheist. Doubt does not make you anything. It simply makes you an inquirer. And that is the dignity of man.

I teach doubt because I know if you can doubt to the very end you will realize the truth of your own being, and simultaneously the truth of the whole existence. And that will be liberation, that will be freedom.

Doubt is neither Christian nor Hindu, nor American nor German. Yes may be Hindu, yes may be Mohammedan, yes may be Christian; no may be communist, no may be fascist — but doubt is simply a quest, an individual quest.

Yes and no both belong to the crowd. Doubt makes you assert your individuality. You start finding your path on your own. You don't accept the maps given you by others.

It is cheap to believe, it is cheap to disbelieve. But it is really a dangerous journey to know. I would like you neither to be negative nor to be positive, but open, available, with a quest, a question mark, and to go on searching. Many times your mind will say it is good to believe — because the journey is arduous, and one never knows where one is going, whether one is going to find anything or not. But don't listen to the mind. Mind has created all these "yes" philosophies, "no" philosophies.

Doubt has never created any philosophy; doubt has created science. And doubt is going to create religion. They are exactly the same — the same application of doubt in different fields. About objects, the outside world that spreads to millions of stars, doubt has given tremendous insight just within three hundred years. You are carrying another world within yourself, which is in no way smaller than the world you see outside; perhaps it is bigger. Why do I say that perhaps it is bigger? I am including the word `perhaps' so that you should not believe. I *know* it is bigger, for the simple reason that you know the stars, you know the sun, you know the moon — but the moon does not know you, the sun does not know you. The stars are great, the universe is vast, but you are the only knower. You have something more than the whole universe. That's why I say inside you are carrying something bigger than the universe, more than the universe. Just inquire.

One of the most beautiful men of the 20th century was Maharishi Raman. He was a simple man, uneducated, but he did not accept the ideology, the religion in which he was born. When he was only seventeen years of age he left his home in search of truth. He meditated for many years in the hills of Arunachal in south India, and finally realized himself. After that his whole teaching consisted only of three words, because those three words had revealed to him the whole mystery of existence. His philosophy is the most concise. What are those three words? Whoever came to him — because as he became known, people started coming to him from all over the world — his whole teaching was to sit silently and ask only one question: "Who am I?" and go on asking that question.

One day the question will disappear, and only you will be there. That is the answer.

Not that you will find the answer written somewhere; you will find yourself. You just go on digging with this question — this question is like digging — but do you see the question? It is a doubt: Who am I? It does not accept the spiritualist who says you are a soul. It does not accept the materialist who says there is nobody, don't waste time; eat, drink and be merry. He doubts. Those three words are followed by a question mark: Who am I?

And this is enough. If you can go on and on and on patiently, one day the question suddenly disappears and what is left is your reality. That is the answer. And the moment you know yourself you have known everything that is worth knowing.

? Are you against God and Jesus both?

I am not against God.

I have been searching and seeking him everywhere, and this is my finding — he is not anywhere. I have looked in, I have looked out; I have done everything that is possible to be done. There is no God. This is a simple statement of fact, with no anger, with no enmity. What can I do if he does not exist? It is not my fault.

But man's mind wants some extreme position. It is worth understanding.

Why does man's mind want some extreme position? Either you have to be a theist or an atheist; either you have to be for or against. It does not allow you a third alternative. The reason is simple: the third alternative becomes the death of the mind. Mind lives on extremism; that is its very nourishment.

Exactly in the middle, where two polarities dissolve and contradictions meet, mind simply goes out of function. The mind cannot conceive how contradictions can meet, how polarities can be one. But in existence they are meeting, they are one. Have you seen life and death separate? It is your mind that makes the categories and words separate. But look into existence — it is life turning into death, death turning into life. There is no division, they are part of one whole.

It is the mind that has created the idea of beauty and ugliness. But in existence... do you think that if all human minds for a moment disappeared from the earth — would there be beauty in anything, ugliness in anything? Would the rose still be beautiful? No, as the mind is not there, there is nobody to judge and beauty and ugliness are mental judgments.

The rose will be there, just as the thorn will be there, but there will be no evaluation because the evaluator is not there. They will both exist without any hierarchy. The rose will not be higher than the thorn. The flower of the marigold will not be a poor flower and the rose, a rich flower; they will be on the same plane.

All hierarchy is created by the mind: the lower, the higher, for and against.

Think in another way: for a moment, let the mind be there but drop judgment — which is a little more difficult. You can visualize a state where all minds have disappeared and certainly you can see there is no possibility of anything being ugly, beautiful. Things will be there just as themselves, with no comparison, no judgment, no labeling.

Now try the other, which is a little more difficult. Let the mind be there — so all the minds are there but nobody is judging — for one hour, no judgment. Can beauty be there, can ugliness be there? Can something be moral and something immoral? Can there be a sinner and a saint? For that one hour, all these categories will disappear and you will have, for the first time, a real contact with reality as it is, not as projected by you, manufactured by your mind. Your mind is continuously manufacturing reality; otherwise, who is a saint and who is a sinner?

Man's mind is easily ready for any extreme because the extreme is its life force. And when two extremes meet, they cancel each other and they leave a vacuum. That's the meaning of the middle way: let the extremes come to a point where they cancel each other and suddenly you are left neither atheist nor theist. Those questions become irrelevant. But the mind is not ready to drop — in religion, in philosophy, or even in science.

Recently I watched a documentary film on the history of mathematics. The whole history of mathematics can be seen as the problem of the human mind. For two thousand years or more in the West, and for five to ten thousand years in the East, mathematicians have been trying to find the ultimate science. One thing is certain in their eyes, that only mathematics can become the ultimate science, for the simple reason that there are no mathematical things around you. It is a pure science. You don't see mathematical objects: this is a mathematical chair and that is a mathematical house. Mathematics is just a pure ideological game. It consists not of things but ideas. And because ideas are properties of your mind, you can refine them to their ultimate purity. So it has been accepted that mathematics can become the purest science possible. But there have been problems. Those mathematicians were not aware that your mind itself is the problem, and the mind is going to try to create a science that will have no problems, no contradictions, no paradoxes.

You can play the game. You can make a great edifice but whenever you look at the base, you will know that at the very base the ultimate problem remains unsolved. For example, Euclid's geometry.... I could not go much into it for the simple reason that I could not agree with the basic hypotheses. My teacher of geometry simply told me, "Your problem has nothing to do with me. Find Euclid — get out of the class, find Euclid and settle things with him! I am a poor teacher, I just get my salary; I have nothing to do with his fundamental axioms. Whatever is written in the book, I teach. I am not interested at all whether his fundamental hypotheses are right or wrong. You get out!" He wouldn't allow me in the class.

I said, "But how can you go on teaching year after year knowing that the basic points are absurd?"

He said, "I never knew; it is you who is hammering on my mind that they are absurd. I have never bothered; I am neither a scientist nor a mathematician, just a poor teacher. And I never wanted to be a teacher. I tried to apply for other jobs; everywhere there was no vacancy. It is just out of compulsion that I am a teacher here. So don't torture me. Your problem is with Euclid — don't bring me in. If you want to read what is written in the book, I am ready. But if you tell me that the fundamentals are wrong...."

I said, "I cannot go on unless I am certain about the base, because this is dangerous: the foundation of the house is missing and you tell me to go on up in a skyscraper? I cannot move a single inch. First I have to be certain about whether the foundation exists that can support this skyscraper. You are going to fall — that is your business — but I am not going to fall with you. If you want to commit suicide, go ahead."

He said, "This is strange! With Euclid, nobody commits suicide. What are you talking about?"

I said, "I am talking about exactly what I said. It is suicide. Not a single hypothesis of Euclid's is explainable."

And yet for two thousand years Euclid has been the foundation, not only of geometry but of all other sciences, because he has to be used in other sciences too. For example, he says about a line that it has only length — only length.

I asked my teacher, "Draw a line that has only length. The moment you draw it, it will also have some breadth, howsoever tiny." And a point, according to Euclid, has no length, no breadth. I said, "Make a point that has no length and no breadth. And the same Euclid says a line consists of points — one point after another point, in a row. Now, a line has only length the point has no length, no breadth — then how can the line have length? because it has only points standing in a queue. From where does the length appear?"

He just folded his hands to me and said, "Leave me alone. I have told you that I am just a poor teacher and you are beyond me."

I said, "This is not the answer. You can simply accept that these axioms are not explainable."

But the mind has some difficulty in accepting the idea that something is there which is not explainable. Mind has a mad urge for everything to be explained...if not explained, then at least explained away. Anything that remains a puzzle, a paradox, goes on troubling your mind.

The whole history of philosophy, religion, science, mathematics, has the same root, the same mind — the same itch. You can scratch yourself one way, somebody else may do it differently, but the itch has to be understood. The itch is the belief that existence is not a mystery: mind can only feel at home if somehow existence is demystified.

Religion has done it by creating God, the Holy Ghost, the only begotten son; different religions have created different things. These are their ways to cover up a hole that is uncoverable; whatever you do, the hole is there. In fact the more you cover it, the more emphatically it is there. Your very effort to cover it shows your fear that somebody is going to see the hole.

It used to happen in my childhood every day because I love to climb the trees: the higher the tree, the greater the joy. And naturally I fell many times from the trees; I still carry on my legs and knees and everywhere, scratches. Because I was continually climbing the trees and falling, every day my clothes were torn, and my mother would say, "Don't go out with that hole in your clothes. Let me do a little patchwork."

I said, "No, no patchwork."

She said, "But people will see that you are the son of the best cloth merchant in the town, that you are always roaming around the whole town with torn clothes; and nobody takes care."

I said, "If you patch it then it becomes ugly. Right now anybody can see it is fresh. I did not come out of the house with this hole. This is fresh, I have just fallen from a tree. But with your patchwork... this is an old thing that I have been hiding.

"Your patchwork will make me look poor, my torn shirt simply makes me look courageous. Don't be worried about it."

But the whole history of mind, in different branches, has been doing this patchwork — particularly in mathematics because mathematics is purely a mind game. There are mathematicians who think it is not, just as there are theologians who think God is a reality. God is only an idea. If horses have ideas, their God will be a horse. You can be absolutely certain it will not be a man, because men have been so cruel to horses that they can only be conceived as devils, not as gods. But then every animal will have its own idea of God, just as every human race has its own idea of God.

Ideas are substitutes for where life is mysterious and you find gaps that cannot be filled by reality. You fill those gaps with ideas; and at least you start feeling satisfied that life is understood.

Have you ever thought about this word "understand? Anything that you can make stand under you, that is under your thumb, under your power, under your shoe, you are the master of. People have been trying to understand life in that same way, so that they could put life also underneath their feet and declare, "We are the masters. Now there is nothing which is not understood by us."

But it is not possible. Whatever you do, life is a mystery and is going to remain a mystery. Even if you come to understand the whole of life, a new problem will arise: "Who is this person, this mind, this consciousness, which has understood everything? From where does it come?"

In that documentary film they talked about one of the mathematicians in the beginning part of the 20th century — a very famous mathematician, one of the greatest in the whole history of mathematics. His name was Freger, and he had devoted his whole life to creating a mathematical system that would dissolve all paradoxes, all mysteries, all puzzles, and solve everything — the ultimate solution. He was just going to publish it — it is published now, and it is a tremendous task that he has done. But Bertrand Russell — a young man at that time, not very famous, just a known by a few people as a philosopher — was also interested in mathematics. Later on, Russell wrote one of the monumental books on mathematics, *Principia Mathematica*, in which three hundred and sixty-two pages are devoted only to proving that one plus one is equal to two. The book is just impossible — to try to read it is enough to drive anybody crazy! Even Bertrand Russell admitted, "After writing that book I have never been so sharp again; my whole sharpness got lost." Certainly he put too much energy into it, and a strange kind of energy; nobody reads that book.

Bertrand Russell was interested in mathematics. Knowing that Freger was going to publish a book that was going to solve all paradoxes, mysteries, and mathematical problems, he sent Freger a paradox — a simple paradox. When he received it, Freger was devastated, he felt all enthusiasm gone. The books were ready — two volumes, his whole life's work — and this man sends a brief letter with a small paradox saying, "Before you publish your book, please think about this paradox." That paradox has become famous as Bertrand Russell's paradox.

It is very simple, but Freger had no answer for it He did not publish his books in his lifetime; they were published after his death. They are monumental, but he failed in the purpose of resolving all paradox. He could not solve the single paradox that Russell had sent him.

The paradox is very simple: All the librarians in the country are ordered to make a catalogue of all the books in their library and send their catalogues to the national library. One librarian made his catalogue, and as he was going to pack and send it to the national library, a question arose in his mind: "Should I also include this catalogue in my catalogue or not? — because this too is now a book in my library. And the order is clear that all the books in the library should be catalogued. So what am I to do about this? This is a book in the library, so to include it seems to be right according to the order."

This problem must have arisen in many a librarian's mind. So what happened was that two types of catalogues arrived in the national library. The national librarian made two piles, one which included catalogues with the catalogue itself included, and another pile which did not. The national librarian was ordered to make a catalogue of all the catalogues that didn't include the catalogue in themselves. So he made a catalogue of all those catalogues which did not include the catalogue in themselves. But when he was finishing, he was puzzled what to do about his own catalogue. If he did not include it, then one catalogue that did not include itself would be left out of his catalogue. If he included it, then this would not be a catalogue of only those catalogues that did not include themselves.

So Russell sent this simple paradox: "What is this librarian supposed to do? Before you go on solving other, bigger problems, please solve this one! This librarian is in difficulty."

Now, whatever you do is wrong. If you don't include this catalogue, then one catalogue that does not include itself is missing from your catalogue: all catalogues that do not include themselves are not included in it. If you include it, then this is not a catalogue of only those which do not include.... You follow me?

I don't see any problem. But Freger was finished; Russell also had no answer for it. And every science, every philosophy, every religion, comes to the same point: somewhere or other something comes to the point where either you have to accept it unquestioningly, blindly... that's what religion calls faith, belief.

It is a patchwork. By asking you to believe in it, to have faith in it, it means you shouldn't try to take away the patch because there is a hole — abysmal, bottomless — cover it! But by covering it, it is not dissolved. Nothing is solved; nothing is helped by covering it — except that you remain blind. So why cover it? Just close your eyes.

That's why all followers are blind followers — because if they have eyes, then there is going to be trouble. Then they are going to find problems that are unsolved, questions that are unresolved. Why has God been created? — just to solve the unresolved question of who created the universe. From that question, all the religions take the plunge into some hypothesis—"God created the world".... But the question is exactly the same as Bertrand Russell's paradox. It is no different. One is mathematics and the other is religion but the problem is the same. The axiom is that anything that exists has to be created by somebody. How can it come into existence by itself? This is the problem. Everything that is, has been created; otherwise how can it come in the first place? So they bring in God to help you solve the problem of who created the universe.

But what are you going to do with God? Does God exist? If God exists, then who created him? If he does not exist, then how could he create the universe? If God himself does not exist, how can he create existence? And if he exists, then what about your basic maxim that anything that exists needs a creator? No, don't ask that. That's what all the religions say — don't ask who created God. But this is strange — why not? If the question is valid about existence, why does it become invalid when it is applied to God?

And once you ask who created God, then you are falling into a regress absurdum. Then you can go on: God one, God two, God three, and you go on numbering them... but finally the question will be the same. After thousands of Gods you will find the question stands clean, clear, untouched. Not even a dent has been made in the question by all your answers. Who created existence? — it is the same question.

To me, existence is a mystery. There is no need for it to stand under our feet, there is no need for existence to be understood. Live it, love it, enjoy it — be it. Why are you trying to understand it?

I am not against God, I am only against a stupid hypothesis that leads nowhere.

And you ask, am I against Jesus Christ too? Why should I be against that poor fellow? I feel sorry for him, sad for him. I don't think that he deserved to be crucified. Yes, he was a bit crazy — I cannot deny that — but just because somebody is a little bit crazy, that does not mean he needs crucifixion. Crucifixion is not a cure for craziness.

In fact, in crucifying Jesus you have created Christianity and you have driven so many people crazy. It is the crucifixion which is responsible for all this nonsense that has been going on for two thousand years and is still continuing. It is the crucifixion which made Christ — without his knowledge — the founder of Christianity. I am not against that poor guy. In fact, he deserved a little better treatment. If we can find him somewhere, there is no need to crucify him; he needs a few therapies to put him right, to put him together. A little deprogramming: "You are not the son of God — drop this idea. This is what is making you look unnecessarily a clown. It does not prove that you are a messiah, it simply proves you are nuts."

We have put many nuts together who were falling apart. Just a few people's nuts get loose, a few people's bolts get tight — we just have to fix them a little bit. Jesus was nothing dangerous. He was a nice fellow, but just to be nice is no protection against going crazy. He was nice, and gullible. He heard this idea continually proclaimed, "The messiah is going to come who will save the whole of humanity," and it got into his head; he had a swollen head. Just a little bit of treatment and he would have been perfectly all right. I am not against him, I feel for him. This was too much, to put him on the cross; he had not committed any crime. And freedom of speech allows it; anybody can say, "I am the son of God." I don't think it harms anybody, or it takes away anybody else's rights. You can say you are also the son of God, there is no problem in it.

Why did they make so much fuss about him? There was no need at all. All that he needed was to be ignored. If nobody had taken note of him he would have come to his senses by himself even without any therapy. But because people started taking note of him and people started getting angry at him, he became more and more obsessed with the idea.

It is a natural conclusion: "If people are annoyed, irritated, then there must be something in it, otherwise why should they bother? If I was just a madman they would have laughed and gone home." But the whole of Judea, all the rabbis, were disturbed. That was enough proof for Jesus that whatever he was saying must have had some significance. Those old fools, those rabbis, destroyed that young man. By giving him importance, attention, they spoiled him. In fact, *they* needed to be punished, and *he* was punished. I feel sorry for him. I am not against him. I am all for his treatment, cure, and a long, healthy life.

…I have been explaining to you continually that I want existence to be accepted as a mystery, because only as a mystery is it beautiful, liveable, loveable, blissful, ecstatic.

It is good that existence cannot be demystified.

There is no way to demystify it, and I am the last person to demystify anything. My purpose is just the opposite. That's what I have been doing my whole life — mystifying everything. It is not a difficult job because people have forced demystifications on things; I simply remove the cover, the patchwork, and I give you the raw life, as it is.

There is no answer anywhere which is ultimate. And there will never be any answer which will solve all the problems; hence, God is an impossibility because God means the ultimate answer.

And it is good that there is no God, otherwise we would be condemned. Then there would be no possibility of any joy, freedom, exploration, ecstasy — God would have killed everything. So I say to you, even if God was there then I would have trained you in how to kill him. But fortunately he is not there, so we are saved from being in any way violent; otherwise that one violence I would have allowed. Even though I am for vegetarianism, if God was there I would have told you, "Finish him! because with him, life is impossible."

You have not thought about the implications: Only without God are you free. Then your inner being has freedom. Then your essence has all possible potentialities to grow. Then there is nobody to dominate, nobody to dictate, nobody to manipulate. You are not responsible to anybody except to yourself. Nobody can question you, why you did this; nobody can punish you or reward you. There is no way of somehow manipulating you into a certain way of life, because there is no God.

And because there is no God how can there be a messiah and the son of God? That's why I call Jesus nuts. It is just out of love and compassion that I call him nuts, but I am not against him. If I had been there I would have told the Jews and Pontius Pilate, "What are you doing? You are creating a religion — of nuts! By crucifying this man you are committing a crime against the whole of humanity for centuries to come. Just leave him alone, let him talk. What harm is in it? It is just pure entertainment. People enjoy, they gather and they listen to him — there is no harm in it. And he is not saying anything against the scriptures. Let him be free so that no religion is created."

Jesus himself was incapable of creating Christianity, you can see that perfectly well. All that he could manage were twelve uneducated dodos; they became his apostles. But in this world it is very difficult to figure out who is the greatest dodo — very difficult. Those dodos were great, but there are even greater dodos today. There are dodos and dodos.

Jesus would have been unable in any way to create Christianity. He had no organizational power, he had no capacity to influence the cream of the society. How was he going to create a religion? But the crucifixion achieved everything.

In this world things function in a very strange way. Once he was crucified, thousands of people who had never bothered about him felt sympathy for him. The same people who would not have even gone to listen to him if he had passed their way felt sympathy for him. And it was natural. Even the Jews felt this was is too much. The man was innocent... maybe talking in an outrageous way, but it was only talk, hot air, nothing much in it. There was no need to crucify the fellow.

It created a great wave of sympathy. Such sympathy is a natural phenomenon. And those twelve dodos for the first time found that people who had never listened to their master were listening to *them*. Slowly, people started gathering. They created the Bible, they created the church. They made up stories, miracles — which is easier when the person is gone. In those days, these things were just rumors. But a rumor from one mouth to another ear has a tendency to become bigger because everybody wants to add something to it, some spice. Over three hundred years Jesus became a thousand times bigger than he ever was; by then he was a myth. The real person was just an ordinary carpenter's son talking off the wall. But in three hundred years' time people's imagination did the whole work.

And then over these two thousand years, scholars, professors, theologians, philosophers — they are all going to increase the myth as much as they can and bring out of Jesus meanings, words, philosophies, and ideologies of which that poor fellow was never aware.

I am not against God, or against Jesus Christ — or against anyone.

But I am for the truth. If it goes against anybody, I am helpless.

? When you say there is no God, does that mean you are an atheist?

There is no God, but that does not mean that I'm an atheist. Certainly I am not a theist — I am saying there is no God — but that does not mean that you should jump to the opposite, the atheist. The atheist also says there is no God, but when I say it there is a tremendous difference between my statement and the statement of the atheist — because I say at the same moment that there is godliness.

Charvaka will not agree on that point; Epicurus, Marx, other atheists will not agree on that point. To them, denying God means denying consciousness. To them, denying God means the world is simply matter and nothing more, and whatever you see as consciousness is only a byproduct of certain aspects of matter put together, just a byproduct. Take those things apart and the byproduct disappears.

It is just like a bullock cart: you take the wheels away, you take other parts away, and each time you can ask, "Is this the bullock cart?" When you take the wheels away, certainly the answer will be, "It is not." No part is the whole. You can take each part away, piece by piece, until you have removed the whole, and no single part will be the bullock cart. In the end you can be asked, "Now where is the bullock cart? — because we have not removed it; you have never said at any point that the bullock cart has been removed."

"Bullock cart" was only a combination. It had no existence of its own, it was a byproduct. That's what Marx means when he says consciousness is an epiphenomenon: remove the body, remove the brain, remove all that constitutes a man's being and you will not find anything like consciousness. And once you have removed everything, it is not that consciousness will be left behind; it was only a combination. You have taken the combination apart.

So when I say there is no God, I am not agreeing with Marx or Epicurus. I am certainly not agreeing with Jesus, Krishna, Moses, Mohammed, when they say there is a God, because they see God as a person. Now, to think of God as a person is just your imagination. The God of the Chinese has a Chinese face, and the God of the Africans has an African face, and certainly the God of the Jews must have a Jewish nose; it can't be otherwise. This is just projection. Giving personality to God is your projection.

When I say there is no God, I am denying personality to God. I am saying God is not, but there is tremendous godliness. That is an impersonal energy, pure energy. To impose any form on it is ugly. You are imposing yourself on it.

The Christian god will disappear the moment Christianity disappears, the Hindu gods will disappear the moment Hinduism disappears. Do you see what I mean to say? It is your projection. If you go on projecting it, it is there. If you are not there to project it, if the projector is not there, the god disappears. I am not in favor of such gods, which have been projected by the tiny mind of man. And of course the tiny mind of man is bound to give qualities to God that are its own qualities.

The god in the Talmud says, "I am an angry God. I am not nice; I am not your uncle." Now, this is perfectly meaningful in a Jewish context, but to a Hindu, God saying that, "I am an angry God" is a sheer impossibility. Anger and God? — they cannot meet. The Jewish god is perfectly angry; it is very human. And if you don't worship him, if you go against him, he will destroy you. This will not appeal to a Hindu, it is impossible. It will not appeal to the Mohammedan, because the Mohammedan prays every day, "God, the compassionate one...." Compassion is the very innermost quality projected by him towards God. Now, God can only be compassion, nothing else. The Mohammedan says that just accepting your sin is enough, because God is compassionate. You will be forgiven.

Omar Khayyam, one of the great poets of Persian literature, says, "Don't prevent me from drinking wine, enjoying women, because God is compassionate. Don't tell me that I am committing sin, let me commit as many sins as possible. His compassion is far greater than all my sins combined together. To stop a certain activity in fear that you will be punished by God is to disbelieve in his compassion." Now, this is a different attitude — but these are all human attitudes.

So when I say there is no God, I am saying there is no person as God; all personality is human projection. I want you to take away the personality and let God be free, free from the bondage of personality that you have imposed upon him.

I am not an atheist. To me, the whole universe is full of the energy of God and nothing else.

You have to understand one thing which is very fundamental. The world consists of verbs, not of nouns. Nouns are a human invention — necessary, but after all, a human invention. But existence consists of verbs, only of verbs, not nouns and pronouns. Look at this. You are seeing a flower, a rose. To call it a flower is not right, because it has not stopped flowering, it is still flowering; it is a verb, it is a flow. To call it a flower you have made it a noun. You see the river. You call it a river — you have made it a noun. It is rivering. It will be more accurate to the existential to say that it is rivering, flowing. And everything is changing, flowing. The child is becoming a young man; the young man is becoming old; life is turning into death; death is turning into life. Everything is in continuity, continuous change; it is a continuum. There never comes a stop, a full stop. It comes only in language. In existence there is no full stop.

Do you remember when you stopped being a child? — when, at what point came the stop and you became a young man? There is no place, no demarcation, no full stop. The child is still flowing in you. If you just close your eyes and look within, you will find everything that has been is still there, flowing. You have been absorbing more and more, but all that has been is still there. The river is becoming big, new rivulets are joining it, but the original is still there.

If you have seen the Ganges in India, one of the most beautiful rivers, you can understand it. The point where it arises is so tiny that the face of a cow — of course of stone, stone carved into the face of a cow — is enough. Through that cow's face the Ganges falls, starts its journey... so small. And when you see it near the ocean, when it is reaching to meet the ocean, it looks almost like the ocean itself... so vast. But that small current falling in Gangotri, far away, thousands of miles away in the Himalayas, from a stone mouth of a cow — that current is still there. So many rivers have come and fallen into it and have made it oceanic. It is still alive. Even while it is falling into the ocean it will remain alive, it will go on moving. Perhaps it will become a cloud; perhaps it will rain again. It will go on and on. Existence goes on and on and on; it never stops. There is no rest period. There is no place where you can mark that something has come to its end. Nothing comes to its end. You cannot find the beginning, you cannot find the end. It is an ever flowing process.

When you say "God" you are using a noun, something static, dead. When I say "godliness" I am using a word for something alive, flowing, moving. So these points have to be clear to you. I am not a theist like Jesus or Mohammed or Krishna, because I cannot agree with the idea of a dead god.

God — perfect, absolute, omnipotent, omniscient, omnipresent; these are the words used for God by all the religions — is dead, cannot be alive, cannot breathe. No, I reject such a god, because with such a dead god, this whole universe will be dead.

Godliness is a totally different dimension. Then the greenness in the tree, then the flowering of the rose, then the bird in flight — all are part of it. Then God is not separate from the universe. Then he is the very soul of the universe. Then the universe is vibrating, pulsating, breathing... godliness.

So I am not an atheist, but I am not a theist either.

Chapter 1
God is dead and man is free ... for what?

Responsibility belongs to someone who has the freedom to act.
Either God can exist or freedom, both cannot exist together.
That is the basic implication of Friedrich Nietzsche's statement,
"God is dead, therefore man is free."

*On their first meeting, Seigen asked Sekito, "Where do you come from?"
and Sekito replied, "I come from Sokei."
Seigen held up a whisk and said, "Did you find this over there?"
Sekito replied, "No, not only was it not over there, but it was also not in
the Westland."
Seigen asked, "You reached the Westland, didn't you?" to which Sekito replied,
"If I had reached, I could have found it."
Seigen said, "Not yet enough—speak further."
Sekito replied, "You should also speak from your side. How is it you urge only me?"
Seigen said, "There's no problem for me in answering you, but nobody would agree
with it." Seigen continued, "When you were at Sokei, what did you get there?"
Sekito replied, "Even before going to Sokei, I hadn't lost a thing."
Then Sekito asked, "When you were in Sokei, did you know yourself?"
Seigen said, "How about you? Do you know me now?"
Sekito answered, "Yes, I do. How can I know you any further?"
He continued, "Osho, since you left Sokei, how long have you been staying here?"
Seigen replied, "I do not know either. And you, when did you leave Sokei?"
Sekito said, "I don't come from Sokei."
Seigen responded, "All right—now I know where you come from."
Sekito said, "Osho, you are a great one—do not waste time."*

Friends, a new series of talks begins today: *God Is Dead, Now Zen Is The Only Living Truth*. The series is dedicated to Friedrich Nietzsche, who was the first man in the history of mankind to declare, "God is dead, therefore man is free."

It was a tremendous statement; its implications are many. First I would like to discuss Nietzsche's statement.

All the religions believe that God created the world and also mankind. But if you are created by someone, you are only a puppet, you don't have your own soul. And if you are created by somebody, he can uncreate you any moment. He neither asked you whether you wanted to be created, nor is he going to ask you, "Do you want to be uncreated?"

God is the greatest dictator, if you accept the fiction that he created the world and also created mankind. If God is a reality, then man is a slave, a puppet. All the strings are in his hands, even your life. Then there is no question of any enlightenment. Then there is no question of there being any Gautam the Buddha, because there is no freedom at all. He pulls the strings, you dance; he pulls the strings, you cry; he pulls the strings, you start murders, suicide, war. You are just a puppet and he is the puppeteer.

Then there is no question of sin or virtue, no question of sinners and saints. Nothing is good and nothing is bad, because you are only a puppet. A puppet cannot be responsible for its actions. Responsibility belongs to someone who has the freedom to act. Either God can exist or freedom, both cannot exist together. That is the basic implication of Friedrich Nietzsche's statement: God is dead, *therefore* man is free.

No theologian, no founder of religions thought about this, that if you accept God as the creator, you are destroying the whole dignity of consciousness, of freedom, of love. You are taking all responsibility from man, and you are taking all his freedom away. You are reducing the whole of existence to just the whim of a strange fellow called God.

But Nietzsche's statement is bound to be only one side of the coin. He is perfectly right, but only about one side of the coin. He has made a very significant and meaningful statement, but he has forgotten one thing, which was bound to happen because his statement is based on rationality, logic and intellect. It is not based on meditation.

Man is free, but free for what? If there is no God and man is free, that will simply mean man is now capable of doing anything, good or bad; there is nobody to judge him, nobody to forgive him. This freedom will be simply licentiousness.

There comes the other side. You remove God and you leave man utterly empty. Of course, you declare his freedom, but to what purpose? How is he going to use his freedom creatively, responsibly? How is he going to avoid freedom being reduced to licentiousness?

Friedrich Nietzsche was not aware of any meditations—that is the other side of the coin. Man is free, but his freedom can only be a joy and a blessing to him if he is rooted in meditation. Remove God—that is perfectly okay, he has been the greatest danger to human freedom—but give man also some meaning and significance, some creativity, some receptivity, some path to find his eternal existence. Zen is the other side of the coin.

Zen does not have any God, that's its beauty. But it has a tremendous science to transform your consciousness, to bring so much awareness to you that you cannot commit evil. It is not a commandment from outside, it comes from your innermost being. Once you know your center of being, once you know you are one with the cosmos—and the cosmos has never been created, it has been there always and always, and will be there always and always, from eternity to eternity—once you know your luminous being, your hidden Gautam Buddha, it is impossible to do anything wrong, it is impossible to do anything evil, it is impossible to do any sin.

Friedrich Nietzsche in his last phase of life became almost insane. He was hospitalized, kept in a mad asylum. Such a great giant, what happened to him? He had concluded, "God is dead," but it is a negative conclusion. He became empty, but his freedom was meaningless. There was no joy in it because it was only freedom *from* God, but *for* what? Freedom has two sides: from and for. The other side was missing. That drove him insane.

Emptiness always drives people insane. You need some grounding, you need some centering, you need some relationship with existence. God being dead, all your relationship with existence was finished. God being dead, you were left alone without roots. A tree cannot live without roots, nor can you.

God was non-existential, but it was a good consolation. It used to fill people's interior, although it was a lie. But even a lie, repeated thousands and thousands of times for millennia, becomes almost a truth. God has been a great consolation to people in their fear, in their dread, in their awareness of old age and death, and beyond—the unknown darkness. God has been a tremendous consolation, although it was a lie. Lies can console you, you have to understand it. In fact lies are sweeter than the truth.

Gautam Buddha is reported to have said, "Truth is bitter in the beginning, sweet in the end, and lies are sweet in the beginning, bitter in the end"—when they are exposed. Then comes a tremendous bitterness, that you have been deceived by all your parents, by all your teachers, by all your priests, by all your so-called leaders. You have been continuously deceived. That frustration brings up a great distrust in everybody. "Nobody is worthy of trust..." It creates a vacuum.

So Nietzsche was not insane in this last phase of his life, it was the inevitable conclusion of his negative approach. An intellect can only be negative; it can argue and criticize and be sarcastic, but it cannot give you any nourishment. From no negative standpoint can you get any nourishment. So he lost his God, and he lost his consolation. He became free just to be mad.

And it is not only Friedrich Nietzsche, so it cannot be said that it was just an accident. Many intellectual giants find themselves in mad asylums or commit suicide, because nobody can live in a negative darkness. One needs light and a positive, affirmative experience of truth. Nietzsche demolished the light and created a vacuum in himself and in others who followed him.

If you feel deep down a vacuum, utter emptiness with no meaning, it is because of Friedrich Nietzsche. A whole philosophy has grown in the West: Nietzsche is the founder of this very negative approach to life.

Soren Kierkegaard, and Jean-Paul Sartre, and Marcel, and Jaspers, and Martin Heidegger—all the great giants of the first half of this century—were talking only about meaninglessness, anguish, suffering, anxiety, dread, fear, angst. And this philosophy has been called in the West existentialism. It is not. It is simply non-existentialism. It destroys everything that has consoled you.

I agree with the destruction because what was consoling man was only lies. God, heaven, hell—all were fictions created to console man. It is good they are destroyed, but you are leaving man in an utter vacuum. Out of that vacuum existentialism is born, that's why it talks only about meaninglessness: "Life has no meaning." It talks about no significance: "You are just an accident. Whether you are here or not does not matter at all to existence." And these people call their philosophy existentialism. They should call it accidentalism. You are not needed; just by accident, on the margin, somehow you have popped up. God was making you a puppet, and these philosophers from Nietzsche to Jean-Paul Sartre are making you accidental.

And there is a tremendous need in man's being to be related to existence. He needs roots in existence, because only when the roots go deep into existence will he blossom into a buddha, will he blossom into millions of flowers, will his life not be meaningless. Then his life will be tremendously overflowing with meaning, significance, blissfulness; his life will be simply a celebration.

But the conclusion of the so-called existentialists is that you are unnecessary, that your life has no meaning, no significance. Existence is not in need of you at all!

So I want to complete Friedrich Nietzsche's work; it is incomplete. It will lead the whole of humanity to madness—not only Friedrich Nietzsche, but the whole of humanity. Without God certainly you are free, but for what? You are left with empty hands. You were with empty hands before also, because the hands that looked full were full of lies. Now you are absolutely aware that the hands are empty and there is nowhere to go.

I have heard about one very famous atheist. He died, and his wife brought his best clothes, best shoes, before he was put in the coffin—the best tie, the costliest possible. She wanted to give him a good farewell, a good send-off. He was dressed as he had never dressed in his whole life.

And then friends came, and neighbors came. And one woman said, "Wow! He's all dressed up and nowhere to go."

But this is the situation any negative philosophy is going to leave for the whole of mankind: well-dressed, ready to go, but nowhere to go! This situation creates insanity.

It was not an accident that Friedrich Nietzsche became insane, it was the outcome of his negative philosophy. Hence, I call this series of talks, *God is Dead, Now Zen is the Only Living Truth*.

I absolutely agree with Friedrich Nietzsche as far as God is concerned, but I want to complete his statement, which he could not do. He was not an awakened being, he was not an enlightened being.

Gautam Buddha also does not have a God, nor does Mahavira have a God, but they never went mad. All the Zen masters and all the great Tao masters—Lao Tzu, Chuang Tzu, Lieh Tzu—nobody went mad, and they don't have any God. They don't have any hell or heaven. What is the difference? Why did Gautam Buddha not go mad?

And it is not only Gautam Buddha. In twenty-five centuries hundreds of his people have become enlightened, and they don't even talk about a God. They don't even say that there is no God, because there is no point. They are not atheists. I am not an atheist, nor am I a theist. God simply is not there, so there is no question of atheism or theism.

But I am not mad. You are my witnesses. It does not create a vacuum in me; on the contrary, there being no God, I have gained the dignity of an individual who is free—free to become a buddha. That is the ultimate goal of freedom. Unless your freedom becomes your very flowering of awareness, and the experience of freedom leads you into eternity, leads you into the roots, into the cosmos and existence, you are going to be mad. Your life will be meaningless, with no significance. Whatever you do it does not matter.

Existence according to the so-called existentialists, who are all following Friedrich Nietzsche, the founder, is absolutely unintelligent. They have taken away God, so they think—according to logic it seems apparently true—if there is no God, existence also becomes dead, with no intelligence, with no life. God used to be the life, God used to be the consciousness. God used to be the very meaning, the very salt of our being. With God no longer there, this whole existence becomes soulless, life becomes just a by-product of matter. So when you die, everything will die, nothing will remain.

And there is no question of being good or bad. Existence is absolutely indifferent, it does not care about you. God used to care about you. Once God is removed, a great strangeness starts happening between you and existence. There is no relationship, existence does not care, *cannot* care because it is not conscious anymore. It is no longer an intelligent universe, it is simply dead matter, just as you are. And the life that you know is only a by-product.

A by-product disappears immediately when the elements that were creating it separate. For example, some religions believe that man is made of five elements: earth, air, fire, water, sky. Once these five elements are together, life is produced as a by-product. When these five elements separate in death, life disappears.

To make it clear to you...in the beginning as you learn to ride a bicycle you fall many times. I have also learned, but I did not fall while learning, because first I watched the learners and why they fall. They fall because they don't have confidence. To be on two wheels you need tremendous balance, and if you hesitate...it is just like walking on a tightrope. If you hesitate just for a moment those two wheels cannot keep you on your seat. Those two wheels can keep you in balance only at a certain speed, and the learner is bound to move slowly. Obviously—it seems to be rational—if you are a learner, you should not go with great speed.

I watched all my friends learning to bicycle, and they always said to me, "Why don't you learn?"

I said, "I am watching first. I am watching why you fall, and why after a few days you stop falling." And once I got the point, the very first time I went as fast as possible!

All my friends were puzzled. They said, "We have never seen a learner go that fast. A learner is bound to fall a few times, then he learns how to balance."

I said, "I have been watching, and I got the clue. The clue is you are not confident, not alert that a certain speed is needed to keep the bicycle moving. You cannot stop it and sit on top of it without falling, a certain momentum is needed, so you have to go on pedaling."

Once I knew exactly what the problem was, I simply went so fast that my whole village wondered, "What will happen to him, because he does not know...and he is going with such speed!"

It was difficult for me to know how to stop; if I stopped, the cycle was going to fall. So I had to go to a place where there was a huge bodhi tree near the railway station, almost three miles from my house. Three miles I rushed so fast that people gave way, stood aside. They said, "This is absolute madness!"

But my madness had a method in it. I was going directly to that tree, because I knew the tree had become hollow. I rode my bicycle into the hollow tree so the front wheel was inside the tree. Then I could stop, there was no problem about falling.

One villager who was working in his field saw this. He said, "This is strange." He asked me, "If there is no tree like this how are you going to stop?"

I said, "Now I have learned how to stop, because I just did it; I will not need a tree anymore.

But this was my first experience. I had not seen the other people stopping, I had seen them falling. So I had no experience about stopping, that's why I was riding so fast to reach to the bodhi tree." One part of it had become completely hollow, and it was a huge tree, so I knew that it would be right to put my wheel inside and be held up by the tree. But once I had stopped, I had learned how to stop.

When I came to learn driving, I learned from a man whose name was Majid, he was a Mohammedan. He was one of the best drivers in the city, and he loved me very much. In fact, he chose my first car. So he told me, "I will teach you."

I said, "I don't like to be taught. You just drive slowly so I can see and watch."

He said, "What do you mean?"

I said, "I learn only by watching. I don't want any teacher ever!"

He said, "But it is dangerous! A bicycle was okay. At the most you could have hurt yourself or one other, and not much. But a car is a dangerous thing."

I said, "I am a dangerous man. You just drive it slowly and tell me everything about where is the pedal, where is the accelerator, where is the brake…you just tell me. And then you slowly move, and I will be walking by your side, just watching what you are doing."

He said, "If you want it this way, I can do it, but I am very much afraid. If you do the same thing with the car as you have done with the bicycle…"

I said, "That's why I am trying to watch more closely." And once I got the idea I told him to get out. And I did the same thing as I had done with the bicycle.

I went so fast. Majid, my teacher, was running behind me, shouting, "Not that fast!" And in that city there was no limit on speed, because in Indian streets you cannot go above fifty-five. There is no need to put a sign everywhere that the speed limit is fifty-five miles per hour, you cannot go above fifty-five anyway.

But that poor fellow was very much afraid. He came running after me. He was a very tall man, a champion runner, there was every possibility that he could have become champion of the whole of India, and he might perhaps someday have participated in the Olympics. He tried hard to follow me, but soon I disappeared from his vision.

When I came back, he was praying under a tree, praying to God for my safety. And when I stopped by his side, so close that he jumped, he forgot all the prayer.

I said, "Don't be worried. I have learned the whole thing. What were you doing here?"

He said, "I followed you, but soon you disappeared. Then I thought, the only thing is to pray to God to help him, because he knows nothing about driving. He is sitting in the driver's seat for the first time, and he has gone nobody knows where. How did you turn? Where did you turn back?"

I said, "I had no idea how to turn, because you were just moving straight and I was walking by your side. So I had to go around the city. I had no idea how to turn, what signals to give, because you had not given any signals. But I managed. I went round the whole city so fast, the traffic was simply giving way. And I came back."

And he said, "*Khuda hafiz*." It means, "God saved you."

I said, "Don't bring God in."

Once you know that a certain balance is needed between the negative and the positive, then you have your roots in existence. It is one extreme to believe in God; it is another extreme *not* to believe in God, and you have to be just in the middle, absolutely balanced. Atheism becomes irrelevant, theism becomes irrelevant. But your balancing brings a new light, a new joy, a new blissfulness to you, a new intelligence which is not of the mind. That intelligence which is not of the mind makes you aware that the whole existence is tremendously intelligent. It is not only alive, it has sensitivity, it has intelligence.

Once you know your inner being is balanced and silent and peaceful, suddenly doors that have been closed by your thoughts simply move, and the whole existence becomes clear to you. You are not accidental. Existence needs you. Without you something will be missing in existence and nobody can replace it.

That's what gives you dignity, that the whole existence will miss you. The stars and sun and moon, the trees and birds and earth—everything in the universe will feel a small place is vacant which cannot be filled by anybody except *you*. This gives you a tremendous joy, a fulfillment that you are related to existence, and existence cares for you. Once you are clean and clear, you can see tremendous love falling on you from all dimensions.

You are the highest evolution of existence, of intelligence, and it is dependent on you. If you grow higher than the mind and its intelligence, towards no-mind and its intelligence, existence is going to celebrate: one man again has reached to the ultimate peak. One part of existence has suddenly risen to the highest possibilities of the intrinsic potential in everybody.

There is a parable that the day Gautam Buddha became enlightened, the tree under which he had become enlightened, suddenly without any wind, started moving. He was amazed because there was no wind, no other tree around was moving, not even a single leaf was moving. But the tree under which he was sitting was moving, as if it was dancing. It does not have legs, it is so rooted in the earth, but it can at least show its joy.

It is a very strange phenomenon that certain chemicals which make you intelligent, which give you a better mind, are found in the bodhi tree in greater amounts than in any other tree. So it is not just coincidence that the tree under which Gautam Buddha became enlightened is still called according to his name. *Bodhi* means enlightenment. And the tree, scientists have found, has a larger amount of intelligence than any other tree in the world. It has so much of those chemicals it is overflowing.

When Manjushree, one of Gautam Buddha's closest disciples, became enlightened, the story is that the tree under which he was sitting suddenly started showering with flowers, and it was not the season for the tree to bring flowers.

It may be just a parable. But these parables indicate that we are not separate from existence, that our joy will be shared even by the trees, even by the rocks, that our enlightenment will be a festival for the whole of existence.

It is meditation that fulfills your inner being and takes away the vacuum that used to be filled by a great lie, God. And many lies have grown around him.

If you remain with the negative you are going to be insane sooner or later, because you have lost all contact with existence, you have lost every meaning, every possibility of finding meaning. You have certainly dropped lies, which is good, but that is not enough to find the truth.

Drop the lies and make some effort to go inwards to find the truth. That is the whole science of Zen. That's why I have entitled the series, "God Is Dead, Now Zen Is the Only Living Truth." If God is dead and you don't come close to the experience of Zen, you will become insane. Your sanity depends now only on Zen, that is the *only* way to find the truth. Then you are absolutely related with existence, and you are no longer a puppet, you are a master.

And a man who knows his relation, his deep relation with existence, cannot commit anything against existence, against life. It is simply impossible. He can only pour as much blissfulness, as much benediction, as much grace as you are ready to receive. But his sources are inexhaustible. When you have found your inexhaustible sources of life and its ecstasy, then it does not matter whether you have a God or not. It does not matter whether there is a hell or a heaven. It does not matter at all.

So religious people when they read Zen are simply puzzled, because it is not talking about anything they have been taught from the very beginning. It is talking about strange dialogues which have nothing...*no* place for God, no place for paradise, no place for hell. It is a scientific religion. Its search is not based on belief, its search is based on experience. Just as science is objectively based on experiment, Zen is based subjectively on experience. One science goes outward, another science goes inward.

Nietzsche has no idea how to go inward. The West has been a wrong place for people like Friedrich Nietzsche. If he had been in the East, he would have been a far greater master, a man of absolute sanity. He would have been in the same category, in the same family, as the buddhas.

But unfortunately the West has not learned the lesson even now. It goes on working so hard on objects. Even one tenth of our energy will be enough to find the inner truth. Even an Albert Einstein dies in deep frustration. The frustration was so great that before he died he was asked, "If you are born again, what are you going to be?" He said, "Never again a physicist. I would rather be a plumber."

The greatest physicist the world has known dies in such frustration that he does not want anything to do with physics, anything to do with science. He wants a simple job like plumbing. But even that is not going to help. If physics has not helped, if mathematics has not helped, if such a great intelligence like Albert Einstein dies in frustration, being a plumber is not going to help. Still you are outside. A scientist may be too deeply involved; a plumber may not be that much involved, but he is still working outside. Being a plumber is not going to give him what he needs. He needs the silence of meditation. From that silence flowers meaning, significance, a tremendous joy that you are not accidental.

I say to you that what I am teaching you is authentic existentialism, and what in the West is thought to be existentialism is only accidentalism. I am teaching you how to come in contact with existence, how to find out where you are connected, wired with existence. From where are you getting your life moment to moment? Where is your intelligence coming from? If existence is unintelligent, how can you be intelligent? Where will you get it from?

When you see the rose flowers blossoming, have you ever thought that all this color, all this softness, all this beauty was hidden somewhere in the seed? But the seed alone was not enough to become a rose, it needed the support of existence—the soil, the water, the sun.

Then the seed disappeared into the soil and the rosebush started growing. Now it needs air, it needs water, it needs the earth, it needs the sun, it needs the moon. All these together transform the seed which was almost like a dead piece of stone. Suddenly a transformation, a metamorphosis. These roses, these colors, this beauty, this fragrance, cannot come from it unless existence has it already. It all may be hidden, it may be covered in the seed. But anything that happens means it was there already—maybe as a potential.

You have intelligence...

I have told you the story of Ramakrishna and Keshav Chandra Sen. Keshav Chandra was one of the most intelligent people of his time. He founded a religion just on his intellectual philosophy, brahmasamaj, the society for God. And he had hundreds and thousands of intelligent people, a very intelligent group, as his followers. And he was puzzled that this uneducated Ramakrishna, who had not even completed the primary school—in India the primary school, the lowest school, takes four years; he had done only half.... Why were thousands of people going to this idiot? That was in Keshav Chandra Sen's mind.

Finally he decided he had to go and defeat this man, because he could not think that the man could not be defeated by argument. That was impossible for him to imagine. This idiot from a small village is collecting thousands of people every day! From far and wide people are coming to see him, and to touch his feet!

Keshav Chandra with his followers informed Ramakrishna: "I am coming on such and such a day to challenge you on every point in which you believe. Be ready!"

Ramakrishna's followers were very much afraid. They knew Keshav Chandra was a great logician; poor Ramakrishna would not be able to answer anything. But Ramakrishna was very joyful, he danced. He said, "I have been waiting all this time. When Keshav Chandra comes that will be a great day of joy!"

His disciples said, "What are you saying? That will be a day of great sadness, because you cannot argue with him."

Ramakrishna said, "Wait. Who is going to argue with him? I don't need to argue. Let him come."

But his disciples were shaky, very shaky, very much afraid that their master was going to be defeated, completely crushed. They knew Keshav Chandra. In that century there was no parallel to Keshav Chandra's intelligence in this country.

And Keshav Chandra came with one hundred of his topmost disciples to see the argument, the debate, the challenge. Ramakrishna was standing on the road to receive him, far away from the temple where he used to live. And he hugged Keshav Chandra. And Keshav Chandra felt a little embarrassed, and that embarrassment went on growing.

Ramakrishna took his hand in his hand and took him inside. He said, "I have been waiting and waiting for years. Why did you not come before?"

Keshav Chandra said, "He seems to be a strange man, seems not to be afraid at all. Do you understand? I have come here for a discussion!"

Ramakrishna said, "Of course."

So they sat near the temple by the side of the Ganges, a beautiful place, under a tree.

And Ramakrishna said, "Start."

So Keshav Chandra asked him, "What do you say about God?"

Ramakrishna said, "Have I to say anything about God? Can't you see God in my eyes?"

Keshav Chandra looked a little puzzled—"What kind of argument is this?"

And Ramakrishna said, "Can't you feel God in my hand? Come closer, boy."

And Keshav Chandra said, "What kind of argument…?"

He had been in many debates, he had defeated many great scholars, and this villager… In Hindi the word for idiot is *ganwar*, but it actually means the villager. *gaon* means village, and ganwar means from the village. But ganwar is used as stupid, retarded, idiot.

Ramakrishna said, "If you can understand the language of my eyes, if you can understand the energy of my hand, you are proof enough that existence is intelligent. Where have you got your intelligence from?"

This was a grand argument. He was saying, "If you have got this great intelligence—and I know you are a highly intelligent person; I have always loved you—tell me from where it comes? If existence is without intelligence you cannot get it. From where? You are the *proof* that existence is intelligent, and that is what I mean by God. To me God is not somebody sitting on a cloud. To me God simply means existence is not unintelligent. It is an intelligent universe; we belong and we are needed. It rejoices in our rejoicings, it celebrates in our celebrations, it dances with our dance. Have you seen my dance?"—and he started dancing.

Keshav Chandra said, "What to do!"

But he danced so beautifully. He was a good dancer, because he used to dance in the temple sometimes from morning till evening—no coffee break! He would dance and dance till he would fall on the ground.

So he started dancing with such joy and such grace that suddenly there was a transformation in Keshav Chandra. He forgot all his logic, he saw the beauty of this man, he saw the splendor of this man, he saw a joy which he had never felt.

All that intellect, all those arguments were just superficial, inside there was utter emptiness. This man was so overflowing. He touched the feet of Ramakrishna and said, "Forgive me. I was absolutely wrong about you. I know nothing, and I have been just philosophizing. You know everything, and you are not saying a single word."

Ramakrishna said, "I will forgive you only on one condition."

Keshav Chandra said, "*Any* condition from your side. I am ready."

Ramakrishna said, "The condition is that once in a while you have to come to discuss with me, to debate with me, to challenge me."

This is the way of a mystic; and Keshav Chandra was completely finished. He became a totally different man; he started to come every day. Soon his disciples deserted him: "He has gone mad. That madman infected him so much. There was only one madman, now there are two. He is even dancing with him."

But Keshav Chandra, who had been a sad man, grudging, complaining about everything, because he was living in a negative space, suddenly blossomed, flowers came to his being, a new fragrance. He forgot all logic. This man helped him have a taste of something that is beyond mind.

Zen is the method to go beyond mind. So we will be discussing God and Zen together. God has to be negated, and Zen has to be planted deep in your being. The lie has to be destroyed and the truth has to be revealed. That's why I have chosen to speak about God and Zen together. God is a lie, Zen is a truth.

Now your questions.

? Is God really dead? The very idea of his death creates intense anxiety, fear, dread and anguish.

The way I look at things, God has never been there, so how can he be dead? He was never born in the first place. It was invented by the priests, and it was invented for exactly these reasons: because man was in anxiety, man was in fear, man was in dread, man was in anguish.

When there was no light, no fire—just think of those days of humanity—wild animals all around, and the dark night, no fire, the intense cold, no clothes, and the wild animals searching for their food in the night, and people were hiding in caves, sitting on the trees just to avoid... In the day, at least they could see that a lion was approaching, they could make some effort to escape. But in the night, they were completely in the hands of the wild animals.

And then they found that a time comes, people become old for no reason, and one day somebody dies. They could not understand what was happening. This man was talking, breathing, walking, was perfectly okay. Suddenly he was no longer breathing, he was no longer talking. It was such a shock to the primitive man that death became a taboo: Don't talk about it. Even talking about it created fear, fear that sooner or later you would be standing in the same queue, with the queue becoming smaller and smaller every moment. Somebody dies and you come closer to death; another dies, you come even closer to death.

Even to talk about death became a taboo, and not only to ordinary primitive people, even to the most sophisticated. The founder of psychoanalysis, Sigmund Freud, could not tolerate the word "death". No one was allowed to mention the word in front of him, because just at the mention of the word 'death' he would fall into a fit, he would become unconscious and start foaming. Such was the fear of the man who founded psychoanalysis.

Once Sigmund Freud and Carl Gustav Jung, another great psychoanalyst, were traveling from Europe to America to deliver lectures on psychoanalysis to many universities. On the deck of the ship, Carl Gustav Jung mentioned death. Immediately Sigmund Freud fell on the deck. That was the reason Sigmund Freud expelled Jung from the psychoanalytic movement, and he had to found another school. He called it analytical psychology. Just a different name, but it is the same process. But the reason for his expulsion was the mention of death.

Two things have been taboos in the world, and those two things are two polarities of the same energy. One is sex, which has been taboo, "Don't talk about it"; another is death which is taboo, "Don't talk about it." Both are connected: in the beginning is sex, in the end is death; it is sex that brings death in.

Only one animal does not die, that is the amoeba. And you know that perfectly well because Pune is so full of amoebas. I have chosen this place specially, because amoebas are immortal beings. And their immortality depends on the fact that they are not sexual beings. They are not the by-product of sex, so there is no death. Sex and death are absolutely connected. Just try to understand.

Sex brings you into life, and life finally ends in death. Sex is the beginning, death is the end. In between is what you call life.

The amoeba is a non-sexual animal, the only celibate monk in the whole world. It reproduces in a very different way. God must be immensely happy—if he is there—with the amoebas; they are all saints. They simply go on eating and becoming fatter and fatter, and at a certain point they divide into two. When one amoeba becomes so fat that it becomes impossible for him to move, he divides in two.

This is a different way of reproduction. But because there is no sex involved, there is no male, no female. Both the amoebas start eating again. Soon they will be fat enough to divide again. So it is by a very mathematical method that they create. There is no death, an amoeba never dies—unless he is murdered! He can live from eternity to eternity if medical science does not murder him. But their immortality depends on the fact they are not the by-product of sex. Any animal who is born of sex is going to die, he cannot be immortal in the body.

So these two things have been taboos in the world: sex and death. Both have been kept hidden.

I have been condemned all around the world, simply because I talked about every taboo without any inhibition, because I want you to know everything about life from sex to death. Only then can you rise beyond sex and death. In your understanding you can start approaching something which is beyond sex and beyond death. That is your eternity, that is your life energy, pure energy.

By sex your body is born, not you.

By death your body dies, not you.

So it is absolutely unnecessary to make those taboos. But religions have a great investment in creating in you anxiety, fear, dread and anguish, and nature was already producing it.

Religions, and particularly the priests all over the world, whatever their denomination, have exploited man's fear, have given him God, a fiction, a lie—which at least temporarily covers the wound. "Don't be afraid, God is taking care of you. Don't be in any dread or anxiety, there is God, and everything is okay. All that you have to do is believe in God and believe in the representative of God, the priest, and believe in the holy scripture that God has sent to the world. All that you have to do is to believe." And this belief has been covering your anxiety, fear, dread, anguish.

So when you hear God is dead, the very idea of his death creates intense anxiety. That means your wound has been uncovered. But a covered wound is not a healed wound; in fact for the healing process it has to be uncovered. Only then in the sun's rays, in the open air, will it start healing. A wound should never be covered, because covering it you start forgetting about it. You want to forget about it. Once it is covered, not only do others not see it, you yourself don't see it. And under the cover it goes on becoming a cancer.

Every wound has to be healed, not covered. Covering is not the way. God was the cover, that's why the very concept that God is dead creates fear. Whatever comes to your mind, intense anxiety, fear, dread, and anguish—these were the things priests were covering with the word "God".

But by their covering, they have stopped man's evolution towards buddhahood, they have stopped man's healing process, they have stopped man's search for truth. A lie was handed to you as truth; naturally you need not search for truth, you have it already.

It is absolutely necessary that God should be dead. But I want you to know my understanding. It was good of Friedrich Nietzsche to declare God dead. I declare that he has never been born. It is a created fiction, an invention, not a discovery. Do you understand the difference between invention and discovery? A discovery is about truth, an invention is manufactured by you. It is man-manufactured fiction.

Certainly it has given consolation, but consolation is not the right thing! Consolation is opium. It keeps you unaware of the reality, and life is flowing past you so quickly—seventy years will be gone soon.

Anybody who gives you a belief system is your enemy, because the belief system becomes the barrier for your eyes, you cannot see the truth. The very desire to find the truth disappears.

But in the beginning it is bitter if all your belief systems are taken away from you. The fear and anxiety which you have been suppressing for millennia, which is there, very alive, will surface immediately. No God can destroy it, only the search for truth and the experience of truth—not a belief—is capable of healing all your wounds, of making you a whole being. And the whole person is the holy person to me.

So if God is removed and you start feeling fear and dread, and anxiety and anguish, that simply indicates God was not the medicine. It was just a trick to keep your eyes closed. It was a blinding strategy to keep you in darkness, and to keep you hoping that beyond death there is paradise. Why beyond death? It is because you are afraid of death, so the priest creates a paradise beyond death, just to take away your fear. But it is not taken away, it is only repressed in your unconscious. And the deeper it is repressed the more difficult it is to get rid of it.

So I want to destroy all your belief systems, all your theologies, all your religions. I want to open all your wounds so they can be healed. The real medicine is not a belief system; the real medicine is meditation. Do you know that both the words come from the same root: medicine and meditation? Medicine heals the body, meditation heals your soul. But their function is the same, healing.

Once you drop the God, you are certainly free. But in this freedom you will be filled with anxiety, fear, dread, anguish. Unless you start moving inwards to find your authentic being, your original face, your buddha, you will be trembling, your whole life will be destroyed, you may become insane, the way Friedrich Nietzsche became insane.

And he is not the only person who became insane. There are many philosophers who have committed suicide because they found there was nothing in life, and they never looked inwards. Because they found there was no meaning, no sense…why go on living?

One of the great novels, perhaps the greatest novel in all the languages, is Fyodor Dostoevsky's, *The Brothers Karamazov*. It is far more important to read it than the Holy Bible, or holy Koran, or holy Gita, or all three combined. *The Brothers Karamazov* has such a deep insight into everything…but Fyodor Dostoevsky became mad.

He created the greatest novels in the world, but he himself lived a very miserable, very sad, very afraid life. He was not a man of joy, but he had tremendous insight—intellectual—into every problem that man is bound to face. All problems he has tackled. *The Brothers Karamazov* is such a big novel that nowadays nobody reads it; people like just to watch the television. It is perhaps nearabout one thousand pages, and with intense argument.

The youngest brother—there are three brothers—is very pious, believing, god-fearing, and wants to become a monk and move to a monastery. The second brother is absolutely against God, absolutely against religion, and in a discussion with his younger brother they are continuously discussing all these problems. He says, "If I ever meet God, the first thing I am going to do is to give him the ticket back, and tell him, 'Keep it. I don't want your life, it is meaningless. Just show me the way out, I don't want to be in the world. I just want to get out of existence; death seems to me to be more peaceful than your so-called life. Just take the ticket back, I don't want to travel in this train. And you never asked me; it is against my wishes. You have forced me on this train, and now I am suffering unnecessarily. I had no freedom of choice. Why did you give me birth?'"

That's what he said he was going to ask if he met God: "On what grounds did you give me birth? Without my permission you created me. Now this is perfect slavery. And one day, without asking me, you will kill me. You have planted every kind of sickness in me, you have planted every kind of sin in me for which I am condemned, and you are the reason."

Who has planted sex in you? It must be God, who created man, and who told Adam and Eve to go into the world and multiply, create as many children as you can. Obviously he has made them sexual, and he created the couple.

Ivan Karamazov, the atheist brother, says, "If I find him"—and who knows, he may still be living and Friedrich Nietzsche may be wrong—"then I am going to kill him. I will be the first to make the whole of humanity free from this dictator who on the one hand implants sex, violence, anger, greed, ambition, all kinds of poisons in man, and on the other hand, whose representatives go on hammering at you that sex is sin, you should be celibate. Strange."

George Gurdjieff used to say, "All religions are against God." There is meaning in his statement. He was not a man to make any statement without a deep, intense understanding. When he says all religions are against God, he is saying God gives you sex, and religions teach you celibacy. What do they mean? God gives you greed, and religions teach you no greed. God gives you violence, and religions teach you no violence. God gives you anger, and religions say no anger. It is such a clear-cut argument, that all religions are against God.

Ivan Karamazov said, "If I meet him anywhere I am going to kill him, but before killing him I am going to ask all these questions."

The whole novel is a tremendous argument. The third brother is not their real brother. He is born of a woman who was not the wife of their father, who was only a servant. The third brother is kept out of the eyes of society, so he remains retarded. He is almost like an animal: he eats, drinks, and lives in a dark place in the vast palace of the Karamazovs. Certainly his life is absolutely meaningless.

And Ivan Karamazov said, "Think about our cousin-brother, illegitimate, who God also created. What is the meaning of his life? He cannot even come out in the sun, in the air. Our father keeps him shut in darkness. Nobody ever comes to see him, nobody ever comes to greet him. Nobody is his friend in this whole earth. He knows nobody else. He cannot speak well because he has never spoken to anybody. His whole life is just like an animal: eating, drinking, sleeping; eating, drinking, sleeping.... He will never know any woman, he will never know any love. What will happen to his sex instinct?"

It is a very intense argument about all the problems any intelligent man is going to face. Ivan is bringing all those problems: "What do you believe God says about my cousin-brother? What is his meaning? Why has he created him this way? If anybody is responsible, he is responsible, and I am going to take revenge. Just let me find him! And I hope," Ivan Karamazov says, "that Nietzsche is not right, that he is not dead. Otherwise I will miss the chance to murder him. I want to murder him so that the whole of humanity becomes freed from him."

But once you make humanity free...freedom for what? For fear? For death? For suicide? For murder? For theft? Freedom for what?

One of the existentialist novels says that a young man is brought before a court because he has killed a stranger on the beach, someone whose face he has not even seen. He came up behind this man, who was sitting looking at the sunset, pushed a knife in his back and killed him. And he has not even seen who he was.

It was a very strange case. You don't kill unless you have some enmity, some anger, some revengefulness. But they were not even known to each other, they were not even friends. You can kill friends—friends are always killing each other—but he was not even a friend, what to say about an enemy? You can make somebody an enemy only if you make him first your friend. That step is necessary: first friend, then enemy. You cannot make somebody an enemy directly. Some acquaintance, some friendship is needed to create an enemy.

The court was at a loss. The judge asked the man, "Why did you kill a stranger whose face you had not seen, whose name you did not know?"

The man said, "It does not matter. I was feeling so bored I wanted to do something, something that would get my photograph in all the newspapers. It has happened; I feel a little less bored. And anyway there is no meaning in life. What was that idiot doing? What was he going to do if I had not killed him? Just repeat the same things that he has done already many times. So what is the fuss? Why have I been brought into the court?"

The magistrate seemed absolutely puzzled: there is no eyewitness, except this man himself who says, 'I have killed that man, but without witnesses you cannot punish me. I may be lying, who knows? There are no witnesses."

Then circumstantial witnesses were brought into the court. One neighbor said, "This man is strange. His mother died on Sunday, and when he was informed he said, 'That woman would always create trouble—and inevitably on a Sunday. Sunday is a holiday, could she not die on Saturday or Friday? But I knew perfectly well from the very beginning that that woman, who has been a torture my whole life, was going to destroy one of my holidays. And it has come true.'

"And when asked, 'Why are you feeling so angry?' he said, 'I am feeling angry because I have purchased tickets for my girlfriend and me, to go to the movie, and this woman could have died any other day. What is the point of dying on a Sunday? I don't understand at all. But I know her mind.'"

Another man came and said, "He buried his mother and then he was dancing in a disco that very evening with a very young, beautiful woman. And when someone said, 'Your mother has died just this morning. It does not look right that you should dance in the evening in a disco,' he said, 'What do you mean? Now every time I dance it will be after the death of my mother, so what does it matter whether it has been twelve hours, twelve days, or five years? It will always be after the death of my mother. Do you want me never to dance because my mother has died?'"

He is absolutely logical, but inhuman.

So these witnesses went on saying things about him: "This man is strange. He can do anything, without relevance." But the man said, "I don't see any relevance in life itself. What is the crime in killing a man? I am simply freeing him from bondage. I am not committing a sin, I am not committing a crime. I am simply helping a man who was too cowardly to commit suicide."

A negative philosophy will bring these results. A negative philosophy basically will lead humanity into madness, and its ultimate conclusion can only be to commit suicide.

A great negative philosopher of Greece, Zeno, actually preached his whole life that suicide is the only way out. Thousands of his disciples committed suicide. He said, "Life is meaningless, of no significance. It is only through cowardice that people continue to live. They cannot gather courage enough to take a jump and be finished. Don't be a coward. Only suicide can prove that you are not a coward."

He was very convincing. It seems convincing if somebody says to you, "Only suicide can prove that you are not a coward, because what is the point of living? What have you done up to now? Half of life you have lived, with what result? What is the outcome? You will live the same way the remaining half, and will die like an animal. At least have the dignity to commit suicide!"

That man was saying that birth was not in your hands, but at least don't let death also be your master. Be master of your death, commit suicide. His arguments are very profound. He was saying, "You were helpless as far as birth was concerned, you could not do anything. It has to happen, but about death there is a possibility: either you die like an animal, or you commit suicide like a man. Suicide gives the dignity to man that he is free to choose his death." He convinced many young people and they committed suicide.

Just before he died at the age of ninety somebody asked, "Thousands of people have committed suicide according to your philosophizing and argumentation, why have you not committed suicide? Why have you lived a long life?"

The man said, "I had to live, just to teach my philosophy. It was a burden, but out of compassion I had to live! Otherwise, who was going to teach? The only right approach towards life is death. I have suffered my whole life. I have dropped my own dignity by not committing suicide, because I had to take care of my fellow citizens, particularly my disciples. I am perfectly happy that they have all committed suicide. Now I can die in peace, I have done my work."

Negative philosophy is going to bring such conclusions. Zen is the only living alternative, positive alternative, because it gives you a sense of direction, a sense of fulfillment, a sense of eternity, and a sense of going beyond birth, death, body, and of being one with this beautiful existence which is immensely intelligent.

? Is it possible for man to live without God?

Yes. In fact, it is only possible for man to live without God. A man with God does not live, he hesitates on every point of living, he is just half-hearted.

He is making love and worried about hell. How can he love a woman when the Bible goes on saying that the woman is the gateway to hell? He is making love, and thinking about the Bible and the sermon on Sunday: "The woman is the gateway to hell. What are you doing?" So neither can he love, nor can he live without love. God has made man very schizophrenic, half-hearted in everything.

You are earning money, and at the same time you know that your greed is a sin. If you don't earn money you starve. Your whole nature rebels against starvation, forces you to earn something to feed yourself. Nature pulls one way, God and his representatives pull you the other way. You are in a strange position.

In Hindi we have a beautiful proverb. In India donkeys are used by the washerman to carry clothes to the river. And then after the washing he again puts the clothes on the donkey and takes them to every house he collected them from in the morning. So the proverb is: "Your life is just like the donkey of a washerman." He is never at the house nor even at the river, always in between, going from the house to the river, going from the river to the house.

The washerman's donkey simply means schizophrenia. You are always half in every act, but because the whole humanity is schizophrenic you don't realize it. You love but you hate the same person you love. What has created this hate? It is because you love this woman, and this woman is the gateway to hell. You are bound to hate her too. You make friends in the evening, by the morning you become enemies. You go on moving away and you go on coming together. This goes on continuously—the washerman's donkey.

You are asking, "Is it possible for man to live without God?" It is only possible without God to live totally, to live meditatively, to live fully.

Sigmund Freud's statement is worth remembering. Because he worked his whole life on sex, he thought sex was the root of all problems. But he never understood that it is not sex that is the problem, it is the suppression of sex that is the problem. The priest is the problem, the God is the problem, the holy scriptures are the problem; sex is not the problem.

Sex is such a simple thing. All the animals are enjoying sex; none of them go to the couch of a psychoanalyst. I have never met any animal going to the psychiatrist because he is feeling schizophrenic. They are all living and enjoying, there is no problem.

The pagans lived very joyously before religions, particularly Christianity, destroyed them from the earth. They had no idea of any sin. They loved women, they danced, they drank, they played music. Their whole life was sheer joy.

But Sigmund Freud has this one statement I was going to tell you about: "The priests cannot destroy sex." But they have succeeded in poisoning it. They could not succeed in destroying sex, otherwise there would have been no humanity. Sex is there, but they have destroyed the joy in it, they have made it a great sin. So you are committing the sin, and you think the woman is the cause.

The reality is totally different; it is God. But as God is only a fiction he cannot do anything. The priest is the representative, the spokesman of God, who goes on creating all kinds of guilt feelings in you. Those guilt feelings don't allow you to live. Everything is wrong, everything is a sin.

So your question, "Is it possible for man to live without God?"—I say unto you, it is *only* possible for man to live if he is without God. But this is only half. The fictitious God has to be replaced by an actual experience of truth in meditation; otherwise you will go insane.

All the religions are based on God. Their morality, their commandments, their prayers, their saintliness—everything points towards God, and you say that God is dead. Then what will happen to all these other things that are dependent on the concept of God?

All those things that are dependent on the concept of God are bogus; hypocrites are created by all those things. Your morality is not real, it is imposed out of fear, or out of greed. A true morality arises only in a meditator's consciousness. It is not something imported from the outside, it is something arising in your very being. It is spontaneous. And when morality is spontaneous, it is a joy, it is simply sharing your compassion and love.

All the qualities which are dependent on God will disappear with God disappearing. They are very superficial.

You all have back doors. At the front door you are one person, at the back door you are a different person. Have you ever watched it? At the front door you are a great Catholic, so religious, so pious, so prayerful, that anybody could think you were a saint. But this is only in your sitting room. At the back door you are just as human beings are supposed to be, with all their instincts, with all their sex, with all their greed, with all their anger. Just look at your God himself. Different religions have different ideas, but all ideas prove one thing, that God is the original sinner.

The Hindu God created woman and became infatuated—with his own daughter. And the woman became afraid, so she became a cow and God became the bull. She rushed and became somebody else, and God followed her—that's how all the species have been created according to Hindu theology; it was God following the woman into different forms. The woman was changing forms, God was also changing forms. The woman was always the female, the God was always the male. That's why there are so many millions of species. If the woman became a female mosquito, God became a male mosquito. It went on and on, perhaps it is still going on.

Do you think this god is a moral god? And the same is true about all gods of all religions. The Jewish god says in the Old Testament, "I am a very jealous god. I am not the one who is going to forgive you, I am a very angry god. You should not worship anybody else except me. And remember I am your father, not your uncle." What kind of god is this, jealous, worried that you may worship another god? And finally he says, "I am your father, remember; I am not your uncle." Uncles are always nicer people than fathers.

A German theology professor, Uta Ranke-Heinemann, has made the following statement: "The majority of Catholic bishops in the US are sexually disturbed. We must assume that German bishops will soon be calling a commission to see if they are sexually disturbed also."

The Barnsberg church historian, professor George Denzler, commented: "The pope is responsible for a very painful, very terrible sexual morality."

And a German Protestant pastor, Helga Frisch, said, "When celibacy was introduced in the tenth century, the priest killed the pope's ambassador and threatened to murder the archbishop. I am amazed that priests today don't resort to similar tactics."

There is a morality which is imposed from the outside which is never in tune with your heart. And there is a morality that comes from within you, which is always in tune with your heart and in tune with the heart of the universe. That is authentic morality.

I don't give you any discipline, any morality. I simply give you a clarity of vision. Out of that clarity whatsoever comes is good, is divine, is moral.

Now before the sutra a little biographical note:

Sekito Kisen was born in China in 700 and was to die ninety years later. Known also as Shih-Tou, Sekito was a contemporary of Ma Tzu. But where the latter was part of what was to become the Rinzai line of Chinese Zen, Sekito was in the Soto line.

These are the two lineages of Zen: Rinzai Zen and Soto Zen. Both are the same, they just come from different masters; there is nothing basically different. But there have been so many masters, it is really amazing that there are only two lines. There could have been a thousand lines, but Zen is only given to the disciple if he is ready. Sometimes the master never finds a single man who can carry the lineage, so that line is simply finished, comes to a full stop.

Many, many masters have lived, whose lines would go for two generations, three generations, and then would stop; because it is not a question of following, it is a question of a direct transfer between the master and the disciple. Unless the master chooses to transfer, that line is broken.

Only two lines are living still. One is Rinzai Zen—we have talked about almost all the masters of the Rinzai Zen sect. This Sekito Kisen belongs to the Soto line. You will not see any difference. There cannot be any difference between two enlightened people.

It is said that between Ma Tzu and Sekito, Zen took flight.

Ma Tzu was a very strange master—you have heard about him. He walked just like an animal on all fours; he never stood up on his legs—not that there was any problem, not that he was hunchback. He just walked on all fours because he said that is the most relaxed position. It is, because man is standing almost despite nature. No animal stands on two legs, because when you stand on two legs your heart has to pump against gravitation towards the head. This cuts your life in half.

You could live one hundred and forty years if you walked like Ma Tzu. But please don't do it! What will you do living a hundred and forty years? When you are walking like an animal, your blood flow is horizontal, and you are not putting extra stress on the heart. Ma Tzu would never have had a heart attack, that was impossible. No animal ever has a heart attack, only man does, because he has gone against nature.

He used to walk on four legs…. That is the whole theory of Charles Darwin, of evolution, that man one day was an animal. What kind of animal? Maybe there are different opinions, but one thing is certain, at one time he used to walk on four legs. There were no heart attacks. Just see how healthy animals are—except in a zoo; in a zoo they become more human. See the animals in the wild.

Just nearby, a few hundred miles away, there is a beautiful lake, Tadoba. It is a forest reserve, a very big forest surrounding the lake with only one government rest-house. I used to go there many times. Whenever I was passing by, I would stay in that rest-house for at least a day or two. It was so lonely, so utterly silent, and the forest is full of thousands of deer.

Every evening when the sun sets and darkness descends, thousands and thousands, line upon line, of deer will come to the lake. You just have to sit and watch. In the dark night their eyes look like burning candles, thousands of candles moving around the lake. The whole night the scene continues. You get tired, because there are so many deer, they go on coming, go on coming. It is such a beautiful experience. But one thing I wondered about was that they are all alike—nobody is fat, nobody is thin, nobody seems to be sick, hospitalized. They are so full of life and energy.

You cannot beat a deer if you run by his side. No winner in the Olympic races can run the way a deer can run, because the deer has such thin legs and such a proportionate body. And he jumps big hedges without any trouble. And his running is a beauty to see. Just the deer's muscles, their movement, is so healthy that man looks almost sick.

This was the trouble that arose by standing up. Your life has been shortened, your heart is continuously under stress because it has to pump against gravitation. It was not made for that.

So Ma Tzu was a very strange man, perhaps there has never been another man so strange. A unique master in himself, he walked on all fours and always looked like a tiger. Whenever he looked at somebody, people started a deep trembling; he was a dangerous man. He was very healthy; he was bound to be, he was almost like a bull. Just the horns were missing, otherwise….

Between Ma Tzu on one side, Rinzai Zen, and Sekito on the other side, Soto Zen, Zen took flight; both were very powerful people, great masters.

As a young boy, Sekito took a stand against an old custom of sacrificing a bull as a means to placate evil spirits; he made a habit of destroying the shrines devoted to such spirits, and would release bulls from their enclosures so they could escape.

At the age of twelve, Sekito met master Eno. Eno predicted that Sekito would follow the dharma, and advised him to become a monk and go to master Seigen. After Eno left his body, Sekito went to Seigen.

This is just a small biographical note about Sekito.

Now begins the sutra:

On their first meeting, Seigen asked Sekito, "Where do you come from?"
and Sekito replied, "I come from Sokei,"

...where Eno lived, his old master, who has sent him to Seigen because his death was imminent, and who said, "I will not be able to see your enlightenment, but you are bound to be enlightened. Just go to Seigen."

This is the beauty of Zen, no competition at all. The whole thing is that everybody should become enlightened. Where he becomes enlightened is not important. Who is the master who makes him enlightened is not important. Seeing death coming, Eno said to Sekito, "You are bound to become enlightened, but my death is very close. It is better you go to Seigen." And Seigen was his competitor master.

Eno lived in Sokei. So when Seigen asked, *"Where do you come from?" Sekito replied, I come from Sokei."*

In other words he is saying, "I am coming from Eno, your competitor master. He has sent me here."

Seigen held up a whisk and said, "Did you find this over there?"
Sekito replied, "No, not only was it not over there, but it was also not in
the Westland."

The West land, in Japan, is India—"What you are asking me for was not in Sokei, it was not even in India where Gautam Buddha was born and where Mahakashyapa started the Zen tradition. What is it that was not even with Buddha or with Mahakashyapa or with Bodhidharma?"

Seigen asked, "You reached the Westland, didn't you?"
to which Sekito replied, "If I had reached, I could have found it."

Only I was missing, otherwise it was everywhere. Because I did not go there, it was not there. He is talking about his own being. It has been inside him, not in Sokei and not even in India. This is a great dialogue.

He is saying, "If I had gone there, it would have been there. It is within me." But he is not directly indicating that it is within him. That is the way of Zen dialogues. Nothing direct, everything very indirect, and you have to catch the knack of following the indirect indications of what they mean.

Seigen said, "Not yet enough—speak further."

Seigen is testing Sekito whether to accept him as a disciple. Certainly he must be a man of tremendous possibilities; otherwise Eno, his competitor master, would not have sent him to him.

The competition between masters is a very strange phenomenon. There is an ancient story in India that there were two sweet shops. Both were competitors to each other and both were always quarreling because the street was small, as in the past all the streets were very small. They could talk to each other just sitting in their shops, and there was always argument.

One day things came to such a head that they started throwing sweets at each other. And a whole crowd gathered, jumping and catching the sweets and enjoying. The fight went on till both their shops were completely empty, and the whole city enjoyed it because they got all the sweets.

This story is told to indicate that when two masters fight it is just throwing sweets at each other. The disciples enjoy. Both lots of disciples eat the sweets that the masters are throwing at each other.

The competitor masters were not enemies. They were using different methods, but they were working for the same truth from different angles. When Eno thought that his death was coming close, he could not see anyone better then Seigen, although Seigen was his lifelong competitor. But that is immaterial; he is the best man, he knows. His whole life they have been fighting and arguing, dialogue upon dialogue, pulling each other's legs. And they lived close enough, not far away.

Seigen said, "Not yet enough—speak further."

You have not said enough. You are very intelligent—just speak a little more.

*Sekito replied, "You should also speak from your side.
How is it you urge only me?"*

You know perfectly well where I am coming from. I come from Eno—you were both equal competitors; neither could defeat the other—and I am his best disciple. So don't just ask me to speak; you have to speak from your side also. I represent here my master, he has sent me. I owe everything to my master. So it is not going to be a one-sided dialogue. You have to say something also.

This is a beautiful illustration of even disciples having their dignity. Although he has come to be a disciple to Seigen, that does not mean that he has to lose his dignity, his individuality, that he has to surrender. No master would like a man who has no dignity. This proves the man has his own integrity.

Seigen said, "There's no problem for me in answering you, but nobody would agree with it." Seigen continued, "When you were at Sokei, what did you get there?"

A very significant statement he has made without making it look important. He is saying, "There is no problem for me in answering you, but nobody would agree with it." If a master really speaks his mind, if he really speaks that which is beyond the mind, nobody is going to agree with him, except only other masters, and they are very few, very rare.

And he said to Sekito, "You will not agree with it. You are not yet enlightened. You are not yet in that space. You can intellectually argue with me but you cannot understand my answers. Remember, I am ready to answer any question you have, but nobody is going to agree. At any rate you are not going to agree. Perhaps your master would have agreed. But it is very rare to find another enlightened man to talk with where agreement is possible beyond intellect. So it is better, rather than me saying anything, that you tell me when you were at Sokei with Eno, what did you get there? What have you got?"

Sekito replied, "Even before going to Sokei..." This is a very beautiful statement, very deep and profound.

Sekito replied, "Even before going to Sokei, I had not lost a thing."

So there is no question of getting anything from Eno, I have everything within me.

A great thinker, Martin Buber, a Jewish philosopher, was on his deathbed, and this is just a few years back. The rabbi came and said to Martin Buber, "Have you made peace with God?"

Martin Buber's last words were—he opened his eyes and he said to the rabbi—"I have never quarreled with him. What question is there of making peace with God?" And he died.

That's what Sekito is saying, *"Even before going to Sokei, I had not lost a thing."* So there is no question of getting anything there. "I am carrying everything within me."

Then Sekito asked, "When you were in Sokei, did you know yourself?"

Because of his statement that he had not lost anything even before he went to Eno, to his place in Sokei, Sekito asked,

"When you were in Sokei, did you know yourself?"
Seigen said, "How about you? Do you know me now?"
Sekito answered, "Yes, I do. How can I know you any further?"
He continued, "Osho, since you left Sokei, how long have you been staying here?"
Seigen replied, "I do not know either. And you, when did you leave Sokei?"
Sekito said, "I don't come from Sokei."

He has changed his statement completely. First he said he came from Sokei. That was just a superficial answer to the question, "Where do you come from?" Now things are getting deeper.

Sekito said, "I don't come from Sokei."

He means that he comes from eternity. Sokei was just one of the stops on the way; he does not come from Sokei, he comes from eternity. There have been many stops; Sokei was one of the stops.

Seigen responded, "All right—now I know where you come from."
Sekito said, "Osho, you are a great one—do not waste time."

He was saying that you are wasting time unnecessarily in checking to see whether I am of any worth or not, but, before you accept me as a disciple, I have accepted you as a master. That's why he has suddenly started calling him Osho. He is saying whether you accept me as a disciple or not, that does not matter. I have accepted you as my master. *"Osho, you are a great one—do not waste time."* Let us begin the real work.

That is the honest seeker's response. Don't waste time in this dialogue and answering and questioning. Just let us begin the real work. And the real work is following the inner path to your very center.

Taneda wrote:

Searching for what?
I walk in the wind.

He is saying that I don't know what I am searching for. How can I know before I have found it? Truth is just a word. How can I say what I am searching for? Before I have found it, I cannot say what I am seeking. This is a very strange but beautiful statement. He is saying before you find the truth, you cannot even say you are searching for truth. You are simply searching. You don't know for what. If you did know it, there would be no need to search. So you are just groping.

Taneda is perfectly right. A seeker is simply groping in the dark hoping some way must be there. Existence cannot be so cruel.

Searching for what?
I walk in the wind.

I am just flying everywhere, walking in the wind. But I don't know what I am seeking. I will know only when I have found it. He is saying: anybody who is searching for something is believing in something before he has found it, and that is wrong. That's what all the religions are doing, creating beliefs before people have even found anything; before they have known anything they have been turned into believers, into faithful ones. And their whole search has been destroyed.

I don't ask you what you are searching for. I simply show you the way. I simply insist, "Go on, go on, go on." You are bound to find it because it is there somewhere inside you. If you search deep enough with urgency and totality, you are bound to find it. And only by finding will you know what you were seeking. This is a totally different, diametrically opposite standpoint to all the belief systems of the world.

? Is not the fantasy of an omnipotent, omnipresent, omniscient God simply a covert expression of man's will to power?

It is two things. First, it is a deep fear of life and death, a fear of ignorance, a fear of not knowing oneself. But out of this fear also arises a desire for power. In fact the desire for power is always based on an inferiority complex.

That's why I say all politicians and all so-called great religious leaders are suffering from an inferiority complex. That inferiority complex is a torture to them. They want to be on some great pedestal with great power. That power will help them to get at least a temporary relief from the inferiority complex. Now they know they are known worldwide. Now that millions of people are following them, how can they be inferior? They can convince themselves, "If I have so much power, how can I be inferior?" But it does not matter whether you have power or not, your inferiority cannot be dissolved by power, it can only be covered.

So there is God on the one hand covering fear, dread, death. While on the other hand to be a believer of a god who is omnipotent, all powerful, omnipresent, everywhere present, omniscient, all knowing, to have belief in such a god helps you somehow to be identified with the god. You are a Christian, you identify yourself with Christ—and he is the son of God. You have come very close as far as relationship is concerned.

You believe in Krishna and he is the reincarnation of God, the perfect reincarnation. Believing in him you have come very close to power. You may not have power, but you believe in a person who has power. So it is also a longing for power. But why do you want power? It is because you feel weak, you feel powerless, you feel inferior.

So religions create inferiority, they create fear, they create greed and out of this creation you are ready to accept a god as all-knowing, everywhere-present, all-powerful, and you are so close to him in your faith, in your belief, in your prayer that you are also sharing some of the power of God. You become a mini-god. But it is all psychological sickness, and God is not the cure.

A Zen Haiku — Taneda wrote:

Searching for what?
I walk in the wind.

He is saying "I don't know what I am searching for. How can I know before I have found it? Truth is just a word. How can I say what I am searching for? Before I have found it, I cannot say what I am seeking." This is a very strange but beautiful statement. He is saying before you find the truth, you cannot even say you are searching for truth. You are simply searching. You don't know for what. If you did know it, there would be no need to search. So you are just groping.

Taneda is perfectly right. A seeker is simply groping in the dark hoping some way must be there. Existence cannot be so cruel.

Searching for what?
I walk in the wind.

I am just flying everywhere, walking in the wind. But I don't know what I am seeking. I will know only when I have found it. He is saying: anybody who is searching for something is believing in something before he has found it, and that is wrong. That's what all the religions are doing, creating beliefs before people have even found anything; before they have known anything they have been turned into believers, into faithful ones. And their whole search has been destroyed.

I don't ask you what you are searching for. I simply show you the way. I simply insist, "Go on, go on, go on." You are bound to find it because it is there somewhere inside you. If you search deep enough with urgency and totality, you are bound to find it. And only by finding will you know what you were seeking. This is a totally different, diametrically opposite standpoint to all the belief systems of the world.

Now for some laughter… laughter is a better cure than God.

It is little Albert's first day at school, and as soon as his mother brings him to the classroom and leaves, Albert bursts into tears.

Despite the combined efforts of his teacher, the principal, the school nurse and even the janitor, Albert just goes on crying and crying. Finally, just before lunch-time, the teacher gets fed up.

"For heaven's sake, child," she shouts. "Just shut up! It is lunchtime now, and in a couple of hours you will go home and see your mommy again!"

At once, Albert stops crying.

"Why didn't you say so before!" he exclaims. "I thought I had to stay here until I was sixteen!"

Paddy and Seamus are walking home from the pub through the park one day, in deep, philosophical discussion. For over an hour, they have been talking abut whether God rules over their lives or not, when Paddy gets fed up and says, "Ah, God can't tell me what to do — I am going to the beach for a holiday!"

"You mean," replies Seamus, "that you are going to the beach — God willing?"

"No!" snaps Paddy, stubbornly. "I am going to the beach, God willing or not!" But just at that moment, there is a loud crash of thunder in the sky. Seamus covers his head in fear, and falls to the ground.

When he opens his eyes again, he looks around, and finds that Paddy has been changed into a slimy, green frog.

For seven weeks, Paddy, the frog, is forced to live in the park pond, and every day Seamus brings a handful of dead flies for him to eat.

Finally, after his penance is completed, Paddy is changed back into his old self. He immediately walks home and begins packing his bags.

"Hey, Paddy!" cries Seamus, with surprise. "My God, you are back! But where are you going now?"

"Like I said," shouts Paddy, "I am going to the beach!"

"You mean," replies Seamus, "that you are going to the beach — God willing?"

"No!" shouts Paddy, furiously. "I am going to the beach or I am going back to that goddam frog pond!"

The chief executive of a big sausage manufacturing company calls his clerk into the office. "Let us get straight to the point," he snaps. "Your work has been lousy lately. You are late every day and your accounting errors are ridiculous. You have been working for me for fifteen years, but recently you don't seem to know a pork sausage from a bunch of bananas!"

"Well, sir," replies the clerk, "I have tried not to let it affect my work, but things have been going very badly for me at home."

"Oh! I am sorry to hear that," apologizes the boss. "I hope I am not interfering, but if you tell me what is on your mind, perhaps I can help?"

"That's very kind of you, sir," sniffles the unhappy clerk. "You see, I have been married for two years, and about six weeks ago my wife started to nag me constantly. You know: Nag! Nag! Nag! I just don't know what to do. She is driving me nuts!"

"Ah!" cries the boss. "I am sure I can help you. You see, women need to feel that they are wanted. You have probably been neglecting her needs. For example, when I get home from work, I embrace my wife, kiss her passionately, remove her clothing piece by piece and carry her upstairs to bed."

"That sounds great!" cries the clerk.

"It is " replies the executive. "Why don't you give it a try? Take the afternoon off; she won't be expecting you, and the element of surprise will make it even better!"

"That is really kind of you, sir," says the clerk. "What is your address?"

And now... the meditation:

Be silent, close your eyes, and feel your body to be completely frozen.

This is the right moment to go in. Gather your life forces—your totality is needed—and rush towards your very center of being with absolute consciousness, and with an urgency that this moment could be your last moment on the earth. Only such urgency can bring you to the deepest center of your being.

Rush faster and faster, deeper and deeper.

As you are coming closer to the center, a great silence descends over you, almost like soft, cool rain. You can feel it, it is tangible.

A little closer and you find all around you flowers of peace blossoming.

A little more...and a great ecstasy makes you drunk with the divine.

Just one step more and you are at the very center of your being. For the first time you see your original face. Your original face is the face of the buddha.

I use the word "buddha" as a symbol of total awakening, of absolute enlightenment.

A great luminosity will surround you, a strange light that you have never seen before.

The only quality you have to remember at this moment is witnessing. That constitutes the buddha's whole being.

Witness that you are not the body.

Witness that you are not the mind.

Witness that you are only the witness.

To make this witnessing deeper…

Relax…

Let go, but keep remembering you are a buddha, and the buddha consists only of one energy, and that energy is witnessing.

At this moment, you start melting like ice in the ocean. This Gautama the Buddha Auditorium is becoming an ocean of consciousness. Ten thousand buddhas are disappearing into the ocean.

All separation is illusory, only oneness is the truth.

You must be the most blessed people on the earth, because everybody is worried about trivia. You are searching for the ultimate, the eternal, and you are very close to it.

A great blissfulness settles in your very center, flowers start showering on you. The whole existence is rejoicing with you.

Gather all these experiences.

You have to bring them to your day-to-day ordinary life—the peace, the serenity, the silence, the ecstasy, the music, the dance. Your life has to become a constant ceremony. Only then are you whole.

And don't forget to persuade the buddha to come a little closer still. He has come very close. It is your nature.

These are the three steps of meditation.

First, the buddha comes behind you like a shadow, but very solid and golden, with great splendor, and creating a new atmosphere around you, of benediction, of compassion, of bliss.

Second step: you become the shadow and the buddha is ahead of you, and your shadow is slowly slowly disappearing.

The third step: you have disappeared into the buddha, and only buddha is there, you are not. When this happens you are at the highest peak of existence, you have come home, you have arrived.

Now there is nowhere to go.

You become one with existence itself.

That's why I call my philosophy more authentically existential than the negative philosophies of the West. I am trying to bring the West and East together.

My whole effort is to make man richer, outwards and inwards, in a tremendous balance. This balance is Zen.

And remember: God is dead, and now Zen is the only living truth.

You are the pioneers of a new age, of a new man, of a new humanity.

...Now before you come back, persuade the buddha, because this is the fundamental step. He has to become your shadow.

Come back...but come back as a buddha, with the same grace, with the same silence, radiating the same joy.

Sit for a few seconds, just to remember the golden path you have traveled, and the experience of the beyond that has come so close, the mystery of your inner world, the space infinite, the time eternal.

And feel the presence of the buddha behind you.

This makes Friedrich Nietzsche's statement complete.

Without Zen it is incomplete and will drive people insane.

With Zen it becomes complete and will drive people to the uttermost sanity possible to human beings.

Chapter 2
God is an insult to man

When Sekito received the precepts, his master, Seigen, asked him,
"Now you have received the precepts, you want to learn the Vinaya, don't you?"
Sekito replied, "There's no need to learn the Vinaya."
Seigen asked, "Then, you want to read the book of Sheela?"
Sekito replied, "There's no need to read the book of Sheela."
Seigen asked, "Can you deliver a letter to Nangaku Osho?"
Sekito said, "Certainly."
Seigen said, "Go now, and come back quickly. If you come back even
a little late,
you will miss me. If you miss me, you cannot get the big hatchet
under my chair."
Soon Sekito reached Nangaku. Before handing over the letter, Sekito
made a bow
and asked, "Osho, when one neither follows the old saints
nor expresses one's
innermost soul, what will one do?"
Nangaku said, "Your question is too arrogant. Why don't you ask
modestly?"
To which Sekito replied, "Then it would be better to sink into hell
eternally and
not ever hope for the liberation that the old saints know."
Sekito, finding that he and Nangaku were not attuned to each other,
soon left for
Seigen without giving Nangaku the letter. On his arrival, Seigen asked,
"Did they entrust something to you?"
Sekito said, "They didn't entrust anything to me."
Seigen said, "But there must have been a reply."
Sekito said, "If they don't entrust anything, there is no reply." Then he said,
"When I was leaving here, you added that I should come back soon
to receive
the big hatchet under the chair. Now I have come back, please give me
the big hatchet."
Seigen was silent. Sekito bowed down and retired.

Friends, before I answer your questions, I have to answer two letters by very knowledgeable idiots. This distinction has to be remembered. There is a certain ignorance that knows, and there is a certain knowledgeability that knows nothing.

One is a Buddhist scholar, and he writes that "An enlightened man cannot be concerned with the trivia of the ordinary world and its concerns."

It means, according to him, I am an ignorant man. It is a compliment to me because every enlightened man finally becomes as ignorant as a child, or as innocent as a child. Socrates' last words were, "I don't know anything."

This man is a scholar but blind. Does he think that a third world war which is going to erase the whole of humanity is trivia? Does he think that the explosion of the population in this country is trivia when it is going to kill almost five hundred million people in the coming ten years? And if these are trivia then I have to take him back to Gautam Buddha.

He was concerned that no sannyasin of his should have more than three pieces of clothes—that is trivia. He was concerned that no sannyasin of his should wear shoes—that is trivia. He was concerned that no sannyasin should eat more than one time in a day—that is trivia. And still he is enlightened and I am ignorant. This is what I call a knowledgeable idiot.

Buddha has made thirty-three thousand rules for his disciples—all trivia. Where can you find thirty-three thousand truths? Truth is one and inexpressible. But he was concerned with absolute trivia.

One sannyasin was going to spread his message and had come for his last word, because he might not be coming back to him for two or three years. And what was his message? "Don't see a woman." Now, unless you see, you cannot decide whether the person is a woman or a man.

I don't understand what kind of nonsense Buddha was talking. How are you going to know that the person coming towards you is a woman? You have to see first, then you can close your eyes—but you have seen. And once you have seen a beautiful woman and you close your eyes, she becomes more beautiful. Is it not trivia?

And Buddha told him, "You have to keep your eyes just four feet ahead of you. Just look only four feet ahead and keep your eyes down, so even if you come across a woman you only see her feet." This is great spiritual stuff!

The man was a little puzzled. He said, "I will try my best, but if by chance I happen to see a woman accidentally—suddenly a woman comes out of the forest or on a crossroad—what should I do?"

Buddha said, "If you accidentally see a woman, don't talk to her." Is it great spirituality? Don't even say, "Hello," because she is a woman!

And the man insisted. He said, "If the woman says something, will it not be embarrassing to not answer her? Will it not be inhuman?"

Buddha said, "If such a coincidence happens, you can talk to her, but don't touch her." Is this spiritual stuff?

What do you call trivia? The whole humanity is going to die and I should not speak!? And your Gautam Buddha is talking absolute nonsense to his people.

And the man was intelligent enough. He said, "There may be a situation in which I have to touch a woman. Perhaps a woman has fallen in a well, what am I supposed to do? Or in a ditch, what am I supposed to do? Should I just go on without looking at her miserable state, without helping her?"

And Buddha said, "If such a coincidence happens, you can touch. But remember, all that is outside is illusory."

If it is illusory then why make the first point? The woman is illusory and don't touch her! What is the problem if you touch an illusion? Don't talk to the illusion! Don't look at the illusion! This I call absolute trivia.

These Buddhist scholars are going to provoke me. I will pull down Gautam Buddha completely!

My concern for humanity makes me ignorant, and his concern about women and about clothes and about shoes, and about not touching women, not looking more than four feet ahead, makes him enlightened! His enlightenment is rotten! It is a bullock-cart enlightenment.

I am a contemporary man, twenty-five centuries ahead of Gautam Buddha. He is just old hat.

But these Buddhist scholars are provoking me. I will start talking about Gautam Buddha and will pull down the whole house that he has built, because it is built on all these stupid things.

My concern for humanity is absolutely spiritual. My concern for this beautiful planet is sacred. It is my compassion and my love. And I don't care about any Gautam Buddha. I am a buddha in my own right, and your old Buddha is too out of date. I belong to my time, and I speak the language of my time.

Buddha was afraid to allow women in his commune. For twenty years continuously he refused women. What was the fear? He did not trust his own sannyasins; this was distrust. A master distrusting his own people? He was afraid that if women enter into the commune, then what will happen to the celibacy of the monks? But if their celibacy is so thin that the entry of a woman is going to disturb their celibacy, it is not much of a celibacy.

They must have been homosexuals, as we are finding now in every monastery around the world that all kinds of sexual perversions are practiced. It cannot have been otherwise for Buddha's disciples. Only my people are living a natural, sacred, existential life, not against the current, not against the universe.

And without listening to me, without reading me, these idiots go on making their comments.

My whole effort is to bring materialism and spirituality into balance. To me the outside world is as real as the inside world. Naturally this creates trouble for me from both sides. The communists have written books against me, for the reason that I am teaching spirituality and meditation and diverting people from their real concern, a classless society. And I am making people selfish because I am just telling them to go in.

And the spiritualists are against me; they have written books against me, and articles, and every day there are letters. Their problem is that I am taking too much interest in the world. A man of real spirituality should close his eyes, because the world is illusory.

But none of your so-called and self-styled enlightened people have taken the trouble to think twice. When you say the world is illusory, then there is no need to renounce it. Nobody renounces dreams. Do you renounce your dream when you wake up in the morning? A dream is just a dream, there is no question of renouncing it. And if you are having a sweet dream, I say enjoy it.

Make this whole world a sweet dream, not a nightmare. All your politicians and all your priests are trying to make it a nightmare. Then naturally people think to renounce it, it is such a tragedy.

But I am not in favor of renouncing the world, and I don't say that the world is illusory; otherwise, why does Buddha go on begging every day? If the world is illusory why are you going to beg before an illusory house? And when a woman gives you food, she is illusory and the food is real?!

Why do you need three pieces of clothes? This was the criticism of Mahavira, Buddha's contemporary, who lived naked. He did not accept Buddha as enlightened because he did not live naked. Three pieces of clothes were luxury to Mahavira, a man who lived naked in summer, in winter, in rain. Naturally he has the right to say to Buddha, "You are living in great luxury. Three pieces of clothes! You are too materialistic."

Buddha ate one meal a day; to Mahavira that was luxury. In the twelve years before Mahavira became enlightened, he ate on only three hundred and sixty-five days. In twelve years he ate for only one year—not continuously. Two months passed, and then one day he would eat; three months passed, and one day he would eat. That means, on average, that out of eleven days he would eat on one day. Of course, to him Buddha is indulging in luxury. These are relative terms.

And Buddha was criticizing Mahavira for such trivial things, because he could not find answers to Mahavira's criticism that he was living in luxury—daily food, three pieces of clothes. He found another way to criticize him, because the followers of Mahavira were saying that Mahavira is omnipotent, omnipresent, omniscient, with all the qualities of God. And Buddha was laughing at Mahavira, telling his disciples, "This fellow, this guy, says that he is omniscient, all knowing, and I know him…Once he was begging before a house in which nobody lived. And he talks about knowing everything: past, present, future, and he does not know that the house is empty, there is nobody there. For years it has been empty, and this man is omniscient?

"And one day he was passing early in the morning, going to the river, when he stamped on the tail of a dog who was fast asleep on the road. When the dog started barking, then he realized. And this man is omniscient, all knowing, and he does not know that a dog is lying just in front of him?"

Do you think these criticisms are very spiritual? Neither are Mahavira's criticisms very spiritual, nor are Buddha's criticisms very spiritual. Just trivia.

So I want to tell this Buddhist scholar to consider again who is enlightened.

The other is also a Buddhist scholar, and he had said to me, "I have been reading your books on Buddha, and I have appreciated them very much." But he never then wrote any letter to me, nor any letter to the newspapers.

It is a strange thing: when I was saying things in appreciation, nobody ever wrote a single word. They thought what I was saying was really the meaning of Buddha's sutras. It was not!

The meaning was given by me, and I can take it away. I can tear down all your scriptures point by point!

Now he has published a letter in the newspapers. Now he says, that I cannot have *samadhi*—enlightenment—because I don't have *sheel*, I have only *pragya*. He does not understand at all—neither Buddha nor me. Pragya is a by-product of samadhi, of enlightenment. Pragya means wisdom. Unless you become enlightened, you cannot have wisdom, you can have only knowledge. And pragya does not mean knowledge, it means wisdom. It is a by-product of samadhi, enlightenment.

But he has no experience of samadhi, he has just seen the scriptures. And you will see in the coming sutra, an authentic seeker simply denies that he has anything to do with sheel. Sheel means character. Now he is concerned with my character, saying that without character you cannot become enlightened. What does he know about my character? And has he ever thought about the character of Buddha?

For twenty-nine years continuously Buddha was indulging in sex, and not only with his wife, he had many concubines. His father was told when he was born that either he would become a world emperor, or he would renounce the world and become an enlightened one. These were the two alternatives. Of course his father wanted him to become a world emperor.

So he asked how to prevent him from becoming enlightened. "I want him to become the world emperor." He was a small king in a small kingdom. Arun has just brought from Nepal a picture of the palace—which is in ruins—where Buddha was born. Even in ruins you can see the kingdom was not great. The palace looks like just an ordinary big house. And it was in just a small village on the border of Nepal and India. Naturally his father must have had the ambition of Buddha becoming a great world conqueror.

And the astrologers suggested, "If you want him to be prevented from enlightenment, then make every comfort and luxury possible for him. He should grow up in luxury and indulgence. He should not see anybody old, anybody dead. Even the flowers which are going to fall down should be removed before he sees them. All pale leaves which are going to fall should be removed.

"And he should be made to live in different palaces in different seasons, so he never comes to feel any season is a trouble. So three palaces were made in different places: one for the summer, one for the winter, one for the rain. And great gardens were created around the palaces. And his father collected all the beautiful girls from the kingdom, to be his concubines. He was surrounded with women, music, wine for twenty-nine years, and he had a wife and a son. And he became enlightened.

I don't have a son, I don't have a wife, I don't have concubines, I don't even have a girlfriend. And I don't have character? And Buddha has character! No man has indulged more than Gautam Buddha. What character...?

He had five disciples before his enlightenment. They were disciples because he was an ascetic. He was torturing himself fasting and had become just a skeleton. And these five disciples were immensely impressed by his self-torture. The whole of humanity lives with this idea: if you torture yourself you are a saint.

The day he became enlightened, he dropped all self-torture; it was absolutely useless. All the five disciples left him immediately: he has fallen, fallen from saintliness. He had become enlightened, and those five disciples who had been with him for many years, respecting him as a great saint, just left him, saying, "He has fallen. He has started eating, he has started having warm clothes."

Perhaps these Buddhist scholars don't understand anything at all except the scriptures.

Character arises out of enlightenment, it is not vice versa. It is not character that produces enlightenment, otherwise enlightenment would have a cause to it. Enlightenment is your nature; it has no cause. It is already there, you just have to discover it. It does not matter what kind of character you have. If you go inwards the sinner will find the buddha just as much as the saint. And after you have found your enlightenment, the radiation of the enlightenment becomes your character, your *sheel*.

Your enlightenment becomes your innocence, and out of that innocence arises wisdom. But wisdom is not knowledge, it is simply transparent clarity about everything, inner or outer.

But these knowledgeable idiots simply prove one thing that I have been continuously telling you: don't get involved in scholarship, don't get involved in knowledgeability. That is the greatest barrier to enlightenment, because you are so full of knowledge, and all knowledge is of the mind.

Enlightenment is not of the mind, it is the fragrance of no-mind. No-mind is not based on any character. Just the contrary: all character arises out of the clarity of no-mind. So it is not imposed from outside as a discipline. It arises as a spontaneous response. You simply cannot do any evil. It is not a question of your deciding not to do evil, you simply cannot do it. You are so full of light, how can you behave like a blind man? You are so full of light, how can you behave like a man stumbling in darkness?

So character arises, wisdom arises, and a thousand other things: blissfulness, ecstasy, benediction, compassion. There is no end; more and more flowers go on flowering.

But this is the difficulty of the knowledgeable person. He has accepted a certain fixed formula.

I want you to know absolutely clearly that just as everything goes on expanding and growing, even enlightenment becomes clearer, deeper, higher as time passes. After twenty-five centuries, I am not going to be a replica of Gautam Buddha. I have nothing to learn from him. If anything has to be, he has to learn something from me. Twenty-five centuries have not been a mere wastage. Just as everything is progressing and evolving, so is consciousness.

But every scholar gets completely fucked-up! He thinks only in terms of his scripture, and the scripture is twenty-five centuries old. I am a contemporary man, and I do not belong to any category. I am a category in myself. I decide according to my spontaneous response, not according to any commandments, not according to any discipline. Whether the discipline is given by Buddha or Mahavira or Christ or Krishna, it does not matter; they are all old. But these people are living in the past.

I am moving moment to moment into the future. I have left Gautam Buddha twenty-five centuries behind. His enlightenment also is twenty-five centuries old. So much dust has gathered on it. But my mirror of consciousness is absolutely fresh, and I am not going to listen to anybody. Nobody is my master! And nobody has the right to tell me what character is and what is wisdom and what is enlightenment. Nobody has that right.

I am a man absolutely free. I live my life according to my own light. I am nobody's follower, and I don't live my life according to any scripture. These idiots should shut up! Because of them I will be provoked to condemn Buddha and Mahavira and Krishna and everybody! And they won't have any argument against me.

How can these people say that Buddha was not concerned with trivia? He was concerned. And my concern is not trivia.

My concern is a third world war that is hanging just on the horizon. Any moment there will be no life on earth, and no possibility of any buddha! And you call it trivia?

Beware of scholars. They are the most idiotic people in the world.

Now your questions.

God is dead, but that creates the question: Who began this universe?

There is no need for anybody to begin it, because there is no beginning to this universe, and there is no end.

This question has been exploited by all the religions, because everybody wants to know who began the universe. Your minds are so small that they cannot conceive a beginningless universe, an endless universe, just eternity to eternity. Because you cannot conceive that vastness, your question arises, "Who created the universe? Who began it?" But if there was somebody to begin it, there already must have been a universe. Do you see the simple arithmetic? If there was somebody already to begin it, then you cannot call it "the beginning," because somebody was already there.

If you think that a God is necessary…it gives you consolation that God created the world, so you have a beginning. But who created God? Again you fall into the same problem.

But all the religions have said that God exists eternally; there is no creator of God. If that can be true for God, why can it not be true for existence itself? It is autonomous, it exists on its own. There is no need of any creator because that creator will require another creator, and you will fall into an absurd regress. You can go from A to Z. But who created Z? The question remains standing, you simply go on pushing against it. But the problem is not solved because you have asked a wrong question.

The universe has no beginning. It is not a creation by anybody. It has no end. And remember, if it had any beginning, then there would certainly be an end. Every beginning is a beginning of an end; every birth is the beginning of death. So it is good! Get rid of God, because if he can create the world he can destroy the world also, and any world that is created is bound to be destroyed sooner or later. If there is birth, there is death. Only a beginningless universe can be endless.

So your problem is just because the capacity of the mind is very limited. That's why I want you to go beyond mind. Only no-mind can conceive the beginningless, the endless. The incomprehensible becomes absolutely clear; there is no problem at all. Those who have risen beyond mind have also risen beyond God simultaneously. God is a need of the mind because the mind cannot conceive of infinite, eternal things. It can only conceive of very limited things.

The question arises because of your mind's incapacity, its impotence.

You ask, "God is dead, but that creates the question: Who began this universe?" But have you ever considered that the existence of God will not solve the question? On the contrary, the question will be pushed a step back: Who created God? Any hypothesis that does not destroy the question is absolutely useless. Any answer that keeps on pushing the question further back but does not touch it at all, is not the answer.

The only answer you will find is in your own experience of eternity. Then you will know nobody has created it. It has no beginning, no end. *You* don't have any beginning, you don't have any end. When you experience it within your own self, you know existence is autonomous, it is not created.

A created thing cannot be more than a mechanism; it cannot be an organic reality. A car is created, man is not created. If man is also created then he becomes a mechanism, a robot. You can dismantle a car, take all the pieces apart, the wheels and everything, and you can put them back together and the car will be perfectly okay. But cut a man into pieces and then join them together—still the man will not be restored.

An organic phenomenon cannot be dissected. The moment you dissect it, its very mystery disappears. Then you can rejoin those parts, but you will have only a corpse, not a living human being.

It is the dignity of existence that it is not created. It is the dignity of man that he is not created. God is an insult to existence, to man, to consciousness, to everything. God is a humiliation. God is not a solution for any problem; in fact, he creates more problems in the world. He does not solve anything. There are three hundred religions in the world and all are fighting with each other. These are all created because of the concept of God, because they have all invented their own concepts.

The Hindu god has three heads. Just think of the poor fellow! Imagine if you had three heads; I don't think you would be able to stand up. One head will be falling to this side, one head will be falling to that side, this head will be falling to another side, the very weight... I have seen statues and pictures of the Hindu god. His body seems to be like a man's body, and a man's body cannot manage three heads.

I have seen children in circuses that are freaks of nature. I have seen children with two heads, but they cannot even sit up; they are just lying down. The circus is enjoying their tragedy, earning money from it. They have to carry them around on trolleys.

The Hindu god must be living in a trolley. One head will always be pushed into the pillow, breathing will be difficult. Walking is out of the question. And all the three heads, who have one body, have wives. Just see the tragedy! Each head is joined with two other heads, and each has a separate wife. Three wives to one man, because the sexual machinery is only one. I have never heard that the Indian god has three sexual machineries. Now, I cannot figure out how things are managed.

... These fictions create three hundred religions, because everybody is free to have his own fiction. Why borrow anybody else's fiction? There are religions that think God has a thousand hands. One thousand hands? They must be growing all over the body just like branches in a tree. I don't think he can manage to do anything. One thousand hands? From the back they will be growing backwards, from the front they will be growing…there will be no space left for anything else!

There are gods that have a thousand eyes — I cannot conceive it. Even with no-mind I cannot conceive it! A thousand eyes in one head? Then there is no space for ears, no space for the nose, no possibility for the mouth, no possibility for anything—not even hair. He must be bald, with eyes all over the head. Even then I don't think he can manage one thousand eyes. How will he move? According to which eye will he see? Even if he winks at a woman, which eye to use? One thousand eyes winking at one woman? That will be real romance!

The existence of God has not solved any problem. On the contrary, God has created thousands of problems. And every religion has its own idea, because it is a fiction. You don't have different ideas about the sun. You don't have different ideas about the rose. You can have only different ideas about a fiction. It is then up to you, whichever way you want to imagine it.

The Bible says God created man in his own image. The reality is just the opposite: Man has created God in his own image. And he has been trying to refine the image of God, finding explanations for all kinds of absurdities. He needs a thousand hands because he has to care for five billion people. But if you have to care about five billion people, you need five billion hands. One thousand hands won't do. At least, if you want to shake hands with the whole of humanity, you will need five billion hands. Just hands and hands and nothing else! You go on shaking hands with God, and nobody is there!

They go on finding explanations: he has one thousand eyes because he has to look after the whole universe. Can't he move his head, just the way I am moving mine? I can see ten thousand people without any difficulty, just with two eyes. Does he not move backwards and go in reverse? He has eyes all over his head, so when he wants to go backwards, the front eyes are closed, the backward eyes are open. When he wants to go sideways, three sides are closed, the right side is open. Is it a god, or some kind of toy to entertain children?

The very idea of God is because our minds cannot comprehend eternity. Once you rise beyond your limited mind to an unlimited no-mind, you can conceive all that was inconceivable before. No God is needed.

? Is there any place for prayer in religion if there is no God?

There is no place for prayer, because prayer is God-oriented. If there is no God, to whom can you pray? All prayers are false because there is nobody to answer them, nobody to hear them. All prayers are humiliations, insults, degradations. All prayers are disgusting! You are kneeling down to a fiction which does not exist.

And what are you doing in your prayers? Begging. "Give me this, give me that"—utterly beggarly—"God, give me my daily bread!" Can't you ask once for all? Why do you have to ask every day? And five billion people asking, with only one person listening — do you think he will remain sane? "Give me my daily bread!" Why not ask for the whole of your life and be finished? One prayer will do.

But every day you are bothering him, nagging him like a wife, morning and evening. And there are Mohammedans who do five prayers a day. They are the great naggers.

I used to go to conduct meditation camps in Udaipur. It was a long journey from the place where I lived, in Jabalpur. It took thirty-six hours because there was no plane between the two places at that time. In Jabalpur there was an airport, but it was a military airport and they were not allowed to open it for the public. So I had to go in a train and change at many junctions. First I would have to change at Katni, then I would have to change at Bina, then I would have to change at Agra. Then I would have to change at Chittaurgarh, and finally I would reach Udaipur. It would be evening when the train reached Chittaurgarh, and Ajmer is very close to Chittaurgarh. Ajmer is one of the strongholds of the Mohammedans, so in the train there were many Mohammedans. And the train had to stay at the station for one hour for some other train to arrive, which was bringing passengers to go on to Udaipur.

So for one hour I used to walk on the platform. All the Mohammedans lining the platform were sitting in prayer, and I was enjoying them. I would just go near somebody and say, "The train is leaving," and he would jump up. Then he would be angry at me, "You disturbed my prayer!"

I would say, "I did not disturb anybody's prayer. I am simply doing my prayer. This is my heartfelt desire that the train should be leaving. I was not talking to you; I don't even know your name."

He would say, "This is strange…in the middle of my prayer?"

I would say, "It was not prayer, because I was watching — you have been looking again and again at the train." The person would admit, "That is true."

And it was the same all over the platform. I would go near a few people further up the platform and just whisper, "The train is leaving," and again another person would jump up and would become very angry: "What kind of person are you? You look religious, and you disturb people in their prayer?"

I said, "I am not disturbing anybody. I am just praying to God that the train should leave now."

What are your prayers? Begging for this, begging for that. Your prayer reduces you to a beggar. Meditation transforms you into an emperor.

There is nobody to hear your prayers; there is nobody to answer your prayers. All religions go on making you extrovert so that you don't turn inwards. Prayer is an extrovert thing: God is there, and you are shouting to that God. But it is taking you away from yourself.

Every prayer is irreligious.

I have often told a beautiful story by Leo Tolstoy.

The archbishop of the Orthodox Church of Russia—it is a story set before the revolution— became very worried when many people from his congregation started going towards a lake, where there were three villagers. They lived on a small island in the lake and they sat under a tree, together with thousands of people who thought they were saints.

In Christianity you cannot be a saint on your own account. The word "saint" comes from "sanction." It has to be sanctioned by the church that you are a saint; it is a certificate.

It is such an ugly idea that the church can give you a certificate that you are a saint. Even a man like Francis of Assisi, a beautiful man, was summoned by the pope: "People have started worshipping you like a saint, and you don't have any certificate."

That's where I feel Francis missed the point. He should have refused, but he knelt just like a Christian and asked the pope, "Give me the certificate." Otherwise he was a nice man, a beautiful man, but I don't mention his name because he acted in a very stupid way. This is not the way of a saint.

I don't need anybody's certificate for my enlightenment or for my buddhahood. I declare it! I don't need anybody's certificate. Who can give me the certificate? Even Gautam Buddha cannot give me the certificate. Who gave *him* a certificate?

But the idea of "sainthood" in English is very wrong. It comes from *sanctus*.

So the archbishop of Russia was very angry: "Who are these saints? I have not certified anybody in years. Where have these saints suddenly come from?" But people were going to see them, and the church was becoming more and more empty every day.

Finally the archbishop decided to go and see who these people were. He took a boat and went to the island. Those three villagers…they were uneducated, simple people, utterly innocent. And the archbishop was a powerful man; next to the czar he was the most powerful man in Russia. He was very angry at those three villagers and he told them, "Who made you saints?"

They looked at each other. They said, "Nobody. And we don't think we are saints, we are poor people."

"But why are so many people coming here?"

They said, "You have to ask them."

The archbishop asked them, "Do you know the orthodox prayer of the church?"

They said, "We are uneducated and the prayer is too long; we cannot remember it."

"So what prayer do you say?"

They all looked at each other. "You tell him," said one. "*You* tell him," said another. They were feeling embarrassed. But the archbishop became more and more arrogant, seeing that these were absolute idiots: They don't even know the prayer. How can they be saints?

So he said, "Any of you can tell me — just say it!"

They said, "We are feeling very embarrassed because we have made up our own prayer, not knowing the authorized prayer of the church. We have made up our own prayer, very simple it is. Please forgive us that we did not ask your permission to use it, but we were feeling so embarrassed we did not come to see you."

They said, "God is three and we are also three, so we have made up the prayer like this: 'You are three and we are three, have mercy on us.' This is our prayer."

The archbishop was really angry now: "This is no prayer! I have never heard this kind of thing." Then he started laughing.

Those poor fellows said, "You teach us what the real prayer is. We thought it was perfectly all right: God is three, we are three, and what more is needed? Just have mercy on us."

So the archbishop recited the orthodox prayer, which was very long. By the time he ended, they said, "We have forgotten the beginning." So he recited the beginning again. Then they said, "We have forgotten the end."

Now he was getting irritated. He said, "What kind of people are you? Can't you remember a simple prayer?"

They said, "It is so long, and we are uneducated, and such big words. We cannot…please just be patient with us. If you repeat it two or three more times perhaps we will get the knack of it." So he repeated it three times. They said, "Okay, we will try, but we are afraid that it may not be the complete prayer…some things may be missing…but we will try."

The arrogant archbishop was very much satisfied that he had finished off these three saints and he could tell his people, "They are idiots. Why are you going there?" He left in his boat.

Suddenly he saw that behind his boat those three people were running on the water, coming after him. He could not believe his eyes! He rubbed his eyes… and by that time they had reached the side of his boat, standing on the water. They said, "Just one time more, we forgot."

But seeing the situation—"these people are walking on water and I am going in the boat"— the archbishop understood. He said, "You continue your prayer. Don't bother about what I have said to you. Just forgive me, I was arrogant. Your simpleness, your innocence is your prayer. You just go back. You don't need any certificate."

But the three fellows insisted, "You have come so far. Just one time more? We know we might forget it, but one time more so we can try to remember it."

But the archbishop said, "I have been repeating that prayer my whole life, and it has not been heard. You are walking on water, and we have heard only in the miracles of Jesus that he used to walk on water. This is the first time I have seen the miracle. You just go back. Your prayer is perfectly all right!"

The prayer was not the thing, because there is nobody to hear it — but their utter innocence and trust transformed them into totally new beings, so fresh, so childlike, just like rose flowers opening in the early morning sun in all their beauty. Now that his arrogance was dropped, the archbishop could see their faces, their innocence, their grace, their blissfulness. They went back over the water, running hand in hand, and reached their tree.

Leo Tolstoy was denied the Nobel Prize because of such stories. He was nominated. The Nobel Prize committee opens its records every fifty years. When they were opened in 1950, researchers rushed to see in the records whose names were nominated and canceled, and what the reason was. Leo Tolstoy was nominated but he was never given the prize. And the reason written was that he is not an orthodox Christian. He wrote such beautiful stories, such novels…Although he was a Christian, he was not an orthodox Christian, so the Nobel Prize could not be given to him.

But it was never made public to the world that the Nobel Prize exists only for orthodox Christians. Leo Tolstoy was one of the most simple-hearted, innocent people, one of the most creative persons the world has ever known. His novels have such a beauty. His life was also very simple, although he was a count. His forefathers had belonged to the royal family and he still had a vast estate and thousands of acres of land and thousands of slaves, peasants.

His wife was angry with him—for his whole life this was a trouble—because he lived like a peasant and worked like the peasants in the fields. He was very friendly with the peasants. He slept in their poor huts and ate their food. They could not believe it. They said, "Master, you are our owner."

He said, "No. We are all sharing. I work with you, I can eat with you, I can sleep here."

His wife was really angry. She was a countess; she herself belonged to a very rich family, another count's family, and she could not believe he was this kind of man. "He lives with those dirty people, he eats their food. He goes to work in the field. He does not need to do that!"

And such a simple man, innocent man, creative man was denied the Nobel Prize on the grounds that he was not of the Orthodox church, he did not belong to the orthodox line of fanatic Christians. Even I was amazed when I read that statement. So the Nobel Prize was just for orthodox and fanatic Christians, politicians, not for creative artists.

You are asking, "Is there any place for prayer in religion?" None at all.

In an authentic religion, meditation has a place, but not prayer. Prayer is extrovert, meditation is introvert. Meditation makes you a buddha, prayer simply makes you a beggar. And prayer is fiction-oriented, meditation is truth-oriented. Meditation is Zen, and prayer is nothing but part and parcel of the fiction called God. Avoid prayers. They are taking you away from your own existential reality. Go deeper into meditation. That is the only religiousness possible.

Now the sutras:

When Sekito received the precepts, his master, Seigen, asked him, "Now you have received the precepts, you want to learn the Vinaya, don't you?"

Vinaya is one of the scriptures of Gautam Buddha. The whole name is *Vinaya Pitak*.

Seigen asked Sekito, "You are initiated into sannyas, do you now want to learn the scriptures called *Vinaya*?" The word *vinaya* means humbleness. It is one of the series of discourses of Buddha.

Sekito replied, "There is no need to learn the Vinaya."

There is no need to learn the scriptures because truth is never found in any scripture. Truth is not a philosophy or a theology. There is no need.

Sekito was sent to Seigen by his master, Eno. He was already ripe, but because Eno felt his own death was coming too fast—he was very old—and perhaps he would not be able to see the enlightenment of Sekito, he felt it was better to send him to a master who could help him in the last stages of his evolution. So he sent Sekito to Seigen, who had been his lifelong competitor. But both recognized each other in their hearts as enlightened.

Sekito was not a beginner, so when Seigen asked, "Would you like to learn the scriptures?" He said, "There is no need to learn the scriptures."

Seigen asked, "Then, do you want to read the book of Sheela—the book of character? If you don't want to learn scriptures about humbleness, would you like to know the scriptures that deal with character and morality?"

Sheela means character. This is what the Buddhist scholar has raised in his question against me: without *sheela* how can you become enlightened?

Sekito replied—and this is the reply of a man who was coming very close to enlightenment—"There is no need to read the book of Sheela, because all these things will follow enlightenment.

They don't precede it, they succeed it."

Enlightenment contains immense treasures. You just become enlightened and everything follows. You don't have to learn, you don't have to discipline yourself, you don't have to make any effort. Everything spontaneously follows you. Just first become a buddha.

So Sekito said, "There is no need to read the book of character and morality."

Seigen asked, "Can you deliver a letter to Nangaku Osho?"

Nangaku was another famous master, and this was just a strategy of Seigen. He was trying to figure out where Sekito was. All these questions were not for the sake of any answers; Seigen was trying to figure out the newly-arrived person who had lived with a great master, Eno — how far has he reached? How deep has he reached He was trying to figure Sekito out from every nook and corner, so that he could know how ripe he was, and know how much ripening he needed. So this was another methodology. He failed when asking about the *Vinaya* scriptures; Sekito answered exactly as if he was already enlightened. He asked about the *Sheela* scriptures, and he answered exactly as if he was already enlightened.

Then he tried a different way. He said,

"Can you deliver a letter to Nangaku Osho?"

Nangaku lived in another mountain monastery nearby.

Sekito said, "Certainly."
Seigen said, "Go now, and come back quickly. If you come back even
a little late, you will miss me. If you miss me, you cannot get the big
hatchet under my chair."
Soon Sekito reached Nangaku. Before handing over the letter, Sekito made
a bow and asked, "Osho, when one neither follows the old saints nor ex-
presses one's innermost soul, what will one do?"

His question is very important. He is saying—with absolute respect—he is saying,

"Osho, when one neither follows the old saints nor expresses one's
innermost soul, what will one do?"
Nangaku said, "Your question is too arrogant."

Nobody asks such a question immediately. You entered into my temple and you started asking me questions. First, you need initiation. First, you have to be a disciple. I am not here to waste my time on anybody who passes by and asks any type of question. This is arrogance."

It was not arrogance, but that was part of the strategy of Seigen. Nangaku was a very different kind of master.

Nangaku said, "Your question is too arrogant. Why don't you ask modestly?"
To which Sekito replied, "Then it would be better to sink into hell eternally
and not ever hope for the liberation that the old saints know."

"If you call my question arrogant, then I would rather suffer eternally in hell than ask you any question modestly."

No question is ever modest. Every question has to be, in a certain way, arrogant. When you are questioning, you are showing doubt, you are interfering in the silence of the master. Obviously, every question is arrogant, no question can be modest. Only silence is modest. But that is not a question. That is the answer.

But Sekito was really a man with a spine, with guts. He said, "Forget all about the question. I will not ask the question modestly, because no question can be asked modestly. The very question is arrogant. Any question is a doubt. *Any* question is interfering in the energy field of the master.

"Only silence can be modest. But then I wouldn't have to come to you. I could be silent anywhere. I could be silent even in the eternal fire of hell."

Sekito is really a man of great intelligence and great courage. Nangaku could not put him down. He was sent specially to Nangaku, who was known to be very hard. Seigen wanted to know Sekito's response, what response he would make to Nangaku. And he really made the right response! He said, "Forget all about the question. I would rather fall into hell eternally than ask you a question with modesty. No question is modest, howsoever put. I have asked it very respectfully. I have called you 'Osho' and you call my question arrogant? Rather than answering it you are insulting me.

"No master insults his disciples, and I am not even a disciple. I am just a stranger, and you are not being nice to me. I am just a guest. You should welcome me. Rather than welcoming me, you are humiliating me. I am not going to ask any question."

Sekito, finding that he and Nangaku were not attuned to each other, soon left for Seigen without giving Nangaku the letter.

That man does not deserve even the letter. He did not stay there, he immediately left.

On his arrival, Seigen asked, "Did they entrust something to you?"
Sekito said, "They did not entrust anything to me."
Seigen said "But there must have been a reply."
Sekito said, "If they don't entrust anything, there is no reply." Then he said,
"When I was leaving here, you added that I should come back soon to
receive the big hatchet under the chair. Now I have come back, please
give me the big hatchet."
Seigen was silent. Sekito bowed down and retired.

The silence of Seigen was his acceptance of Sekito, his courage. He knew that the letter had not been delivered, that there had not been any reply, although Sekito had not mentioned the letter. Sekito simply said, "They did not entrust anything to me, so how can there be any reply?"

Seigen saw the man, he saw that he has the quality and deserves to be enlightened. Seigen's silence was his hatchet. He was saying, "When you come, I am going to cut off your head with a hatchet."

And now Sekito reminded him, "Now I have come back, please give me the big hatchet. Cut off my head. Do whatsoever you want to do, I am ready."

Seigen was silent. In that deep silence is the transfer, the transmission of the lamp. It is not a question of language; it is a question of a transfer of energy. Just simply in that silence the flame jumped from Seigen to Sekito. And because he received the flame, the fire, he immediately bowed down and retired. Now there is no need to disturb the master. He has been accepted, not only accepted; the last step for which he had come has been delivered.

Eno was dead before Sekito became enlightened. In fact, the moment Sekito left Eno, before he reached to Seigen, Eno died. He was absolutely aware that his death was coming close, and that Seigen was the right person to whom Sekito should be handed over. He was absolutely correct in his judgment; it was Seigen who finally managed Sekito's enlightenment.

But enlightenment happens in silence. That's why my whole effort is to make you as silent as possible. Then you don't need even a Seigen. Sitting anywhere—in your room, under a tree, in the garden, by the side of the river, anywhere—if your silence deepens, existence itself gives you the initiation into buddhahood. And when it comes directly from existence itself, it has a far greater beauty than when it comes through a master.

I teach immediate, sudden enlightenment. The meditation that you are practicing is just preparing you for that great silence in which existence will become a flame inside you.

Etsujin wrote this haiku:

Falling
but with easy hearts –
poppies.

The flowers are falling with easy hearts. They are not even looking back to the plant they have been blossoming on, the plant that has been their home for so long, the plant that has been their nourishment for so long. Now they are going back to the earth from where they have come.

Falling, but with easy hearts…There is no regret. They enjoyed the sun, they enjoyed the moon, they enjoyed the stars. They danced in the wind, they danced in the rain, they danced, celebrated. What more does one need? It is time to go into eternal rest. That's why their hearts are easy, no tension, no anxiety. They lived totally, they are dying dancingly. They are falling very easily toward the earth where they will disappear again. They came from the earth, they are going back to the earth; the round is complete.

Just as flowers arise from the earth and go back to the earth for eternal rest, you come from existence and you return to existence if you have an easy heart. Then you will not be coming again into the imprisonment of a body. You will simply go back to the very source you have come from, to eternal rest.

That eternal rest is *nirvana*, that eternal rest is *moksha*, that eternal rest is liberation. That eternal rest is *samadhi*, truth, enlightenment—different names for the same experience. You have come back home, and you have come back home dancing, with no regret, with no complaint, with easy hearts, peacefully and silently to disappear. This is the most exquisite experience, when you are on the verge of disappearing with an easy and relaxed heart, a simple and pure let-go.

> **In his book, The Antichrist, Nietzsche states: "People who still believe in themselves still also have their own God. In him they venerate the conditions through which they have prospered, their virtues—they project their joy in themselves, their feeling of power, onto a being whom one can thank for them." Would you like to comment?**

Nietzsche wrote his book *The Antichrist* in the insane asylum. But he was such a genius that even though he was declared insane by all the psychiatrists, his books prove they were wrong. Even in his insanity he was far saner than your so-called sane psychiatrists. Even in his death—he wrote his last letter to a friend—he did not forget...He had always signed his name, "Antichrist, Friedrich Nietzsche". Even at the moment of death he did not forget to write "Antichrist" first, then his name.

And in that insane asylum he wrote many things which are of tremendous importance. The Antichrist is one of the books that will help you to understand Nietzsche's depth. Although he never went beyond the mind, he managed even with his mind to reach to great heights and to great depths.

He was anti-Christ his whole life. He said, "Christ's teachings are a humiliation to humanity because he calls humanity sheep and calls himself the shepherd. He says humanity has committed the original sin, and he calls himself the savior. Just believe in him and he will save you? This is the ultimate insult to anyone who understands."

That's why Sekito said, "I would rather suffer eternal hell than ask you the question again. We don't fit with each other. There is no harmony between my heart and your heart. My journey to you has been futile."

In *The Antichrist*, Nietzsche says many, many things. His whole teaching is concerned with the superman. God is dead and man is free to be a superman, now he need not be a slave. Now he can declare his freedom, and in his freedom he will become superman. With God he was just a slave kneeling down before statues and sculptures and scriptures, and praying to God like a beggar, believing in saviors, prophets, messiahs, who were nothing but arch-egoists. The whole of humanity has been directed toward a great spiritual slavery.

Nietzsche was against Christ because he was telling lies: "Blessed are the poor for they shall inherit the kingdom of God." This is a lie. He is simply consoling the poor. And to console the poor is to destroy any possible revolution. That's what all the Christians are doing. They are protecting capitalism, they are protecting the people who are in power and they are giving empty words as consolation to the poor: "Blessed are the poor." Nonsense!

And just to give them a deeper consolation, Jesus condemns the rich. He says, "It is possible that a camel can pass through the eye of a needle, but no rich man will ever pass through the gates of paradise." This is just to make the poor feel great: their poverty is spiritual, it is a gift of God, they are blessed. These people like Jesus have created poverty, and have destroyed the possibility of revolution, of changing the social structure, of creating a better society without classes and finally, an ultimate society where the state also withers away.

People like Jesus are not saviors, but consolers. They are functioning, perhaps not knowingly, as agents of the vested interests. That was the reason why Nietzsche continuously wrote in front of his signature, "Antichrist." He was very clear about it.

Jesus says, "If someone slaps you on one cheek, you give him your other cheek." Nietzsche does not accept it, and I agree with Nietzsche, not with Jesus. The reason? Nietzsche gives a perfect argument for it. He said, "If you give your other cheek to the person, you are insulting him. You are telling him, 'I am holier-than-thou. You are just subhuman.'" Nobody before Nietzsche has seen that this statement is an insult; that's why I call him an original man. He just missed one thing: meditation. Otherwise, we would have had a greater buddha than Gautam Buddha himself, because he would have been absolutely contemporary.

Do you understand what he is saying? When you give your other cheek you are rejecting the man, his humanity. You are saying, "I am a saint, and you are just an ordinary human being." Nietzsche says, "When somebody hits you on the cheek, hit him back as hard as you can. That makes you equal." You accept the man's dignity as a human being, and you also say, "I am also a human being; I am not superior to you, I am not holier than you." A strange argument, but absolutely perfect.

In this book, *The Antichrist*, he says, "People who still believe in themselves still have their own God." Now they have become gods themselves. But he does not know anything about meditation; that is the difficulty. In meditation you enter as if you are a self, but the deeper you go the more the self starts withering away. When you finally reach your center you are no more. The question of being a god does not arise. You are certainly godly, because the whole of existence is godly. But it is not a power trip, because a power trip needs others to be lower than you; it needs you to be higher.

In deep meditation you know that even trees are equal to you, that even animals and birds and rocks are equal to you. The whole existence lives in tremendous equality. That's what I have been saying again and again. Only a spiritual, meditative person can be authentically communist and anarchist, nobody else, because as you go deeper into yourself you disappear; you are no more. So there is no question of any power trip, any ego number. The whole existence suddenly becomes just as you are. The ego is absent, the "I" is absent; there is only a presence of light, of consciousness, of witnessing. And the whole existence seems to be as silent as you are, as ecstatic as you are. There is no higher, no lower.

Both the movements—the movement of communism and the movement of anarchism—have failed in a way, because they missed the basic point of equality. Only a meditator knows everything is equal, because we are all part of one organic cosmos. Different shapes and different forms create the beauty because they create variety. But deep down in the roots is the same juice; it is the same nourishment that is flowing in the tree, that is becoming a flower, that is flowing in you and becoming a buddha. Your unfoldment into a buddha is exactly the unfoldment of a lotus flower, there is no difference at all. Nobody is higher, nobody is lower.

Nietzsche is right. If people are not meditative and they drop the idea of God, they themselves will become gods, because who will prevent them? Their egos will become absolutely inflated, they will become more and more egoist. When God was there, they were humble, they were afraid of punishment, of hell. Now there is no God—who is going to prevent them from becoming great egos?

Once somebody objected to Napoleon Bonaparte, "What you are doing goes against the constitution of the country. Napoleon said, "I am the law. Throw away the constitution. Whatever I say is the constitution." Now this is bound to happen. The egoists become the very law. Egoistic people become gods.

The Second World War was such a shock to the Japanese people not because of Hiroshima and Nagasaki, but because of the defeat of the Sun God. They believed that their emperor was a Sun God, he was not a human being, he could not be defeated. Because he was never defeated the concept continued and became more and more ingrained: "He cannot be defeated, there is no power which can defeat him. He is no longer just a human being, he is a god, a Sun God." But all great kings and emperors have believed that they share power with God. If there is no God, your kings, your emperors, the people who have power will start thinking, "We are gods and everybody else is just an ordinary human being."

So Nietzsche is right. If you are not acquainted with meditation, mind is a dangerous phenomenon. Without God, it can become very inflated. It can start thinking of itself as God.

I am reminded of a beautiful incident. It happened in Baghdad in the times of a certain Caliph Omar. A man declared that he had come with a new message from God, and that it was a great improvement on the Holy Koran. He was immediately caught and brought to Caliph Omar, to his court. "This man is proclaiming that he comes from God and has brought a new message to humanity, more refined than Mohammed's Holy Koran."

Mohammedans cannot accept any refinement on the Holy Koran, that is the last word of God. Every religion says the same. Mahavir is the last word for the Jains, nothing can be changed, nothing can be refined. So is the Buddha the last word for the Buddhists. So is Jesus, so is Moses — every founder of a religion in the world has tried to establish that "I am the final stop. Everything stops with me; no more evolution." But evolution does not care about these people, it goes on and on.

Omar was very angry. He said, "You are a Mohammedan and you are claiming that you are a better prophet than Mohammed?"

The man said, "Of course, because I come after so many centuries have passed. The world has changed, the times have changed; we need a new Koran. I have brought it."

Omar was very angry. He told his soldiers, "Give him good treatment. Bind him naked to a pillar in the prison and beat him for seven days. Don't allow him to sleep, and no food. After seven days I will come and see whether he has changed his mind or not."

The man was tortured for seven days continuously: no sleep, no food, and continual beatings. When on the seventh day Omar went to the jail, the man was simply covered with blood, the whole body was bruised and bleeding.

Omar asked, "What do you think now? Have you changed your mind or not?"

The man laughed. He said, "When I was coming from paradise, bringing the new message to humanity, God told me that I would be tortured. Every prophet has been tortured. These seven days have proved completely that I am the prophet. God was right."

Omar could not believe his ears. And at that moment, suddenly, from another pillar came the voice of a man who had been brought there a month before. He had been declaring, "I am God himself!" So he had been tortured in the jail for one month. Omar had completely forgotten about him—he had become interested in this prophet—but the man suddenly shouted, "Omar! I am God! Beware! After Mohammed I have never sent any prophet to the world! This man is lying!"

What to do with these people? They are just insane.

No psychoanalyst, if he is true to his scientific analysis and scientific approach, can say that Jesus was sane. The man is calling himself the "son of God." He needs hospitalization! He does not need crucifixion; that is absolutely wrong. He has not committed any crime, he is simply declaring his insanity. And you don't put insane people on the cross, you have compassion for them; they need psychiatric treatment. But unfortunately there was no psychiatry and no psychology at the time. It was waiting for another Jew, Sigmund Freud, to invent it. But he came too late, two thousand years after the first Jew, Jesus, was crucified.

It is really megalomania. If God is not there, there is every possibility that anybody who has an egoistic mind will move to the other extreme. First he was kneeling down before God. Now, knowing there is no God, he moves to the other extreme. Now he declares, "I am God." Either way, God has to be there.

But this statement of Nietzsche's is the experience of one who only knows the mind and not anything beyond it. As you move beyond the mind, you are no more. There is no one to declare, "I am the son of God," or, "I am God." There is no one to declare, "I am the savior of mankind," or, "I am a prophet," or, "I am the reincarnation of God." All these people are simply insane. You have been worshipping insane people because they declared themselves to be God. All these so-called founders of religion needed psychiatric treatment.

There are still people…When Jawaharlal Nehru was the prime minister of India, there were at least a dozen people all over India who believed they were Jawaharlal Nehru. One person I knew, because he used to live in a nearby town and I used to go there once in a while to lecture in that town's college. I met him there, because he had come to the lecture. The school's principal laughingly introduced him to me: "Here is Pandit Jawaharlal Nehru, our prime minister." And the man was dressed exactly like Jawaharlal Nehru.

I said, "He looks like Pandit Jawaharlal Nehru." The man said, "Looks like? I am!"

The principal later on told me that this man kept sending telegrams to government circuit houses informing them that the prime minister would be coming on such and such date, so they should keep the best room for him: "He will be staying for two days. Inform all the officials." And many times he deceived people, because in a small village nobody knew Jawaharlal

Nehru directly. They had only seen his pictures, and that man was dressed exactly like him. He had the same hairstyle, the same cap, the same vest, the same Mohammedan-style pajama— everything was perfect. And, because of his mind perhaps, his face was also becoming similar to Jawaharlal Nehru. He believed it absolutely, there was no doubt about it in his mind. He behaved the way Jawaharlal behaved, he walked the way Jawaharlal walked. Finally he died in a car accident.

Another man, who used to think that he was Jawaharlal Nehru, was in the biggest madhouse in India, in Barelli. After three years there he finally recognized that he was not Nehru, perhaps because of the torture or the continuous hammering on his mind, "You are not him." He got tired, that's my feeling; and what happened later on proves my feeling right.

Jawaharlal Nehru was going to Barelli for some celebration, and was going to visit the madhouse also, to open a new wing that had been newly constructed for more mad people to be accommodated. So the officers of the madhouse thought that since now the man was cured, it would be good to give him his release from Jawaharlal's own hands.

When Jawaharlal came, they brought the madman. They introduced him, "This is Pandit Jawaharlal Nehru, our prime minister."

The man looked at Jawaharlal Nehru, and he said, "Don't be worried. It will take three years at least. I used to think exactly the same as you think, but these people are such torturers. Finally I had to accept that I am not, although I know I am. In three years' time you will also accept that you are not Jawaharlal Nehru. Just go in. I am going out, you go in! Don't be worried, it takes only three years to be cured."

The man was being perfectly logical. He used to think he was Jawaharlal; then these people had cured him by torturing him. But deep down, he still knew who he was.

It happened in England when Churchill was the prime minister...Because of the Second World War, in London after six o'clock there was a very strict curfew. Nobody should be seen outside their houses, otherwise they might be shot.

Churchill used to go for an evening walk. And that day there was such a beautiful sunset... very rare in England, where the sun appears only once in a while. So he was sitting on a park bench watching the beautiful sunset, and he forgot all about the curfew. Suddenly, as the sun went down beneath the horizon, he realized that he was late. It was already past the time when he should have been inside the house, which was still at least a mile away. And the strict orders, his orders, were that everybody had to be in their house after six o'clock. He would be shot.

He looked to see where he could go inside—anybody would give him shelter knowing that he was Winston Churchill, the prime minister, the savior. So he knocked on the first house, which happened to be a madhouse. A man opened the door and Churchill said, "I am sorry to disturb you. I am Winston Churchill, you must know me, I am the prime minister of England."

The man simply grabbed him. Churchill said, "What are you doing?"

The man said, "There are already six Winston Churchills here. Come in!"

He said, "I tell you, I am *really* Winston Churchill."

The man said, "That's what they all say. I am putting you with the others. Soon you will know who is real."

There was no way to get out. There was a danger of being shot dead, it was better to rest in this madhouse. But he was put with those six fat guys, smoking the same kind of cigar as you always saw Churchill smoking. When the seventh Churchill entered, they all waved to him—the Victory sign. "Welcome, come in!"

They all looked like him, all fat and puffed-up and smoking cigars and giving him the Victory sign. He tried hard to convince them, the whole night the discussion went on. He told them, "You people are mad. I am the real Winston Churchill…" They all laughed. One of them said, "Everybody here is real. Unreal Churchills don't exist."

Churchill tried hard, "Don't you recognize me?"

They said, "Don't you recognize us? We are very happy to have you. Six were already here, you are the seventh. More will be coming! But all are real! Nobody is unreal."

He spent the whole tortured night with those six Churchills continuously smoking and talking the way Churchill used to talk, about war affairs and plans of how to defeat Hitler. Churchill was silent: "What to do with these idiots?" They nagged him: "Why are you sitting silently? If you are the real Churchill, come in and discuss with us the problems of the country. The country is in danger and you are sitting silently? What makes you think you are the real Churchill?"

Churchill said later on, "Once in a while in the night I had a doubt…these people were so certain, who knows? Maybe I was mad? I was certain, they were also certain. In fact, they seemed to be more absolutely certain than me. I sometimes had some hesitation, maybe…"

In the morning he phoned to his secretary: "Send people to convince this jailer." They were all worried, the whole night he had been searched for all over London. "Where had he gone?" The whole of England was dependent on Churchill's methodology to defeat Adolf Hitler. "Where has he gone? Is it some conspiracy? Has Adolf Hitler abducted him?"

So when he phoned, people immediately came and told the warden, "You are an idiot. You tortured our prime minister."

The warden said, "Just come in, and you can see there are seven prime ministers. I am not at fault, they all say the same thing. This man was also saying the same thing. How am I to decide who is real?"

And when those people went in, they could not believe their eyes. They said, "You are right, we are sorry. But this man is the real Churchill. We are taking him out." And they were high officials of the parliament, so the warden agreed.

Those six others said, "What is going on? That phony fellow has been taken out. We are the real Churchills—not one, six!—but nobody takes any notice…"

Ego is insane. If there is no God, the egoist can think of himself as God. But this can happen only if you are not acquainted with meditation. Meditation simply dissolves you into the cosmos. You are no more, only existence is.

It is time for laughter…

A new young priest has just arrived at the monastery. After a couple of weeks he is feeling so disturbed by sexual fantasies that he goes to see the father superior, aged ninety-five.

"Ah, Father," cries the young priest, "I am deeply troubled by impure thoughts, and sexual temptations come crowding into my mind—things like doggie-style and sixty-nine, satin panties with pictures of Jesus on them! The more I try to resist them, the more they crowd into my mind."

"Hmm," says the old priest, adjusting his robe. "So what would you like to know?"

"Well," replies the young man, "you are ninety-five years old and one of the most ancient relics of the church—tell me, how old do you have to be before you are released from the lusts of the flesh?"

"Hmm," says the Father, eyeing the young priest. "It takes many years of self-torture and holy prayer before your mind is cleaned of all such wickedness."

"Really?" asks the young priest. "How many years?"

"Well," replies the old priest with a sigh, "I can tell you that it is more than ninety-five!"

Newton gets into a New York taxi to go across town, and finds himself being thrown around inside the car as the driver races through the streets.

"Hey! Slow down!" shouts Newton, when he finally manages to catch hold of something, "or you will get us both into the hospital!"

"You don't need to worry, mister," replies the driver. "I have just got out of the hospital after being there for eighteen months, and I don't intend going back!"

"Ah! I am sorry," says Newton, feeling reassured. "You were in the hospital for eighteen months—that must have been awful! Were you badly injured?"

"Nope! Not a scratch," replies Dingle. "It was a mental hospital!"

The meditation:

Be silent...

Close your eyes, and feel your bodies to be completely frozen.

This is the right moment to turn in. Gather all your energy, your total consciousness, and with an urgency as if this is going to be the last moment of your life, rush towards your very center of being.

Faster and faster...

Deeper and deeper...

As you come closer to your very center, a great silence descends over you. It is falling like soft rain.

A little more, closer, and a totally new experience...

Flowers of peace, flowers of serenity, flowers of absolute tranquillity are growing all around you.

Just one step more and you are at the very center of your being, absolutely drunk with the divine, surrounded by an aura of ecstasy. You are facing your original face for the first time. The face of the buddha is just a symbol, it is really everybody's face, the ultimate face.

The only quality the buddha has...all the buddhas, past, present, future are bound to have only one quality—witnessing, awareness.

Just witness you are not the body. Witness you are not the mind.

And witness you are only a witness.

You are just a buddha, utterly innocent, beyond mind, a pure space, infinite and eternal.

To make your witnessing deeper…

Relax… Let go, the same way as the flowers fall down from the trees…with easy heart, no tension, no anxiety. Settled at the center you are in tune with existence, your heartbeat is the heartbeat of the whole universe.

At this moment you are the most blessed people on the earth, because there is no other splendor in existence greater than you are in this moment.

Rejoice in this beautiful moment.

Rejoice in this authentic and original experience.

Rejoice that you are so blessed to be so close to existence itself. And gather all these experiences before you come back back.

You have to bring them from the center to the circumference of your life. You have to live a life of grace, beauty, joy, blissfulness, ecstasy—in every moment, around the clock.

Whether awake or asleep you are the buddha and all that belongs to the buddha—the witnessing, the ecstasy, the rejoicing, the blissfulness, the utter drunkenness that comes to you. When you reach your center you have reached to the very center of existence.

You are drowned in the juices of life, and nourished.

Collect all this experience and remember that you have to persuade the buddha to come with you.

These are the three steps of meditation: first the buddha comes behind you as a shadow. But the shadow is fragrant, the shadow has tremendous solidity, the shadow is not a shadow but a presence—very tangible, you can touch it, you can feel it. It is almost behind you; its warmth, its compassion, its light will all be showering on you.

The second step: you become the shadow, and buddha comes in front of you. Your shadow slowly fades away, because your personality is nothing but a false idea, an imagination, a fiction, a lie.

And as your shadow disappears your being becomes one with the buddha. That is the third and the final step.

The moment you become the buddha, you have come back home. That day will be the most fortunate day of all your lives. You have lived for many lives, in many ways, in many bodies, and you have been missing and missing and missing. This time, make it clear to yourself you are not going to miss: you have to become enlightened, you have to achieve the highest peak and the deepest depth of your being.

This is the very purpose of calling your hidden secret, your hidden splendor, to the surface.

God *is* dead, now only Zen is the living truth.

Come back…but very slowly, very peacefully, very silently, as if there is no one here.

Just sit silently for a few seconds to remember the path you have followed, to remember all that great space, those beautiful moments when your heart was in tune with the heart of the universe, those few rare moments when your whole life was eternal.

And feel the buddha, his warmth, his compassion, his presence. It is just behind you.

The day is not far away when you will take the second step and you will take the third step.

You will all become buddhas in your own right.

Chapter 3:
God is just like tomorrow

On one occasion Seigen commented to Sekito, "Some say that an intelligence
comes from the south of the Ling."
Sekito said, "There is no such intelligence from anybody."
Seigen said, "If not, whence are all those sutras of the tripitaka?"
Sekito said, "They all come out of here, and there is nothing wanting."
On Seigen's death, Sekito went to Mount Nangaku. Finding a large, flat rock,
he built a hut, and from thence forward came to be known as "Stonehead,"
and later, when he was a master, as "Stonehead Osho."
Hearing of Sekito living on a rock, the master, Nangaku, sent a young monk to
him, saying, "Go to the east and examine in detail the monk sitting on
the stone-head.
If he is the monk who came the other day, address him. And if he replies,
you recite to him the following song, 'You are sitting so proudly on the stone,
it is better to come to me.'"
The attendant monk went to Sekito and recited this song. Sekito replied,
"Even if you cried tears of sorrow, I would never, ever cross over the hills."
The monk came back and made a report to Nangaku. Nangaku said,
"This monk
will surely make the mouth of the people tremble for generations."

Before we discuss the sutra, a few questions.

? **My deepest pain is that of being an outsider, that I don't belong here in this life,**
that I am essentially wrong, and death is just waiting to claim me unmercifully.
That sense of belonging here, valuing myself and being valued by existence,
and thus letting myself live and celebrate fully eludes me. Is this feeling related
to the influence of a God-oriented religion?

The God-oriented religions are bound to create such a feeling. It is absolutely necessary, because they are giving you lies as consolation. As man has gone beyond his primitive states of consciousness, he has become more intelligent and today he can see the myth of God. He has lived with the lie as if it was the truth, and he was content. But now that he is intelligent, he can see the falsity of the whole religious lie, and a great problem arises for him.

God is dead. Man's consolation is destroyed. He feels utterly empty, in no relationship with existence. God used to be the fulfillment of one's life, somebody who was caring, somebody who was forgiving, somebody who was compassionate. With no God, suddenly you feel yourself an outsider to existence. But this is a good beginning, don't take it wrongly.

Every lie taken away will for some time leave a space empty. You can use this empty space to become miserable; misery will fill it. You can make this space anguish, anxiety, suffering, pain. But it is up to you. You can make this empty space a new beginning, a new door. God is dead, now you have to search for truth on your own; nobody can give it to you. This emptiness should become a door going inwards.

The moment you enter to the center of your being, you are no longer an outsider. For the first time you are an insider! God was keeping you outside the truth, outside existence. God was keeping you simply consoled, but consolations are of no help. You need a transformation of being, you need to use your emptiness joyfully, because it opens a door to the eternal space. It opens a door into your very roots, which are in existence. It suddenly makes you feel at home with the trees, with the birds, with human beings, with stars—with everything around you. The whole cosmos is your very home.

So it all depends how you use your emptiness. The so-called western existentialists are using it wrongly. They are filling it with misery, anxiety, tension, dread, anguish, angst.

First you were full of lies, fictions; at least they were consoling, at least they were giving you some hope, some connectedness with existence. But existentialism is using your emptiness in an even worse way than the religions have used it.

Religions have used it to exploit you. They were giving you consolation, and there is a price to everything. So they were exploiting you, but you were feeling perfectly happy for centuries, because God was in heaven and everything was all right—he will take care of you.

This consolation was false; it was not going to change you, it was not going to make you a buddha, it was not going to make you awakened, enlightened. It was not in favor of your spiritual growth, but at least it was keeping you without anxiety, without anguish, without meaninglessness. You were feeling at home, although that feeling was a dream. Now that the dream is destroyed, you suddenly feel you are alone. There is no God and you don't know any other way of relating with existence. Your old programming has failed.

You need a new insight. You need, instead of prayer, meditation; instead of God, your own consciousness. A pillar of consciousness is going to fill your being, and this will not be a consolation. It will be authentic contentment; it will relate you with existence, you will not feel at all the outsider.

Do you think I feel at all an outsider? I am as deeply involved with existence as one can be. The whole existence has become my very being, my heart is dancing with the heartbeat of the universe.

God was preventing this happening, this tremendous phenomenon of transformation. God was not a friend to you; God was the greatest enemy. And the priests have been exploiting you.

Now that intelligence understands there is no God, there is bound to be a small gap in which you either have to choose western existentialism—which is not authentic, it is accidentalism— or you have to look inwards the same way as every awakened being has looked. You have to stop looking towards the sky. You have to close your eyes and look towards the inner space from where you are connected with existence. Immediately the emptiness will disappear. Not only emptiness, you will disappear. And then only a dance remains, a celebration of this whole universe. And you are absolutely one with it, there is no question of even being an *insider*. There arises a great oneness. You suddenly see yourself in various manifestations: in the trees, in the flowers, in the clouds, in the stars, you are everywhere. The moment you disappear you are the whole existence, blossoming, flying; all the greenness, all the mountains, all the snow, all the rivers, all the oceans—everywhere you are spread. And this state is the state of a buddha. This is true liberation.

So you are feeling yourself an outsider — this is good! This is the transitory period; now you have to be alert not to fill yourself with pain and misery. Now that God is no longer there, who is going to console you? You don't need any consolation. Humanity has come of age. Be a man, be a woman, and stand on your own feet.

For millennia you have been crippled because of God, because of the whole priesthood. They never wanted you to be healthy and whole. Their whole profession was dependent on your misery and pain. They were the people who were covering your misery and pain and giving you hope, and hope is an empty word. Karl Marx is right when he says religion is the hope of the hopeless. But the hope was just like a carrot hanging in front of you. You never reach it, but it is so close it feels you are going to reach—if not today then tomorrow, if not tomorrow then the day after tomorrow. The carrot is always hanging in front of you.

A Sufi story says:

A man has purchased a cow, and he was not accustomed to dealing with cows. So he was trying to drag the cow along holding the cow's horns, and the cow was very resistant—obviously, this man was new. She wanted to go to her home, she wanted to go to her old owner.

A Sufi mystic was watching. He said to the man, "It seems you are very new; you don't know how to deal with cows. This is not the right way."

The man said, "What should I do, because I am not that strong. The cow is stronger; she is dragging me with her."

The mystic gave him some beautiful green grass, and told him, "Let go of her horns. You take this grass and just move ahead of her. Keep the grass very close, but don't allow her to eat it. As she moves towards the grass, you go on moving towards your home." And it worked. The cow came along because the grass was so close, and so green and so fresh. She forgot all about the owner; the immediate problem was how to get this grass. And it is so close, just hanging in front of your eyes! But the man went on moving slowly, so that the distance between the cow and the grass remained the same. And she entered into the barn belonging to the new owner, and he closed the door.

Religions have been hanging carrots in front of you. Those hopes are never fulfilled, they are hopeless. Those promises are empty.

When your hopes and your expectations and your ideas of God and your relationship with the world are destroyed, naturally there is bound to be a small gap before you choose the right path. And the right path is not the existentialism of the West. The right path is the meditation that the East has been using for centuries, and has worked out completely into a science. You move inwards.

God was preventing you because he was outside. Your prayer was directed towards the God who was not there. You *are* here, there is no need of any evidence that you are here. There is no need for any argument to prove that you are here. So why not explore this "hereness," this presence that you *are*, this consciousness that you *are*. Why not explore it?

Those who have explored it have never come back saying they are outsiders. They have not even said that they are insiders, because even an insider is separate. They have come out and declared, "*Aham brahmasmi!*"—I am the whole, "*Ana'l haq!*"—I am the truth, I am existence itself. There is no question of outsider or insider. Those are two sides of the same coin. The whole coin is dropped, suddenly you find yourself one with the cosmic dance, a tremendous rhythm in which you disappear as a separate personality, and you become one with the whole.

Every wave in the ocean for a moment thinks it is an outsider, it does not belong to the ocean. But the next moment it disappears into the ocean. You will disappear in the ocean of consciousness the same way; you are just a wave. It does not matter that you exist for seventy years. Perhaps you have become frozen and all that is needed is melting. Melt, melt, melt like ice melting and become one with the ocean that surrounds you. You are living in the very ocean.

I have told you about a young, very revolutionary fish. She started asking every other fish, "Where is the ocean? I have been hearing so much about it."

No fish could answer. They said, "You will have to find some wise fish, some enlightened fish maybe, but we don't know where this ocean is. We have also heard about it, and we believe it must be somewhere when everybody says so. For centuries our forefathers have been saying the ocean *is*. So we believe in it."

Then an old mystic fish got hold of the young fish and said, "You idiot! You are *in* the ocean. You *are* the ocean! You are born of the ocean, you will disappear in the ocean and you will live in the ocean. You are just a rather more solid wave, but you will disappear in the ocean."

This is the ocean in which you are living. Around you there is, just like air, the cosmic consciousness; you can't see it, but it is continuously nourishing you. Your consciousness is nourished by the cosmic consciousness, just as your heart is beating because of the breathing. The air that you cannot see is continuously giving you oxygen, keeping your body alive.

But you are not only body. Behind the body is your hidden splendor, the consciousness. That too needs nourishment continuously. And all around you just like air…

Once you are empty, just wait a little; don't take any decision. And suddenly you will feel a new rush of energy coming into you, from inside, from outside. You will suddenly feel you are surrounded with consciousness and you are melting into it. And then comes the realization: "I was just ignorant about myself and the existence in which I am living, which has given me birth and which is going to be my ultimate home. I have to disperse in this home."

But it always happens that there is a small period when you are very shaky.

The other night I was talking about Gurdjieff and his method of working on the energy system. He divided energy into the first layer, which is very small, enough for day-to-day affairs… the second layer is bigger. If the first layer is finished and you continue, the second layer will suddenly start functioning. And if you continue to exhaust the second layer—which is very difficult, it takes months, sometimes years to exhaust it—then the third layer which is cosmic, inexhaustible, starts functioning. Gurdjieff's method is very old, very primitive. But the energy of the cosmos is surrounding you. All that is needed is a certain emptiness in you.

So the emptiness is good; don't fill it with beliefs, don't fill it again with another kind of god, another philosophy, some existentialism. Don't fill it. Leave it clean and fresh, and go deeper. Soon you will find from both sides, from outside and inside, a tremendous rush of energy, a tremendous rush of consciousness. Then you disappear. You are almost flooded with the cosmos; you are so small and the cosmos is so vast. You suddenly disappear into it, and that disappearance is the ultimate experience of enlightenment. Then you know you were neither an outsider nor an insider; you are one with existence.

Other than oneness with existence, nothing is going to help you. But that oneness is so easy, so obvious. Just a little relaxation, just a little turning in—not much effort, not much discipline, not much torture for yourself.

It is good that you are feeling like an outsider because God is no longer filling the space, and you are feeling disconnected with the universe. It is good. It only means that false connections have been removed.

It happened one day…

Mulla Nasruddin was sitting in his office waiting for some customers. Finally a man came in, and Nasruddin did not even give the man a chance to say anything. He just waved his hand telling him to sit down, picked up the telephone and started talking about millions.

"One million dollars? Yes, okay I'll take it."

At that moment the man who had just come in said, "Wait a minute. I have come from the telephone company to connect the telephone." The telephone was not connected; that one-million-dollar purchase was just show business!

You are feeling disconnected because your connections were false. In fact, there were no connections, and you were talking to God—on the phone, direct line! I have made you aware that your telephone is not connected. To whom are you talking? All your prayers are on a telephone that is not connected.

The only way to be connected with existence is to go inwards, because there at the center you are still connected. You have been disconnected physically from your mother. That disconnection was absolutely necessary to make you an individual in your own right. But you are not disconnected from the universe. Your connection with the universe is of consciousness. You cannot see it, so you have to go deep down with great awareness, watchfulness, witnessing, and you will find the connection. The buddha is the connection!

? Is monotheism a necessary step in human evolution, or is it just an invention of the priests?

Monotheism is a far more dangerous device of the priests than polytheism. In a monotheistic religion there is no possibility for a buddha to be born. It is not part of evolution; on the contrary, it is preventing your evolution.

All the religions born outside India—Judaism, Christianity, Mohammedanism—are monotheistic. Mohammed gives it perfect definition: one God, one prophet, one holy Koran. This is a very dictatorial type of religion, naturally dangerous because it is very intolerant. The Jewish God himself says, "I am a very intolerant god. I am very jealous, I will not allow you to worship any other god."

Monotheism is a far more efficient way of exploiting people. Hinduism is polytheistic; it has as many gods as you can think of. When Hinduism came into existence, there used to be thirty-three million people in India. Hinduism has exactly thirty-three million gods. This seems to be far more democratic—everybody has a god of his own! Rather than worshipping somebody else's god, it is far better to have your own private god; then there is no conflict.

No Hindu scripture says, "One God, one scripture, one prophet." All the Hindu scriptures say there are as many gods as there are people. That's why Hinduism is very inefficient. It has to be: it is not an army; it does not have a pope; it does not have any organized central body, it is a very disorganized chaos. So there is every freedom for everybody.

Somebody becomes a Mahavira, Hinduism has no objection. Somebody becomes a Buddha, Hinduism has no objection. Both were born as Hindus, and both went against the Hindus. There is no problem, because there is no central body to appoint a court or a grand jury to judge whether Mahavira is authentic since he does not believe in God. His whole effort is that you should develop your consciousness to the ultimate peak: everybody is a god.

Mahavira's interpretation of thirty-three million gods was that there are thirty-three million people, who are all going to become gods one day, when they evolve to the highest peak. He said it was a probability…there are not yet thirty-three million gods, but thirty-three million potential gods. That gives a great freedom, and there is no need of any priest. You have your private god on a direct line.

But Christianity, a monotheistic religion, will not allow any Buddha; hence it has remained poor in consciousness. Its religion looks very primitive and is based on fictions. Nothing has been contributed by monotheistic religions to the world except war, because the Mohammedan God cannot tolerate the Jewish God, nor can it tolerate the Christian God, nor can it tolerate the Hindu gods. It has to kill all those gods and the believers in those gods. "Only one God"…. So when Mohammedans came to India they destroyed millions of beautiful temples that had been made over the centuries by great sculptors. They destroyed millions of statues, beautiful statues of Buddha, Mahavira and other Jaina *tirthankaras*. Whatever is left is a very small amount. Here and there perhaps some temple was left because it was hidden deep in the forest.

In every village you will find that when the Mohammedans came, people just threw their gods, beautiful statues, into the wells — just to protect them from the Mohammedans, who would otherwise destroy their statues. So in every village—it happens often—you will find, in summertime when the water level goes down, suddenly a buddha arising, and people pull the buddha out. For centuries he has been lying in the well, but he has been protected. People had forgotten, because those who had thrown the statues in the wells had died centuries before.

Mohammedans came two thousand years ago, and they destroyed everything. Their God was intolerant, how can they be tolerant?

Monotheism is the ugliest religious form in the world, because it is intolerant. Intolerance creates violence. Christians have crusades, Mohammedans have *jihads*—religious wars. India had never known any religious war. It was everybody's choice to have a god or not to have a god; even the atheists were not harmed.

A great philosophy of charvakas flourished for centuries. Charvakas believe there is no God, there is no soul—the same as what Marx said five thousand years later. They say that the soul is just a by-product of five elements that constitute the body. The founder of the charvaka religion was Acharya Brihaspati—and it is strange that Acharya Brihaspati is mentioned in the Vedas with great respect.

This is tolerance. It is your choice, you are free to choose your path; you are free to choose even a religion that has no God, even a religion that has no soul. Charvakas were the perfect atheists. Their whole philosophy was: eat, drink and be merry, because there is no hell, no heaven, no god. And don't be worried because there is no judgment day and there is nobody to judge. Sinners and saints all disappear into five elements.

In India you will see people chewing *pan*. Brihaspati used the symbol of *pan*. If you chew the *pan* leaf it will not make your lips red, and if you chew separately all the things that are put in the *pan* your lips will not be red. But if you mix them together, your lips become red. The redness of your lips is a by-product of the five elements making up the pan. It is not an independent entity, it is the combination of the five elements together. This was a simple example used by charvakas, and they were respected. Even the Vedas mention Brihaspati as a great master, an *acharya*.

Such tolerance is possible only in a polytheistic religion. When there are so many gods, you have a variety of choice, you have a certain freedom. When there is one god you don't have any freedom.

According to me, monotheism is far worse than polytheism. The polytheism of the Hindus allowed the Buddhas, the Jaina *tirthankaras*, the Charvakas, without any problem. Although they were against Hinduism, still nobody was crucified. Even Brihaspati was not crucified, but is mentioned with great respect in the Vedas. He has the freedom to think, to speak, to create a philosophy of his own.

And the name was not *charvak*, it was *charuvak*. There is a great difference. "Charuvak" means sweet words. The philosophy of Brihaspati was of sweet words. He was taking away all fear—there is no god, no heaven, no hell—he was taking away all kinds of dread. Death is the end, birth is the beginning, in the middle is a small life. Enjoy it, and enjoy it even if you have to borrow money. Don't be worried, because after death nobody is going to tell you, "Give me my money back."

His sentence is: *Rinam kritva ghritam pivet*. Even if you have to borrow money, don't be worried: borrow money, drink *ghee*. Ghee is the most refined part of milk. When butter is refined, it becomes ghee. You cannot go beyond ghee, that is the ultimate thing. And you cannot go backwards either, neither forwards nor backwards. You have come to a full stop.

So, significantly, he is saying that this life is the full stop. You are not going anywhere, so just enjoy it. It does not matter what means you employ; what matters is your enjoyment. Life is so short, don't waste it in unnecessary fears that you will suffer in hell. Don't waste it in unnecessary greed that you will be rewarded in heaven. Don't bother about right and wrong. The only thing that is right is to enjoy! Even this man is respected. But slowly, slowly the word charuvak became in the minds of the masses, "charvak." *Charvak* means one who goes on eating continuously, just chewing like a buffalo—because that was actually his teaching: eat, drink, be merry.

Nor was Gautam Buddha crucified, although he declared that all the Vedas are false. He declared that the whole of Brahmanism, the priesthood of the Hindus, has been exploiting people. He declared that the Hindu caste system was wrong, that every man is born equal. But he was not crucified. Even Hindu philosophers used to go and listen to him. In fact, all his disciples were basically Hindu. From where else could he have found thousands of disciples? Great Hindu scholars came to debate with him and became his disciples, finding that they had only words, whereas this man had experience. There was such a tremendous urge to find the truth, it did not matter from whom it came.

The monotheistic religions—Christianity, Judaism, Mohammedanism—have been the most dangerous religions in the world. Not a single person has been killed in the name of Buddhism in twenty-five centuries. Buddhism has never attacked anybody, and it has spread all over Asia, converted the whole of Asia just by a simple experience.

It was difficult to confront a Bodhidharma. Even the Emperor Wu of China could not manage to stand up straight in front of Bodhidharma. And Bodhidharma said to him, "You are an idiot!" He called the emperor of China an idiot. The emperor asked Bodhidharma: "I have put my whole energy, my whole power and my whole treasure at the disposal of the Buddhist monks. Thousands of monks are here translating scriptures of Buddha into Chinese, and they are all my guests. I have opened many monasteries. I have made many temples for Buddha. What is going to be my reward?"

Just the word 'reward' was enough, and Bodhidharma said, "You are an idiot. If you have been doing all this for a "reward", you will fall into the deepest hell." The emperor was shocked. But Bodhidharma said, "The very idea of reward is nothing but greed. You are more greedy than ordinary greedy people. Those who are collecting money know perfectly well that when they die their bank balance is not going with them, nor is their money going with them. But you are really greedy — so greedy that you are trying to create a bank balance in the other world, of which you know nothing. Obviously you are an idiot and I am not going to enter your empire. I had come with that idea, but when the emperor is an idiot, that is proof enough of what kind of people you must have."

He refused to enter. He remained outside the boundary of China in a small temple. And when he was dying, Emperor Wu said to his people, his prime minister, "Write on my grave that I am really an idiot. I could not understand the great buddha who had come in the form of Bodhidharma. He was right, I have lived a wrong life of greed and fear."

Buddha's word spread all over Asia from Sri Lanka to Korea. There was no clash, there was no fight. At the most there were beautiful discussions, very nice, civilized, cultured.

The sword cannot prove that you are right, nor can crucifixion prove that Jesus was wrong. I always wonder… Judaism had such great rabbis, scholars. Could they not convince Jesus, a young man, only thirty-three years of age? The problem was they were only scholars; there was not a single man who really knew the truth. And this man was claiming something that they could not argue against, because there is no way to argue against it.

Jesus was saying, "I am the prophet you have been waiting for." And they certainly had been waiting; they are still waiting; they will wait forever. It is waiting for Godot.

When for the first time the book came to me, *Waiting for Godot*, I thought, "This Godot seems to be a parody on the word "God"." My oldest German sannyasin, Haridas, was there, so I asked Haridas, "Do you think Godot is German for God?"

He said, "No. The German for God is *Gott!*"

I said, "That's great! Already *gott*, there is no need to wait." I said, "That's perfectly okay. When you have *gott* it, what is the point of waiting?"

I love the idea. God is so far away. *Gott* is very appealing.

You are asking whether monotheism is a necessary step — no, not at all. It is an absolutely *unnecessary* step, and not only unnecessary but dangerous. It has created only violence, murder; living people have been burned in the name of a monotheistic God. One God will not allow you to believe in another God.

Polytheism is also an invention of priests, but far more liberal. Monotheism is the invention of the priests, but dictatorial. It gives you commandments, as if you are an army and you need commandments.

Buddha does not have any commandments, nor Mahavira. They persuade you; they don't command. They don't humiliate you. They respect you, they know that your hidden potential is the same as theirs.

Gautam Buddha relates this about his past life. He heard that one man had become enlightened. He was not very much interested, but just out of curiosity…The man had come to the town where he lived. He was very young and not interested at all in enlightenment or spirituality, but out of curiosity to find out what this enlightenment was, he went to see the man.

He had no desire to bow down to him, but when he saw the man—he was so luminous, had such a grace, such a tremendous presence—in spite of himself he touched his feet. He became aware when he was touching his feet, "What am I doing? I had come just to be a spectator."

When you really face a man who knows, a gratitude arises spontaneously, it is not an effort. It was not an effort at all. He had not even come with touching his feet in mind; he had come just to be a spectator. But seeing this man was enough. He forgot himself. This man's presence was so overwhelming. Such beauty! His eyes so deep like a lake, so clean, so clear. He fell in love with that man immediately as he touched his feet. He thought, while touching his feet, "What am I doing? It has happened on its own."

But a bigger miracle was awaiting him. As he stood up, the man who had become enlightened bowed down and touched this young man's feet. He said, "What are you doing?

You are a great awakened one. It is absolutely right for me to touch your feet, although I had not come with that desire—it was spontaneous, you touched my heart—but why are you touching my feet? I am nobody, I don't know even the ABC of enlightenment."

That man said, "This life you don't know. There was a time I was also just like you. I had no idea who I was. Now I know, I have come to my flowering. And I know you will come to your flowering. Don't forget! I have touched your feet so that when you become a buddha you won't forget that everybody is a buddha. Somebody has blossomed, somebody is waiting for the right season. And everybody's spring comes in its own time."

Buddha reminded his disciples again and again, "Never think for a single moment that you are inferior to me. We are all equal. The only difference is—a very slight difference, which does not mean much—you are asleep, I am awake. But I was once asleep, and you will be awake, so what is the difference?"

The difference is only of timing. In the morning I wake up, in the evening you wake up—just twelve hours difference. That does not create any superiority or inferiority. Everybody has to walk according to his pace. Some people run, some people are really fast runners. Some people go slowly, some people take many stops on the way and have a little rest and a cup of tea, maybe an afternoon nap. But everybody is on the way. Somebody is a little behind, somebody is a little ahead, but that does not create any question of inferiority or superiority.

Buddhism has no priests, Jainism has no priests, because they don't have God. If you don't have God, you can't have priests. Priests are the representatives of the fictitious God; they are the agents between you and God. And priests certainly would like monotheism rather than polytheism.

Hindu priests are trying hard to make Hinduism a monotheistic religion also, but they have failed. There are eight *shankaracharyas*. The original, Adi Shankaracharya, appointed four more shankaracharyas. He was the first man to make some effort to organize Hinduism. Before him there was no leader at all; it was absolute freedom. He appointed four shankaracharyas, one each for the four directions, so that each could rule over one direction. But after his death, four more shankaracharyas popped up — because there are eight directions, not four. So four more people popped up on their own, and now there are eight shankaracharyas.

I was telling one shankaracharya, "You should have two more."

He said, "What?"

I said, "There are ten directions. The eight you have, you need one upwards and one downwards."

He said, "That's a great idea. Then we can afford two more."

But these shankaracharyas have no central body — and they cannot have, because somebody is a worshipper of Shiva, somebody is a worshipper of Vishnu, somebody is a worshipper of Krishna, somebody is a worshipper of Brahma. And there are hundreds of smaller gods that people worship. People worship trees, people worship stones. Put a red color on any stone and just wait by the side. You will soon find some Hindu coming there and bowing down.

When for the first time the British government made roads and milestones, they painted the milestones red because red can be seen from far away. No other color is so sharp or can be seen from far away. So they painted the stones red, and then they were very concerned. Hindu villagers would come, place their flowers and coconuts around the stones, and worship them.

The British said to them, "These are milestones." But the villagers said, "It does not matter. Any red stone represents God."

You will see trees being worshipped, stones being worshipped. There is a complete freedom to worship. It is far better than monotheism, but I don't support it. It may be better than monotheism, but it is still poison, just a little diluted. It will kill you slowly, but it will kill you certainly. Every religion is destructive of your evolution of consciousness. Monotheism is the most dangerous, but religion as such is dangerous.

If you can avoid religion, you can become religious. If you can avoid religion, you can have a direct contact with existence and the cosmos.

Is it difficult for people to drop God because he is their only hope and they focus all their expectations on him? It seems to be very hard to drop an expectation, even when one can see it as such and can guess that most likely it will end up in disappointment.

It is true. It is very difficult to drop an expectation, to drop a hope, because you don't have anything real in your life. You are living only in the hope that tomorrow will be better. You are only living with the expectation that after death you will enjoy the pleasures of paradise eternally. Hence it is difficult to drop the idea of God.

But it is God who is preventing you from all the joys and blissfulness and ecstasy right now. You are missing the present in the hope of the future, and the future is not certain. Tomorrow never comes. Have you ever seen tomorrow coming? God is just like tomorrow, always hanging around. It just seems it is coming, it is coming, but what comes is *today*. Tomorrow never comes. All those hopes never come true. All those expectations finally become frustrations.

Why do you see rich people more frustrated than the poor? Just go into the interior parts of India where real poverty exists, and you will not find anybody disappointed. They are hoping for God. They think their poverty is a fire test, and only the poor will enter into the kingdom of God. That's why Christianity has such great appeal to the poor people of the world. It gives great consolation. It gives you an expectation, which helps you tolerate the present misery, the pain, the present poverty and slavery. Your eyes are focused on the future and the present goes on passing in misery. Because your eyes are no longer focused on the present, the consolation helps to keep you alive — but just "alive," just like vegetables. It keeps you vegetating.

A life that cannot dance is not life. It is living at the minimum survival level. A life that cannot sing the song of love and joy is not life. So your expectations and your hopes may make it difficult to drop God, but you have to gather courage and understanding that your hopes and expectations are destroying your whole life. God is just a fiction. It is not going to fulfill anything. God is nowhere. You *are*, God is not. Existence is, God is not.

So look into the isness of things, look into this moment now and here, into yourself. That is the closest door to the cosmos; it opens in your very center. All your expectations will look so poor, and all your hopes will look so ugly when you come to know your tremendous splendor, your godliness, when you realize your freedom and when you realize that the whole cosmos is related to you, deeply related to you, and you are just a great aspiration of the cosmos to reach to the highest point of consciousness.

Vincent Van Gogh used to paint trees... Nobody liked his paintings because they were very absurd. His trees went beyond the stars. When asked, "Where have you seen these trees?" he said, "I have never seen these trees; I have just heard a whisper. I was lying in the shade of a tree and I just heard the whisper. The earth was saying to the tree, 'You are my ambition. You are my ambition to reach the stars.' Since that moment I have started painting my trees going beyond the stars."

He is really a genius. Certainly trees are ambitions of the earth. And what is man's consciousness? The ambition of the whole of existence to reach to the highest peak, to become a Gautam Buddha.

In your becoming a Gautam Buddha the whole existence rejoices. You have fulfilled the expectation of existence. You don't need to expect anything, you are yourself an expectation of existence. You fulfill it — and you can fulfill it because existence has given you every opportunity and all the potential to fulfill it. Everything is there. You just have to put everything in the right place, and suddenly you will see that life is a sheer dance of ecstasy from birth to death, from death to birth. These are small episodes, birth and death, in the eternal flow of life.

But unless you drop God, you are going to remain miserable. And misery needs some support from hope, expectation, tomorrows. But this is not living. Do you think living in tomorrow can be called living? Life knows only one moment, and that is the present. Life knows only one space, and that is here. Now and here: these two words are the most significant words in the human language. They represent reality.

Friedrich Nietzsche suggests that the hope of happiness is the instrument by which man is manipulated, more than any actual instance of happiness. Do you remember any moment of real happiness in your past? Just go backwards to your childhood. When you were a child, you thought you would be happy when you were older. Every child wants to grow up quickly.

I used to live in a house that was eight or ten houses away from a post office. In front of my house was the public park, so it was a very quiet and silent place. I used to go for a walk early in the morning about three o'clock. One day I saw near the post office a little boy with a mustache. I could not believe it! It was dark, but it was full-moon night, so I could see the mustache. And he was smoking a cigarette.

I thought, "Perhaps he is a pygmy." Seeing me the boy moved behind a big tree by the side of the road. So I went behind the tree.

The boy said, "Don't tell my father."

I said, "I'm not going to tell anybody. I don't know your father. Who are you?"

He said, "My father is the postmaster here; that is the post office."

I said, "What are you doing? You have got a good mustache."

He just pulled the mustache off. He said, "It is not real, but my father has a real mustache and I always want to grow one quickly. But how to grow it quickly? I even shave my mustache when my father is out, but nothing grows. And he shaves twice a day. So I got this mustache from a shop that sells things for people who are playing in a drama somewhere."

I said, "You are smoking a cigarette, too." He was hiding it behind him.

He said, "My father always smokes, and while smoking he really looks like a man. So I just thought to give it a try."

In that small boy I saw all the children of the world. Every child wants to grow fast, because what is childhood? Being ordered by the mother, by the father, being ordered by the teacher, beaten by the parents, beaten by the teacher… Every boy wants, every girl wants, just to grow as quickly as possible. Just remember your own childhood.

It is absolutely false, the saying, "My childhood was the most beautiful period of my life." If your childhood was the most beautiful period of your life, and out of your childhood grows your youth, it should be even more beautiful. Out of your youth grows old age, which should be perfection. But that is not the case. When you become a youth you start looking embarrassed. You are young and where is the happiness? Perhaps it is hidden in a woman, or hidden in a man. Find a soul mate!

Just today I have received information that in Europe there is a great New Age movement for finding your soul mate. In their pamphlet they mention my name, because once I said that you cannot find your soul mate. It is a big world, and I don't think existence creates soul mates. Where are you going to find each other? People find each other just in their neighborhood, or in their college. How is existence going to manage to put you and your soul mate in the same college? So that pamphlet condemns me because I am not saying the right thing: everybody has a soul mate.

That is a good consolation; but just look at those who have found their soul mates… Zareen is sitting here. She has found a soul mate, and since she found the soul mate I have never seen her as happy as she was before. And I know her soul mate. He keeps himself locked in his room, because he wants, poor fellow, some time to himself. But Zareen is not going to let him be alone—you have to be careful when you have found your soul mate—she goes on knocking on his door. She jumps balconies to reach the poor fellow. Not to make a fuss—"Everybody will know"—he has to open the door. Then the meeting of the soul mates begins. Both are miserable since they have met.

My secretary was telling me, because I was asking her why Zareen does not look as happy as she used to. She said, "She has found a soul mate." I said, "She should be happier. If the soul mate is not right, bring a group of men and put them in a queue before Zareen—'Choose your soul mate!'" And you can change every day. Why get bored with one? Just the same dress, the same dress…One gets bored, that is absolutely natural. All soul mates create boredom and nothing else.

And here in this place where freedom is the absolutely total value, ultimate value, where change is accepted as life's way, why should you bother about one soul mate when there are so many soul mates available? Just go on changing, and life will be a joy. Zareen will again be laughing and smiling. Because of this soul mate she has become hard and dictatorial in her work. On whom to take revenge because the soul mate always travels to Bombay? And I know why he goes to Bombay—just to have a little freedom.

Unnecessary misery…

In youth, people start thinking, "Perhaps in old age life will be peaceful." In old age life becomes a constant anxiety. Death is coming closer and closer. So your whole life is wasted just looking ahead.

I am reminded of a famous Greek astrologer. Even kings of the different countries of Europe used to consult him about their fate. One night he was walking, looking at the stars. But when you look at the stars you cannot look at the road. You cannot manage one eye looking up and one eye looking down; I don't think it is possible. They both go up, or they both go down. So he fell in a well, and then he shouted, screamed, "Save me!"

An old woman, living nearby on her farm, came. She was very old, but somehow she managed to pull him out with a rope. The astronomer said to her, "Do you know who I am? I am the royal astrologer. Almost all the kings and queens of Europe come to me. All the richest people discuss with me their fate, their future. My fee is very high, but because you have saved me you can come to me. I will tell your future without any fee."

The old woman laughed. She said, "You cannot even see that the well is ahead of you. You should be ashamed of yourself, and those who have been coming to you must be fools. I am not going to come. If you cannot see the well ahead of you, what can you see about my future?"

The future is just your hope, expectation. And when this life is not fulfilling you start looking further, beyond death. All these are fictions just to enable you to survive somehow. But this survival is not how you are supposed to be. Existence has not given you birth just to live in hopes. You can be really ecstatic this moment, and there is no other moment.

Meditation is, Zen is living now and here.

Now the sutra:

On one occasion Seigen commented to Sekito, "Some say that an intelligence comes from the south of the Ling."
Sekito said, "There is no such intelligence from anybody."

Intelligence arises within you. It never comes from outside, from anybody, from any place, south or north, or east or west. It has nothing to do with outside. It is your inner flowering.

Seigen said, "If not, whence are all those sutras of the tripitaka?"

If you say that intelligence does not come from outside, then what about the sutras of Gautam Buddha called *tripitaka*, three treasures? What do you say about them?"

Sekito said, "They all come out of here...."

Remember this word "here".
We were just talking about it.

Sekito said, "They all come out of here, and there is nothing wanting."

Once you are *here*, there is nothing unfulfilled in you. Everything becomes so fulfilled, such a deep contentment, that you don't need anything anymore. You have actualized your potential. Your flowers have opened their petals, the spring has come.

It all comes from here, it all comes from now. Neither can Buddha give it to you, nor anybody else.

On Seigen's death, Sekito went to Mount Nangaku. Finding a large, flat rock,
he built a hut, and from thence forward came to be known as "Stonehead,"
and later, when he was a master, as "Stonehead Osho."

This Mount Nangaku is the place where he had gone to see Master Nangaku.

In Japan it has been a tradition that whenever a master lives on a mountain the emperor gives the name of the master to the mountain, so the mountain becomes his memorial. For centuries and centuries people will know that this Mount Nangaku once was the temple and the shelter of a great master, Nangaku.

Sekito had gone to see Nangaku to deliver a message, a letter, from Seigen. At that time he must have looked on the beauty of the mountain where Nangaku used to live, at the top. When Seigen died, Sekito went to Mount Nangaku. He must have seen, while he was going there and coming back, that the place was immensely beautiful.

Nangaku was not right for him, which does not mean that the man was wrong. It simply means they could not feel a certain harmony. He might be right for someone else, but he was not right for him. Or perhaps Sekito was not right for Nangaku—it is the same thing, but it is not a condemnation of Master Nangaku. It simply means that two persons did not feel anything as a bridge. But Sekito must have seen the mountain as he came and went; it was a beautiful place. So he found a small place, a flat rock on Mount Nangaku, on the top of which was the monastery. *He built a hut, and from thence forward came to be known as "Stonehead,"* because he was always sitting on this stone. And he used to have, like every Buddhist monk, his head shaved. So his head looked almost like the rock he was sitting on.

Hearing of Sekito living on a rock, the master, Nangaku, sent a young monk
to him, saying, "Go to the east and examine in detail the monk sitting on the
stone-head. If he is the monk who came the other day, address him. And if he
replies, you recite to him the following song, 'You are sitting so proudly on the
stone, it is better to come to me.'"
The attendant monk went to Sekito and recited this song. Sekito replied,
"Even if you cried tears of sorrow, I would never ever cross over the hills."

Sekito was absolutely certain that Nangaku was not the man to be his master. There was no feeling of synchronicity, he had not even delivered Seigen's letter.

The monk came back and made a report to Nangaku. Nangaku said, "This monk will surely make the mouth of the people tremble for generations."

Nangaku was right in his estimation. He encountered this fellow when he came to see him, and you remember what he said? Because Nangaku said, "You should not be so arrogant in asking the question, you should be more moderate, you should be more humble," Sekito said to him, "I would rather go into hellfire for eternity than to change my question." And the reason was that no question can be humble. Every question is deep down a doubt, and every question is an interference in the master's silence. It is arrogant. And he left immediately without delivering the letter.

Nangaku had seen this man, so when he sent the messenger he told him, "Take care. If this is the same fellow who came the other day, recite this sutra. Tell him to come to me rather than stay sitting on that stone, and report to me what he says." And what did he say? He said, "I am not going to leave this place, even if you come with tears in your eyes."

Nangaku must have immediately known that this was the same man who was ready to go to eternal hell, but would not ask his question in a different way. That's why he made this comment:

"This monk will surely make the mouth of the people tremble for generations."

And Sekito became a master of hundreds of people who became enlightened. He was a very hard master, almost dangerous to the disciples, but all his hardness came from a very loving heart, a very deep compassion. He wanted them to become enlightened, he did not allow them to escape. Once in a while a disciple might escape and Sekito would follow him for miles and pull him back, "Where are you going? Come back!" And the disciple would say, "Just forgive me, I am tired,"—because he would beat the disciples, he would jump on the disciples. Once he threw a disciple from the window of a second-story building, and jumped on top of him. The disciple had multiple fractures, and Sekito was sitting on his chest asking, "Got it?" And the disciple really got it, he became enlightened. Who cares about multiple fractures, the real thing is enlightenment. At any cost it has to happen!

People had never come across a man like Sekito, whose compassion was so great. He was ready to do *anything*. Even in his old age he would hit so hard that his own hand would hurt. And disciples would say, "You are getting old now, Master, you should not hit people so hard, because they are young and you are old. You are becoming every day more fragile."

He said, "I know. My hand hurts the whole night, but I cannot bear to see somebody groping in the darkness. If just one hit can make him awake, it does not matter if my hand hurts the whole night. Sooner or later these hands will disappear into the earth, but if these hands can help somebody to wake up...You think I am getting old; that is true, but as far as I am concerned, even when I am dead if I see someone stumbling in the darkness I will jump out of my grave and hit him as hard as I can."

This man was a rare master, apparently very hard but deep down so soft that he was ready to jump out of his grave. My feeling is, if he had done that—he never has done that—just his skeleton would have made the person enlightened. There would not have been any need to hit. The person would have shouted immediately, "Got it! You just go back into the grave."

Issa wrote:

Pearls of the dew!
In every single
one of them
I see my home.

These Zen poets have transcended all the poetry of the world, because all poetry is mind fabrication; only haikus come from no-mind.

Pearls of the dew!
In every single
one of them
I see my home.

And when you can see in every dewdrop your home, how can you feel an outsider or insider? You simply become one with existence.

This whole existence is so deeply one at the center. Only on the circumference are we different.

You draw a big circle. On the circumference of the circle you can put points which are different. Then from every point draw a line towards the center. As those lines start coming closer to the center, you will find they are coming closer to each other also. And at the center all the lines meet.

So when I say go to your center, I am not only sending you to your center, it is the center of the whole existence. There we all meet, there it is only one oceanic consciousness.

Nietzsche's foreword to his book, The Antichrist, begins, "This book belongs to the very few. Perhaps none of them is even living yet. Possibly they are the readers who understand my Zarathustra... Only the day after tomorrow belongs to me. Some are born posthumously."

To understand him, Nietzsche continues, one must have "... New ears for new music. New eyes for the most distant things." Do you find in us the capacity for those "new ears," those "new eyes?"

Everybody has the capacity, but the capacity has to be transformed into reality. It is only a potential. And I am working to give you that transformation where your potential "ears" become your reality, where your potential "eyes" become your reality.

Perhaps Nietzsche is talking about you. This is the day after tomorrow. And your meditation will make your ears sensitive enough, your eyes clear enough.

If you can understand me, there is no difficulty in understanding Friedrich Nietzsche, because Nietzsche is only mind. I am no-mind. If you can understand me, you have far better ears and far better eyes than Nietzsche was thinking about. Your meditation is going to open all your sensitivity, your receptivity. Nietzsche will not be difficult for you to understand.

Meditation will make you capable of understanding not only Nietzsche, but those great buddhas who are not born yet. You will be able to understand all the buddhas of the past, of the present, of the future, because their song is one, their music is one. It is the music that arises out of deep silence.

This place is just a scientific lab to create the new man—in Friedrich Nietzsche's words, the superman. But I use the term "new man" because "superman" implies a sense of superiority. Otherwise the word is beautiful, but it can be misguiding; hence I call it the new man, or the buddha, because the new man is going to be fully awakened. If a fully awakened man cannot understand Friedrich Nietzsche, who else can understand him? You are on the way to understanding even deeper things and greater heights.

It is time from these great heights to roll down laughing.

When Little Ernie gets into mischief, his mother tries to discipline him by saying, "God would not like that!" And when Ernie gets really out of hand, his mother says, "God will be angry!"

But one evening at the dinner table, Ernie takes one look at the plate of prunes put in front of him and says, "*Yuck*! I'm not going to eat these wrinkled old black things!"

"Ernie!" says his mother. "God would not like that!"

"I don't care," snaps Ernie. "I am *not* going to eat them!"

"Ernest!" threatens his mother, "God will be angry."

"*Ah!*" shouts Ernie. "*Fuck* God!"

At this, his mother sends him up to his bedroom.

A few minutes later, a violent thunderstorm blows up and shakes the roof and rattles the walls. Ernie's mother goes upstairs to remind him about God's anger. But to her surprise, she finds Ernie looking out of the window at the terrible storm.

"You see, Ernie," exclaims his mother. "This is what happens when you make God angry!"

"Well," replies Ernie, "if you ask me, it is a lot of fuss to make over a plate of prunes!"

The captain of the LA police receives an order from the police commissioner to raid Madam Fifi's "House of Carnal Delights" in downtown Hollywood. But this order causes the captain and his men some embarrassment, because they are all frequent customers themselves and are friendly with Madam Fifi.

So he calls the establishment on the phone to warn them, but finds that Madam Fifi and all the girls have gone out on a picnic. Only the cleaning lady, is there to answer the phone.

"Listen," says the captain. "Pass this message on to Madam Fifi: Tonight, we have to make a surprise raid on the place. But when we come, we will honk the horn loudly, and drive around the block. We will do this three times—and then we will come rushing in. By that time, we want everybody safely out of the place! Do you understand?"

"Yes, yes!" replies the cleaning lady, and she puts down the phone. But when she has finished her work she goes home and forgets to pass on the message.

That night it is business as usual, and Madam Fifi's "House of Carnal Delights" is packed to capacity. At midnight exactly, the police captain and the boys arrive in their patrol cars. They all honk their horns and screech around the block. When they reappear, they honk their horns and go around again. They honk and circle the block once more and then screech to a halt outside and charge into the building.

As they are racing up the stairs with the captain in the lead, they meet two naked girls coming down, holding a mattress between them.

"What the hell is going on?" cries the captain. "Where are you girls going?"

"Don't blame us!" shouts one of the girls. "Some idiot outside is honking for take-away service!"

Now the meditation:

Be silent.

Close your eyes, and feel your body to be completely frozen.

This is the right moment to turn inwards, with your whole energy, with your total consciousness.

Rush towards the center, with an urgency as if this is going to be your last moment on the earth. Without such an urgency nobody has ever become awakened.

Faster and faster…

Deeper and deeper…As you are coming closer to your center, a great silence descends over you. The whole night starts singing songs for you.

A little more, deeper, and you find flowers of peace, serenity, joy, ecstasy, blissfulness, all growing around you.

Just one step more and you are at the very center of your being. Suddenly you see you are no more, only your original face without any mask, without any personality, is there.

This is the face we have called in the East the face of the buddha. This is everybody's original face, it is nobody's monopoly.

The only quality the buddha at the center of being has is witnessing. Witnessing is the whole of spirituality compressed into one word.

Witness you are not the body, witness you are not the mind, and witness you are only a witness, just a mirror reflecting without any judgment, without any appreciation, without any condemnation—a pure mirror, that's what the buddha is.

The silence becomes deeper. Ecstasy becomes overwhelming. You are drunk with the divine. This center is the connection with existence. From here your consciousness is being nourished continuously.

This is your eternal life, without beginning, without end.

To make the witnessing more clear, and more deep…

Relax, let go completely, but remember one thing constantly, that you are a witness.

This witness is the truth.

This witness is beauty.

This witness is the good.

This witness is the opening of all the mysteries of existence, the ultimate secret of all the miracles.

At this impeccable, silent moment, you are the most fortunate people on the earth. I can see your melting, the ice is melting into the ocean. You are disappearing. Ten thousand buddhas have disappeared into one oceanic consciousness.

Collect as much experience of the center as possible, all the flowers of the beyond, the eternal peace, the ultimate joy.

You have to bring all these qualities to your ordinary day-to-day life. The more your day-to-day life becomes graceful, beautiful, peaceful, silent, loving, compassionate, the closer the buddha will come to you.

So remember to persuade the buddha that you are getting ready, only he is missing. He has to come following you just like a shadow.

These are the three steps of enlightenment: first, buddha comes behind you with all his warmth and grace and beauty and blissfulness and benediction, as a shadow.

Soon he takes over. You become the shadow in the second step.

And in the second step, your shadow by and by starts withering away, because it has been only a shadow and nothing else.

In the third step you find you are the buddha, and the person you used to be is no more to be found anywhere.

That day will be the greatest day of celebration in your life—not only in your life, but in the life of the whole of existence. The whole existence will celebrate: the trees, the stars, the moon, the oceans, the earth—everything around you will have a tremendous ceremony to welcome your coming home.

After a long wandering into different bodies, into different species, finally you have come home.

… Now come back, but come back with the same grace as a buddha comes, with the same silence.

Sit for a few moments, reminding yourself of the golden path you have traveled, and the tremendous space you have been in.

And feel the radiance and the coolness of a buddha behind you.

He is almost touching your body and your heart. He is so motherly, he is so feminine, so fragile—just like a lotus leaf.

Rejoice that you are those chosen few Friedrich Nietzsche speaks of. Soon you will start having a new sensitivity to your ears, and a new light will shine in your eyes, and a new dance will be in your heart.

The spring is coming soon, and you are all going to blossom into buddhas. Less than that is not sufficient.

You *have* to be a buddha; only that experience of the ultimate height and the ultimate depth will bring you home. The very source from where you have come is also the goal where you are going.

And I am immensely happy with you. You are doing so well, with such honesty that any master would have been proud of you.

God is dead, and Zen is the only living truth.

Chapter 4
God is a lie

After Nangaku's comment about Sekito, he once more sent the attendant
monk to Sekito to ask him a question. On arrival, the monk asked Sekito,
"What is liberation?"
Sekito said, "Who bound you?"
The monk asked, "What is the pure land?"
Sekito responded, "Who made you dirty?"
The monk asked, "What is nirvana?"
"Who gave you birth and death?" Sekito replied.
The attendant monk came back to Nangaku and reported Sekito's answers.
Nangaku put both hands together and made a gesture of touching his feet.
At that time, Kengo, Ran and Nangaku were thought to be the three masters
in the country, and all three of them said, "From the stone-head comes
the lion's roar to my ear."
The monk went back to Sekito and said that, if there were anything the monk
could do for him, to let him know. A little later, the master, Nangaku, came
with his monks to see Sekito. Sekito stood up to receive him, and the two
greeted each other. Later, Nangaku had a temple built for Sekito's convenience.

First the questions.

?
Is it not the same to call existence intelligent and loving as to call it God?
It might not be the Christian concept of God, but there are other pantheistic
concepts which see God in everything.

It is not the same. "God" gives a sense of personality, of limitedness, while "existence" gives you an unlimited, non-personal vastness. God cannot be equivalent to existence. God has always been conceived by all religions, monotheistic or polytheistic, as the creator of existence. And existence is not a created phenomenon; it has been here always.

So first the "God" gives you an impression that there is a creator. Then many lies start arising out of the idea of God. Then prayer becomes possible, then worship becomes possible, then statues of God become possible. Then temples and churches and mosques start arising. Then organized religions become possible. God is the center of all organized religions.

Once you accept God as a person, you have limited intelligence, invested intelligence in one person. I am spreading it all over existence. The whole existence is intelligent, caring, compassionate, loving — but it is not a person. It is not limited in any way; it is unlimited, infinite and eternal. There is no beginning, no end. It is continuously evolving towards higher peaks and higher peaks; it is continuously fathoming depths beyond depths. There are skies beyond skies; there is no end to existence, it has no boundary.

God is bound to be limited. God is a fiction of the human mind, existence is not. You have created God in an old image. He is just sitting on a throne, an old man, of course—you cannot conceive of God as young or a child—with a long beard. The beard must be longer than God himself. Since eternity he has never entered a barber shop and I don't think that he has safety razors. Every morning in the bathroom...In fact, I don't think he has a bathroom either, there is no mention of his bathroom in any scripture. So beware of him! He must be using the whole sky as his toilet. When something falls on your head, it is holy shit. Conceiving of God as a person is going to create many troubles.

No, existence is a totally different concept. It is not your fiction; it is really there. When you were not here, it was there. When you will not be here, it will be here. We come and go; we are just waves in this vast ocean of existence. We come and go, existence remains — and to find that which remains is the ultimate truth. You don't have to worship nature, you don't have to pray to nature. Those things are only associated with the fiction of God.

Existence is non-judgmental. I want to emphasize this fact as categorically as possible. God is judgmental. The Christian God has exactly declared that there will be a Judgment Day, when he will choose those who are on his side, the followers of Jesus Christ, his son. And those who are not on his side are against him. They will be thrown into hellfire for eternity. It is because of God that all kinds of moralities arise: this is good, that is bad. What is the criterion? The scripture. And the scriptures were written by primitive people, uneducated; they don't belong to our century.

Existence does not write any scriptures and does not give any commandments. Existence does not tell you what to do and what not to do. Existence is absolutely non-judgmental. It is as compassionate to the sinner as to the saint, it makes no difference, because in the eyes of existence everything that is natural is beautiful. Those who go against nature, the religions call saints. Nature simply feels sad for them. Existence simply feels that they are going astray, and by going astray they will suffer. It is not that existence is giving them suffering and hell, punishment and reward, no. Existence simply is there. If you are in tune with it you will be immensely rewarded. Nobody is rewarding you, it is just that the very tuning with existence is such a peace, such a joy, such a benediction, you are already rewarded. There is no reward beyond this; and those who are not in tune with nature and existence are already punished.

You can see your saints: they can't smile, they can't laugh, they can't enjoy anything. They are the ugliest human beings who have fallen from humanity into some kind of darkness that knows no end. They are self-torturers, masochists, and they are already suffering. Their suffering is not caused by anybody else, it is caused by themselves.

This is the criterion: if you are suffering, that means you are not in tune with nature. If you are miserable, that means you are not in tune with nature. So the moment you feel you are miserable, suffering, in agony, immediately try to make the distance smaller, come closer to existence and suddenly there will be light and there will be joy and there will be song and there will be celebration.

To be in tune with existence is its own reward; not to be in tune is its own punishment. So my approach is very clear and clean. If you create a God, then he is bound to judge you. And his judgment is going to be out of date; he will always be lagging behind human consciousness. And if you follow those scriptures which are creations of the priest, not of God...

There is intrinsic proof of it. Hindus say the Vedas were written by God himself, and I cannot conceive the stupidity. Nobody in thousands of years has objected to the idea. There is intrinsic proof in the Vedas themselves that they were created by the priests. There is no need for any outer proof.

I will tell you just which proofs are intrinsic. Ninety-eight percent of the prayers in the Vedas are from priests. God will not say a prayer. There is no other God; to whom will he pray? Just look at the point. God cannot be a worshipper; God cannot be in prayer; God cannot ask anything from anyone because there is no one beyond him. All the Vedas are nothing but prayers, and the content of the prayers is so idiotic it is a miracle that nobody raises any question. One of the so-called Hindu seers prays, of course to God, that this year, "Just let your clouds rain in my fields and not in the fields of my enemies." Do you think this writing can come from God?

Another asked God, "Let my cows have more and more milk and let my enemies' cows simply stop giving milk at all." These kinds of things God will write? This is intrinsic proof that these are the writings of ordinary worshippers, brahmins, priests, and they have been proclaiming for thousands of years that the Vedas are written by God. All religions try to prove that their holy scripture is written by God. If not written, at least sent through a messenger; but the word is coming from God.

Once you accept the fiction of God, you will have to accept these holy scriptures and you will have to accept his judgment. And his judgment is absolutely against nature, because these scriptures prescribe that you live an abnormal, stupid, insane life: Don't eat according to the needs of your body, fast. Don't live in the world, renounce, go to the Himalayas, live in the caves. With difficulty man has come out of the caves. Thousands of years' struggle has brought man out of the caves, and these so-called holy scriptures are sending him back: "Go to the caves!"

There is a certain psychological reason behind it. If you are fasting, you become more imaginative. Obviously you have to imagine food; that is the first imagination that comes. The whole night you will imagine that you are being invited by the king himself and you are enjoying a great feast. It is bound to happen. If you are sexually starved, you will have sexual dreams. If you are physically starved, you will have dreams about food. If you are thirsty, you will dream about water.

Your dreams show what you need, what you are denying yourself. The dreams are indications from your very nature that you are unnecessarily going against nature and you will suffer. But all religions prescribe fasting as one of the virtues, great virtues. The reason is that fasting helps hallucination, it is a scientific fact. If you fast for three weeks continuously and you are alone in a cave in the Himalayas, you will start hallucinating. By the end of the second week you will start talking to yourself. By the end of the third week you will start talking to God. The actual dialogue you will manage from both sides. You will ask the question and you will answer the question and you will feel that the answer is coming from God. By the end of the fourth week you will be able to see your God, Jesus Christ or Krishna or Buddha, whosoever you have been believing in. By the fourth week you have lost all grip on intelligence, you have lost all grip on reality. You cannot make any distinction what is real and what is dream; you have fallen back into the state of a small child.

The small child in the beginning cannot make the distinction between what is dream and what is real. In the dream he is playing with a toy, and when he wakes up in the morning and the toy is gone, he starts crying, "Where is my toy?" He cannot make the distinction that the toy was a dream. It will take a little maturity, a little growth of intelligence to make the distinction between the real and the unreal. In just four weeks fasting you will lose all the discrimination of your intelligence.

Living alone is absolutely necessary for it, because if somebody else is living with you, you will talk to him. That will be a release. But if you are living alone…and every religion prescribes living alone, in monasteries, in your cells or in caves. Live alone. Why alone? So that you cannot talk to anybody—then your whole mind is so boiling to talk that you start talking to yourself.

You have seen people on the street also. You can see their lips moving, yet they are alone. They are rushing towards their office or their home and their lips are moving. Sometimes they are making gestures, throwing out something. What is happening to them? They are going like robots towards their house because it has become habitual. They don't need to think about where to turn right and where to turn left, this will be done by the legs themselves. I have seen people counting money on their fingers, I have seen people with their lips moving.

I have loved a story very much. A man had become the center of attention of a crowd gathered in a waiting room at a junction railway station. The train was late and all were eagerly waiting for the train, but everything was focused on a person who was resting in a chair. His lips were moving and once in a while he would start smiling, once in a while he would giggle, once in a while he would throw something away. Finally they could not resist the temptation to ask what was going on.

So one man asked him, "What is going on? Sometimes you giggle, sometimes you smile. Sometimes you throw something away."

He said, "Nothing. I am just telling jokes to myself. When I hear a really good joke, I smile. And when a joke is so fresh and new, I giggle. And when I hear some old joke, I simply throw it away."

He is telling jokes to himself … all the jokes must be old. Everybody said, "You are having a great time, while we are unnecessarily worrying about the train that is getting later and later."

In India it happens…

Once I was stuck in Allahabad. First they declared the train was two hours late. I said, "Not much of a problem. I will reach to the place where I am going in time. After two hours, then I went to inquire. They said, "Now it is another four hours late."

I said, "Is it going backwards? How can it be another four hours late when it was just two hours late? Those two hours are gone; the train should be on the platform. It means it is now six hours late. What is happening? Is the train going backwards?"

The man was in shock. He could not answer me, because my question was absolutely logical. "What is happening to the train? I can understand that it was late, but it cannot go on moving backwards. Next time I come after four hours it might be twelve hours late because it is going backwards. You have to answer me."

But in India it happens every day...just to keep people hoping. They don't know exactly how late it is, so they say two hours late. If it comes early, it is good. If it does not come early, then it is still later, but to tell people that it will be twelve hours late will be too shocking. So, make it easy: two hours, four hours, two hours more...it is just coming in an hour. By and by it is twelve hours late. They could not answer me because I knew the reality. What was the reality? The reality was they had no idea how late it was going to be.

Sitting in the waiting room, watching people...I have seen people with nothing to do; they start moving their lips, talking to themselves, just keeping themselves engaged. Otherwise it is an agony to think that you are caught up in this place for nobody knows how long. Sometimes the train is twenty-four hours late, and I have seen it even forty-eight hours late. I don't know how this happens.

But I found out once. I was coming from Chanda to Gondia, in a very small train. Now these small trains have almost disappeared, except in a few places. This train was a passenger train; on that small line there were only passenger trains, and it was stopping at every station. One friend of mine, who has since died, a rich man, had persuaded me to travel. He said, "It is a beautiful place to travel to in this train. On both sides it is scenic—mountains, rivers, wild forests."

So I agreed; otherwise I was going to fly, because this train would take twelve hours while I could fly in fifteen minutes. I said, "Okay, this time let us try it. You have been telling me again and again that it is beautiful country around the train." It is an almost unpopulated area, an aboriginal area, where people live deep in the forest.

At one station he told me, "Get down." It was mango season. And that place! Outside the station, there were such beautiful mango trees, perhaps for miles, and the smell of mangos... and hundreds of cuckoos creating such beautiful songs, such beautiful sounds. He took me out. I said, "What are you doing?"

He said, "Come with me. You will never find such beautiful mangos anywhere."

So he climbed up a tree and told me to come behind him. I said, "But what about the train?"

He said, "Don't be worried. That is my responsibility. Unless I come down, the train will not move."

I said, "This is strange—because you have not told anybody, the stationmaster or the driver."

He started laughing, he said, "Just look up. The driver is above us. Unless I allow him to come down, the train cannot move. Don't you be worried."

And the driver started laughing. He said, "That's right."

So we enjoyed mangos for almost an hour, and whenever the driver tried to come down my friend said, "I will pull you by the leg and throw you down. Just remain there. The train cannot move until we are finished. You eat mangos, there is no harm."

So we kept the driver up the tree and all the passengers on the train were wondering what the matter was. It was the only train on the line. One time it goes, one time it comes. So there was no question of another train coming. The stationmaster was looking to see where the driver had gone. The conductor was looking all around, everywhere…And we saw everybody searching for the driver. The driver was imprisoned completely because he could not pass us. We were there to push him back. "Just go back up!" Then I knew how these trains get so late. It could only happen in India.

All religions preach fasting and, "Go into aloneness and constantly visualize, imagine your God." It is a psychological fact that in four weeks even the most intelligent person will start wavering over what is real and what is imaginary. And what to say about the ordinary masses whose intelligence quotient is not greater than that of a seven-year-old? Their minds remain stuck between the ages of seven and fourteen. The body goes on growing to seventy, eighty, but the mind stays somewhere between seven and fourteen; very rarely does a man pass beyond the mental age of fourteen.

So these people who have a retarded mind—and only a retarded mind can belong to a religious organization, can believe in the fiction of God, can believe in heaven and hell, can pray to the empty sky—these people renounce the world out of fear and greed. And when they are alone they start visualizing, for which fasting is absolutely necessary. It weakens not only you, but also your mind.

Have you ever considered the fact that no vegetarian in India has ever received a single Nobel Prize? And in fact they should be the ones to receive most of the Nobel Prizes, because they think they are eating the purest food. Their minds should be purer and clearer and cleaner than those of non-vegetarians. But not a single Jaina has received a Nobel Prize, and it will never be possible because something which is needed for intelligence to grow is missing in their food. But they won't listen. I have talked at their conferences and they were all angry, they were ready to kill me. But they won't listen. I was telling them that it is perfectly good to be vegetarian, but they should understand that there are a few proteins which are missing in their food for which they have to have a substitute.

The best way is to start eating eggs that are unfertilized. They are just like vegetables, there is no life in them. When the hen has not been hanging around a cock, she is still going to give eggs every day. She is not dependent on the cock. So the egg will be just vegetarian, there will be no life in it. And it has all the proteins and vitamins which are needed for the intelligence to grow.

But just the word "egg" is enough to freak them out: "You are teaching us to eat eggs!"

I said, "You don't understand. I am not teaching you to eat eggs, I am teaching you to eat unfertilized eggs."

They said, "Eggs are eggs."

They will not understand a simple phenomenon: that when it is unfertilized, it is not an egg, it is just the shape of the egg. Otherwise it is pure protein, vitamins, and so cheap and so natural. And it is an absolute necessity for your intelligence to grow.

You will be surprised to know that Jews get forty percent of the Nobel Prizes and the whole remaining world gets the other sixty percent. And there are not many Jews because everybody is killing them. For four thousand years the whole world has been killing Jews. Mohammedans are killing them, Christians are killing them, everybody is against them. So they are a very small portion of humanity, but they get forty percent of the Nobel Prizes. What is the problem? When I worked out what the reason was and I told the Indians, everybody was against me.

I finally stopped talking to the masses because these idiots won't understand. The Jews are some of the most intelligent people on the earth. Just see: Jesus has turned half of humanity to Christianity; Karl Marx, another Jew, has turned the other half to Communism. Sigmund Freud, the third Jew, exploits both. The fourth Jew, Albert Einstein, created atomic energy and nuclear weapons to destroy the whole world.

These four Jews are the most important people in the world. Strange! And the reason is even stranger: it is their circumcision. It is not a laughing matter at all; it has a scientific basis. Even scientists are now agreeing with the fact that circumcision has something to do with Jewish intelligence. As they have been working on the brain, they have found that there are millions of small nerves in the brain. In this small skull millions of small nerves, not visible to the eyes. And they control your whole behavior, your intelligence, your functioning of the body, your digestion, your blood circulation, they control everything.

The intelligence is controlled by a certain center in the brain. By the side of this intelligence center is the center that controls your sexuality. They are too close. The more intelligent a person is, the more sexual he will be. The more sexual a person is the more the possibility of energy for creation, for intelligence. And what happens when the very small child, just born, is immediately circumcised?

The sexual organism is connected with the brain center, and particularly in a small child everything is very soft, flexible. And to cut that small child's unnecessary skin from the sexual organ gives a certain shock. That shock goes not only to the sexual center — because the sexual center is so close to the intelligence center, the shock goes to the intelligence center also. And the shock in a certain way wakes it up.

There was a great debate in the time of the emperor Constantine, whether to continue circumcision for Christians. He was a Roman and the president of the council of Nicaea that was deciding what to do about circumcision. Because they were all Jews converted into Christians, Constantine voted against it. That's why Christians stopped circumcision; now they are starting again.

In America now it is an established thing, it does not matter to what religion you belong. Almost every child born in the hospital is circumcised as a matter of routine.

So the doctor has immediately to circumcise the child. The reason is double: it is hygienic, it prevents many diseases, it keeps you cleaner; and the secret reason is, it gives a shock to your intelligence center, which then certainly starts functioning better than any other center.

I am absolutely in favor of it. The whole world should be circumcised, and immediately after the birth; the more quickly you do it, the better. But to tell people the truth about anything is very difficult. To have eyes in a valley of blind people is not an easy job.

Keeping a person fasting for four weeks destroys all those proteins and vitamins that make his intelligence. You don't know the dynamics of fasting. Why are all religions insisting on fasting? Because it destroys… For four weeks, at the most, one can live on the storage. After the fourth week there is no storage. And immediately, within six minutes, if they are not supplied with the right amount of proteins, oxygen, the right amount of vitamins, those small nerves break down. Once those small nerves break down, you don't have any capacity to discriminate whether Christ is standing before you, or it is your imagination, your projection.

With open eyes you start seeing dreams. It needs aloneness so nobody disturbs your imagination and it needs constant visualization, praying the whole day. In monasteries what are people doing? The whole day praying: *Ave Maria, Ave Maria*...and holding Maria's picture and prostrating themselves and fasting and "Ave Maria"...In a few days' time the picture will start moving its lips. Ave Maria is coming alive and that is a great satisfaction to the stupid mind.

Soon Maria will start coming out of the picture. A great revelation! That's what the person was waiting for. He touches the feet of nobody, but he feels the feet, just as you feel things in your dream. He has destroyed the barrier between dream and reality. To destroy that barrier, fasting and aloneness and constant visualization are used.

You can visualize God, but you cannot visualize existence; and there is no need to visualize it, it is already there. The trees are there, the rivers, the ocean, the mountains, the stars, the whole sky is there. It is not your imagination; it is an objective phenomenon.

You can all agree that it is a full-moon night. But if somebody is seeing Jesus, you will not agree because you will not see Jesus, only he is seeing Jesus. It is a projection. If it were a reality, then there would be no question; others would also see it, as they see the full moon, as they see the sunrise, as they see roses and everybody agrees that, yes, there is a rose flower. Maybe they will have different opinions: a poet may be more sensitive, a painter may look at the rose with different eyes because he has a sensitivity for colors. A man who is an expert in perfumes will have a different sensitivity towards the rose because he will smell more deeply than you can. And for a man like me who has an allergy to perfumes...

My gardener has to keep all the flowers outside my windows, which are never opened, so I can see the roses but the perfume cannot reach to me. And the poor gardener has to work hard because keeping those roses around my room...There are such big, huge trees, so much shadow, and roses cannot blossom perfectly unless they have sunlight. So she has constantly to change the flowerpots.

But she manages for me to see the roses all around me wherever I am in the house. She is deceiving the sun and she is deceiving the roses. She has to continually move them in a rotation; whenever a flower comes to its total blossoming, she brings it around to my side outside the windows. And when she sees that the plant is not happy without the sun, she takes the plant to the sun. So she has to keep a double row rotating. It is a rotary club! But she manages perfectly well. She knows I love the roses but I cannot tolerate their fragrance. I am too sensitive to their fragrance; that immediately disturbs me.

So it may be different to different people, but the existence of the rose will be objective. Everybody will accept it, except a few blind people; but they also can touch the rose, they also can smell the rose. Some idea they can have of the rose except the color. They can feel its softness, its velvety petals and because the blind man has no eyes...

Eyes use eighty percent of your energy. The other four senses have only five percent distributed to each. Twenty percent of your energy is used by four senses, the eyes use eighty percent. So the blind man distributes a hundred percent of his energy to the four senses; twenty-five percent to each. That's why blind people can be such good singers; they have a better ear than other people. Their touch has more energy than a man with eyes because their hands are carrying twenty-five percent of their energy, your hand carries only five percent. So they may not be able to see the flower and the color, but they can touch and their touch will be deeper than yours. They can smell and their smell will be deeper than yours. But we can come to the same conclusion that there is something objective.

Your dream is purely yours; you cannot share it with anybody.

Two friends were talking. One said, "Last night was a great night. In my dream I went fishing. And, my God, I had never seen such a big fish in my whole life. Just to catch one fish and to carry it to the bank, I felt I was not strong enough. The fish was so big. And fish upon fish…I was lying down on the beach, the whole beach was full. You should have seen, you should have been there."

The other friend said, "That's nothing. Last night I dreamt that naked women were lying by my side, one on my left, one on my right. I looked to the right, and I was amazed: it was Marilyn Monroe. And on the other side was Sophia Loren, both naked, and you are talking about fish, you idiot."

The other man also became angry. He said, "If this was the case, why did you not give me a phone call immediately? What were you going to do with two women?"

The man said, "I did. I phoned your wife, and she said, 'He has gone fishing.'"

You cannot share your dreams, you cannot share your hallucinations. So a follower of Krishna will see Krishna, not Christ. A follower of Christ will see Christ, not Krishna, and when he is seeing Christ you can be there but you won't see anything at all. It is just a projection, an open-eyed dream. To make it possible you need to fast to destroy your intelligence and you need aloneness, so nobody disturbs you and tells you that you are an idiot: "There is nobody. I can see a plain wall. Where is your Krishna? I don't see anyone and I can bring other people and prove that nobody sees what you are seeing." So you need to be alone, so nobody disturbs your projection, your hallucination.

God has been one of the greatest disturbances to human evolution because it has made people hallucinate, destroying their intelligence, destroying their possibility of becoming a buddha.

Existence has its own wisdom, existence has its own love. You just have to experiment. And now science is very clear about it. In fact, the first scientist who became aware of the sensitivity and intelligence of trees was so shocked because he felt, "We don't have that sensitivity and that intelligence; it is a totally different dimension which we have never bothered about. We have lived with trees for millennia, millions of years, but we have never bothered to find out whether those trees have any intelligence, any sensitivity." It is just recently that scientists have become aware.

Now they have a special instrument, similar to a cardiogram; it uses the same type of mechanism. They put the cardiogram around the tree and the cardiogram starts creating a graph of how the tree is feeling. The graph is very harmonious — the sun is rising, a cool breeze is blowing and the tree is dancing in the wind, in the sun; she is really happy. The graph is very harmonious, there is no tension in the tree's mind, no trouble, no anxiety. The graph continues harmoniously…and suddenly a gardener appears with an ax in his hand. Immediately the graph starts trembling, it is no longer harmonious, the tree is feeling worried. But this happens only if the gardener is going to cut the tree. It is strange, because they found that the tree is not bothered by the ax; the tree is bothered by the intention of the gardener. When it became clear to the scientist, it was really shocking.

First they thought it was the ax. The tree has no eyes, but it must have some way of perceiving. But finally they discovered that it was not the ax, it was the intention of the person. The first time they brought a gardener with an ax to cut the trees, including the tree that they were studying. The gardener was going to cut off one of its branches, and the tree completely freaked out. The graph showed that the tree was absolutely against what was going to happen. It was shocking…because trees don't have eyes, and how far away was the gardener with his ax? Then they tried having a gardener come with the ax but with no intention of cutting the tree. The graph remained harmonious.

So it was not the ax, it was the desire, the intention of the gardener to which the tree was somehow receptive. Then they researched further. They wired other trees also near the main tree, and they found that it was not only the tree that was going to be cut, other trees also felt sympathy for that tree; their graphs didn't go as crazy, but they did become disharmonious. They knew that one of their friends, one of their neighbors, was going to be cut. But this would happen only if there was an intention. If there was no intention and the gardener came with an ax and passed by, no tree gave any sign of worry, anxiety, anguish.

This whole existence has its own ways of being intelligent. Our intelligence is not the only intelligence. A famous scientist, John Lilly, has been working with dolphins. Dolphins have a very different language. Nobody ever thought that anybody had language except man. And the dolphin's head is bigger than a man's head; it has more nerves than the man's head. Perhaps it has a higher stage of intelligence than man. It uses a certain system which is called sonar, because it creates a certain sound in the water. That sound travels through the water for miles and reaches another dolphin to whom it is addressed—without any wire, this is a wireless system! There are thousands of dolphins in the area, but perhaps the boyfriend or the girlfriend…and the message is a sound we cannot hear, it is beyond the range of our hearing. Only when we magnify it through instruments can we hear it, a certain very beautiful sound. And it must be that the sound is directed to a particular dolphin—perhaps that particular dolphin has a name and address. The sound reaches and soon you find the other dolphin rushing to the spot from where the first dolphin has given the signal, "Come soon!"

Lilly worked almost his whole life with dolphins. Dolphins are very loving animals, very playful, very joyous. They have never attacked any human being or any other dolphin—no fight, no quarrel. If you are swimming, they will swim with you. If you are playing with them, they will play with you. They are perfectly happy with human beings, they have no problem at all. The whole existence…

I used to have a gardener, a very old man. I found that once in a while when he was not aware that I was watching—I may have been inside the house looking at him through the window—he was talking to the trees. I caught him one day red-handed, I said, "What are you doing?"

He said, "Don't tell anybody, they will think I am mad. But the truth is that I feel a certain affinity… My whole life I have worked with trees; I have always talked to them and to my surprise, if I put two plants of equal height and I talk to one plant and not to the other—and I give equal nourishment, equal care, equal water, equal sun, equal manure to both, but to one I talk with great love, I caress with my hands—that tree grows faster. Soon, within a month, it has a height double the other tree. Although everything else is equal, one thing is missing—my love.

Every year he used to win the competition for flowers. He produced the greatest roses I have ever seen, the greatest dahlias I have ever seen. And his strategy was to talk to the flowers: "Don't let me down. The competition is coming closer. You have to give me one big flower, the biggest that you can manage."

I became intimate with him and he knew that I would not tell anybody. I understand him… and I don't think he is mad. He is working perfectly. Poor fellow, if he had been educated and scientific, he would have discovered many secrets about trees. But I have seen it with my own eyes because he was with me for almost nine years. When I left, he wanted to come with me. But I said, "In Bombay I won't have a garden."

He even wrote to me in America, when I was there: "Now you have such a big place there, why don't you call me. Although I am so old, and not much use, still — what I can do with trees, nobody else can do."

Existence has multidimensional intelligence. We are only one section of this vast universe. Don't think for a single moment that I am putting existence in place of God. No! God does not exist, existence exists. That's why we call it "existence."

It is very easy for me to say, "Ah, I have not believed in God since I was a child, and even then I was not so sure." But this habit of the mind to try to turn the mysteries into superstitions is very deep-rooted and slippery. The other night when you were speaking I was reminded of occasions in the past when I have attributed these qualities of omnipotence, omnipresence, omniscience to you, despite the fact you have always told us that way of thinking is nonsense.
It seems this disease of God is hiding deep in the bones and pops out like some obscene intruder when I least expect it and where I certainly don't want it.

It is easy to change your prisons. The new prison looks better. It is easy to change your chains, your slaveries, because any slavery, howsoever different from the old one, is still deep down the same—and that's what people go on doing. Hindus become Christians, Christians become Hindus. They are only changing their slavery. They are only changing their prisons, they are only changing their handcuffs, their chains. Nothing is changed.

So when you hear God is dead and your intellect is convinced that God never existed, he is nowhere to be found…it is simply intellectual conviction. But you are not just intellect; you are emotion, you are sentiment, you are feeling, which is deeper than intellect. And the concept of

God has entered into your emotions, into your sentiments, into your feelings. The intellect is the surface of your mind, and you may be convinced logically, rationally, there is no God.

One of my friends, an old man, very intelligent, used to be a follower of J. Krishnamurti, and was of the same age as J. Krishnamurti. I came into his life when he was very old, but he started coming to me. He was intellectually a giant, convinced that there is no God, no hell, no heaven, no morality, that this is all social convenience.

One day his son came running to me, they lived just five minutes walking distance, and he told me, "My father has had a serious heart attack and the doctors are worried that he may have another attack coming. He is so weak and he has suddenly remembered you and wants you to be there."

So I went, running, with him. As I approached...they had put the whole room in darkness, an air-conditioned room. I stood at the door, I heard some sound. That old man was repeating, "Hare Krishna, Hare Rama." I could not believe it. His whole life he had been denying, denying, denying, and now he was repeating, "Hare Krishna, Hare Rama."

I went very slowly, not to disturb him, sat by his side, listened closely. He was repeating, "Hare Krishna, Hare Rama." I shook him. He opened his eyes. I said, "What are you doing? Just one heart attack, and your whole philosophy is gone?"

He said, "This is not the time for discussion, and this is not the time to take any risk. Just leave me alone; just sit by my side and let me pray to God. I know intellectually there is no God. But who knows? What is the harm? Anyway I am dying. It is better to repeat his name. If he exists, it will be helpful; if he does not exist, what is the harm? I just repeated his name a few times, that's all."

I said, "This is not the question. It is a question of your whole integrity. You are a very split man." It was only intellect. That's what I have been saying to you again and again, that this is intellectual rationality. And that was the failure of J. Krishnamurti. He was only talking to people intellectually, convincing them intellectually, but he had no method, no meditation that people could experience deeper than feeling. People can go deeper than the heart. They can reach to their being, and only then a tremendous light arises which is unwavering; whether death comes or a heart attack comes, it makes no difference.

The man recovered. After a few days he came to see me and he said, "Don't tell anybody."

I said, "I am going to tell everybody and I am going to send the message to J. Krishnamurti."

I did. I said, "These are your followers, lifelong followers. And you have depended on these people."

Krishnamurti's last statement before he died agreed with me. His last statement was, "I am dying a frustrated man. People have used me as entertainment. Nobody has listened." But it was not the fault of the people. It was his own fault. He was just talking to them intellectually; he never gave them any indication to go deeper.

Unless you go deeper, you will shift your projections from one to another. If there is no God, you will make *me* your God. And certainly I am not God. I have never created this ugly mess that you see around the world. I never created Adolf Hitler, Genghis Khan, and Tamerlane, and

Nadirshah and Benito Mussolini. I never created these people. Don't make me responsible! And I am not omnipotent. I am just sitting in my chair, that's all. Omnipotent means I will need a chair in which the whole universe fits. And I am not omnipresent. I am not a peeping Tom to look into your bedroom. That's what God used to do, watching you even in your bathroom through the keyhole.

I am not omniscient either. I don't know what is going to happen the next moment. I am simply human, just awake, just fully alert, conscious and responding to life moment to moment according to my awareness, my consciousness; just a pure mirror reflecting whatever comes in front of me. Don't project anything on me.

But I can understand your trouble. Your trouble is you are convinced intellectually, but you have not known the truth from deeper sources of your being. You have to know through meditation that there is no God; existence is self-sufficient, it does not need any God, any fiction.

Once this happens inside you at the deepest core, you will never project the same old stupid superstitions again. Only meditation can bring a metamorphosis to your being. Krishnamurti died a failure because he never considered that he was only dealing with people's intellect. Intellect is part of the mind, and Krishnamurti never helped anybody to go beyond mind.

I suspect perhaps he himself never got beyond the mind. Otherwise, how could he miss it? If he had gone beyond the mind, then his whole effort would have been a long life of ninety years to help people go beyond the mind. When you start looking beyond the mind, there is no God, but this existence becomes so beautiful, so intelligent, so charismatic, so self-sufficient, it needs nothing else. But only meditation can do that miracle.

? Yesterday I heard you saying that prayer is something directed towards the outside. What about gratefulness? I have the feeling that gratitude does not necessarily have an outer object. Also does gratitude happen only because of a declared or undeclared desire that is fulfilled?

You are not aware that you have changed the word from "gratefulness" to "gratitude". They are two different words. Gratefulness is always towards the outside, and gratefulness is always because deep down you wanted something directly or indirectly and it has been given to you. That's why you are grateful. Gratefulness simply means thankfulness. That will make it clear. You thank the person who has fulfilled a desire which was hidden in you whether you were aware of it or not. Something has been gratified; hence you feel a thankfulness.

Thankfulness is going to be outward. It may be thankfulness towards God which does not exist. It can be thankfulness towards a friend who exists. But thankfulness is a gratification of conscious or unconscious desire being fulfilled.

Gratitude is a totally different phenomenon, though not in the dictionaries. In the dictionaries gratefulness, thankfulness, gratitude—all are put into the same category. Existence is not according to your dictionaries. Gratitude has no outward object, nor inward object. Gratitude is almost like a fragrance arising out of a flower. It is an experience not directed to anybody.

When you reach to the very source of your being where you are completely in the mood of spring, and the flowers are showering on you, you suddenly feel a gratitude not directed to anybody, just like a fragrance arising out of you, just as incense brings ripples of smoke and fragrance moving towards the unknown sky and disappearing.

Gratitude arises out of you just like a fragrance, not as a thankfulness to anybody. It is the shadow, the by-product of your becoming the buddha. It is not a gratification of any desire. If you have any desires, conscious or unconscious, you cannot become a buddha. It is only when all desires have passed on, when you have transcended all desires and demands, that you become a buddha. And out of a buddha, a fragrance radiates. That fragrance has many elements in it. It is gratitude, it is compassion, it is love, it is blissfulness, it is ecstasy—it is manifold, multidimensional.

Now the sutra:

After Nangaku's comment about Sekito, he once more sent the attendant monk to Sekito to ask him a question. On arrival, the monk asked Sekito, "What is liberation?"

Before I discuss Sekito's answer, I will tell you a small anecdote about al-Hillaj Mansoor, the Sufi mystic. A man came to him and asked the same question, "What is liberation?"

He was sitting in a mosque with beautiful pillars all around. Listening to the question, al-Hillaj Mansoor went immediately towards a pillar, and holding on to the pillar with both hands he started shouting, "Help me!"

The man could not understand what was happening. He had just asked about liberation and this man seemed to be mad. Mansoor is holding on to the pillar, and he is asking the man, "Please help me, the pillar is holding me, and it is not letting go. Liberate me."

The man said, "You are mad, you are holding the pillar. The pillar is not holding you."

Mansoor said, "I have answered, now just get out of the place. Nobody is binding you."

That was Sekito's answer. *"Who bound you?"* Why are you seeking liberation? This is the right approach of Zen, to look into your bondage. Don't bother about liberation. Your bondage is false, and it is your own creation. Who has made you a slave? You yourself! And now you are asking, "Liberate me." Nobody can liberate you because nobody has enslaved you. It is your own game.

The answer is very hard, but very clear and very truthful.

Sekito said, "Who bound you?"

First tell me what is your bondage? Who has done it to you? Why are you asking for liberation? Once you look into your bondage, you will simply start laughing. The bondage is your own creation; you can drop it right now. And once you drop the bondage, you see that liberation has been your nature; you don't have to be liberated. You are born liberated, you have been liberated since the beginning, but you get again and again into bondage.

Perhaps the bondage gives you a certain security, a certain safety. The bondage gives you a certain feeling of doing something against the bondage. But you are in your consciousness absolutely liberated, always liberated.

It is as if you lie down and close your eyes and start shouting, "Wake me up!" Now it is very difficult to wake a man who is awake. It is easy to wake up a man who is asleep. You can throw cold water, a bucketful of ice-cold water, on his eyes and he will jump. You can take his blanket and he will immediately shout, "What are you doing?"

But if a man is awake, lying with closed eyes, and says to you, "Please wake me up!"... That's what Sekito is saying to the monk who asked "What is liberation?"

Sekito said, "Who bound you?" You have always been liberated; you are the buddha; you are the awakened one. It is your own fabrication, a fiction of bondage.

You can try a small experiment, just sitting in your room. Clasp your hands tightly together, with the fingers interlocked. Close your eyes and just think that whatever you do, you cannot open your hands. For at least five minutes continue repeating, with closed eyes, "Whatever I do, I cannot open my hands." Then, after five minutes, make every effort to open them. Put your whole energy into opening them and you will be surprised—the more you try, the more it seems to be impossible. You have hypnotized yourself into bondage.

Now the only way to open the hands which you have hypnotized into bondage is not to make any effort of opening them. Just relax, and the hands will be okay without your making any effort. Your effort is going against you because you have hypnotized yourself. Now you cannot; with effort, you cannot open your hands.

We have hypnotized ourselves into all kinds of bondages and then we wonder how to be liberated. Then we make a great effort. Every effort brings more trouble. The hands become tighter, then you start freaking out. My God, what to do? The more effort I make, the tighter they become! It seems impossible because you don't understand the simple process.

Hypnosis can be dissolved only by relaxation. You just relax. You don't make any effort to open. The hands will open by themselves, because closing is an effort but opening is just effortless. You don't have to make any effort. That's why... Have you seen any person dying with closed fists? Can a dead man manage to keep his fist closed? Impossible, because the fist needs effort and the dead man cannot make any effort...so all people die with open hands. All people are born with closed fists. Just watch a small child—the fists! And watch a dead man; the hand is open, because the dead man is completely relaxed. For the first time in his whole life there is no tension.

The monk asked another question: "What is the pure land?" But this is just going roundabout the same thing.

Sekito responded, "Who made you dirty?" Why are you bothering about pure land?

The monk asked, "What is nirvana?"
"Who gave you birth and death?"

They are fictions. Your birth is a fiction, your death is a fiction; your body is born, your body will die. But you have never been born; you are coming, passing through many bodies, many births, many deaths and you are going on and on from beginning to end—eternity to eternity.

You are an eternal light. So what is the point of asking, "What is nirvana?" Nirvana simply means getting rid of birth and death; and birth and death are both fictions.

Even to say 'getting rid of' is not right. What is right is just to look deeply into everything, into your bondage, and you will find that it is your creation. Your idea that you are a sinner, dirty, is your idea. Perhaps you have borrowed it from others, the preachers, the priests, the so-called religious saints. They are making you feel dirty, like sinners, getting ready to fall into hell. They are putting all kinds of humiliations on you. And people go on listening to those humiliations.

From my very childhood I was fighting with every saint who passed through my village. My parents were worried, my family was worried: "You disturb every meeting. Whenever some saint comes, the whole village gathers to listen to him and you stand up in the middle." And my father would beat his head, "Again he is standing, again a disturbance!"

My basic point was, "You are humiliating people by calling them sinners. Just tell me who is a sinner here and what sin he has committed. You are making a generalized statement, 'You are all sinners.' Just point out the person who is a sinner."

These saints were telling people, "Don't be attached to women because they are nothing but bones, flesh, mucus, blood covered in a bag of skin. Why are you getting attached to them?"

I would immediately stand up and say, "What about you? You think you are made of gold? Women are bones, blood, mucus, flesh; okay, what are you? And if blood, mucus and bones hug each other, what is the problem? Rubbing their skin together, what is the problem? Why are you making so much fuss? What else can they do?"

But all the holy scriptures are full of these descriptions in detail — only about women, not about men. Strange! Both are made of the same stuff, and in fact man comes from the woman. The woman never comes from the man.

In America they have allowed in some states lesbian marriages, so a woman can marry a woman. There is no problem now, it is legalized. And there are thousands of babies born out of lesbian marriages. One of the partners who is ready to carry a baby for nine months simply goes to the hospital, gets an insemination, an injection. What is man? Just an injection, a syringe! Any syringe can do that work. So I used to tell the saints, "You only have a syringe, and that syringe is also made of bones and flesh, and is covered with dirty skin. So what are you bragging about? And why are you making these people feel humiliated?" They were all listening with their eyes down because this saint was telling a great truth. All the scriptures were saying it too.

So my father would take me home, "Because you disturb the whole meeting, people have started leaving and the mahatma is very angry."

I said, "I don't care. If he is angry, he is going against his own teachings, he will suffer in hell. He was teaching against anger and now he is angry, so I have shown him his real face."

My father would say, "Just come home. Sometimes I feel worried that they will not even beat you, they will start beating me. And you are such a fellow…Not a single saint can depart the village who has not been disturbed by you. We try to keep the information as secret as possible so you should not come to know that some mahatma, some saint, is delivering a speech. We give you money to go to the movie…"

And the moment they gave me money I would say, "Keep the money. I am coming with you! This money is never given to me for the movie, it is given only to protect the mahatma. I am going to the real show!"

It became so difficult because of the problems that I created for the mahatmas, because it was a simple question: "If two persons are rubbing their skin together, what sin is there? Just tell me. I am rubbing my skin; it's the same, it is just cleaning my hands, warming my hands. If a man and a woman are rubbing their skin together, they will fall into hell? And just look at your belly…"

All the mahatmas in India have big bellies and they are teaching people, "Don't eat for the sake of taste." They themselves… I said, "Where does this belly come from? Stand up! Show your belly to all the people. You are eating too much and the country is hungry. And I know that because of this belly you cannot make love to a woman, so now you are teaching everybody not to make love to any woman. It is because of this belly, not because of your religion."

Such bellies I have seen…you would not believe it. Muktananda's guru was Nityananda. Perhaps he had the biggest belly, it was an Everest. He was always lying down, because with that belly walking was difficult. And lying down, it does not seem that Nityananda had a belly, it seemed the belly had Nityananda. The belly was just like a mountain; on this side a small head, on that side two small legs. These creatures have become great mahatmas! I have never seen such a perfect belly, and he was always lying down and eating sweets. Worshippers were bringing sweets and halwa and puri, and making his belly bigger and bigger.

When I saw him for the first time, I said, "This man some day is going to burst. He is using his belly as a balloon. This man cannot make love to a woman." That is true. Where could you find such an inverted-belly woman? I don't…I can't understand. It just seems to be impossible, a puzzle, a koan. This man can make love only if he can find a woman with an inverted belly, so they can fit together.

Obviously, because he cannot do something, he will say to everybody, "Be celibate." He is having to suffer, and trying to create the same suffering around him. People enjoy other people's suffering because that gives them a chance to demonstrate: "We are higher than you. Look at us. We are always happy, silent, peaceful." And the reality is that they cannot stand up, they cannot walk.

One very famous mahatma, Shivananda, who had many followers in the West, used to be a doctor. That a doctor should do such stupid things to himself makes it more difficult to understand. He was eating so much that he could not walk without two persons holding his arms. He could not even raise his hands. His hands were so heavy, so fat, that one person would take one hand, another person would take his other hand and then the small walk would be done. And he was telling people, "You have to follow the five great principles of Hinduism. The first is ashwad, no taste."

What happened to this man? He was a doctor! I said to him, when I went to Rishikesh and saw him, "What kind of doctor are you? It seems your certificate is bogus. You can't even take care of your body; you have become a monster. You cannot raise your own hands, they have become so heavy."

Everything was out of proportion: a big belly, big fat hands, the legs like elephant legs, and this person is teaching the whole world, "You are not the body, you are the soul." Who are these monsters? Just bodies, with no soul at all. I can't see any space in them; they are so filled up with junk that I don't think they can have a soul too.

What Sekito is saying is absolutely right. There is tremendous truth in small statements.

"What is the pure land?"
Sekito responded, "Who made you dirty?"

You are always pure; that is the Pure Land. Your inner space never has gathered any dirt. That mirror is always clean. No dirt can reach that depth, that invisible beyond.

The monk asked, "What is nirvana?"

He is not understanding at all, because the first question is the last question. All these are repetitions of the same thing. Nirvana is nothing but liberation, liberation from all desires, liberation from all attachments, liberation from all bondage. What is nirvana? Liberation from birth, from death.

And Sekito said, "Who gave you birth and death?" It is you, your desire.

Just try a small experiment. In the night when you are going to sleep, wait, and at the last moment when you think you are just on the verge of falling asleep, just say, "One." Go on saying, "One, one, one…" As you are crossing the border from waking to sleep, "One, one, one…" Perhaps two or three times after the boundary is crossed, you may repeat, "One, one, one…" and then you will be fast asleep. In the morning, watch. As you become aware that you are waking, you will be surprised, you are repeating, "One, one, one…" Strange! After eight hours of sleep that 'one' was continuously being repeated inside you. The last thought when you go to sleep will be the first thought when you wake up. That is an absolutely guaranteed science.

Why am I giving you this example? Because the last thought and desire when you die will be the first desire to enter into a womb. If you die without a desire, without any thought, you will not enter into any womb. Nobody is forcing you into some womb. It is your desire, your last desire when you die. Some ambition, some unfulfillment, some frustration…You wanted to be the prime minister and you missed. You wanted to be the richest man—you missed. You wanted a beautiful woman and you missed. Whatever remains in you will take you into a new womb to fulfill your desire.

Life is very merciful; existence is very compassionate. It gives you chance upon chance, opportunities upon opportunities. If you die meditatively, without any desire, then there is no womb for you, no birth, no death. That's what Sekito is saying. Who has given you birth and death? You yourself. By your desires, by your ambitions you go on perpetuating the circle of birth and death. Stop desiring; that is nirvana, you move from death into the cosmos, not into another womb.

To move into the cosmos, to become one with existence, is nirvana. It is also liberation, it is also freedom, it is also pure paradise—different names for one experience.

The attendant monk came back to Nangaku and reported Sekito's answers.
Nangaku put both hands together and made a gesture of touching his feet.

Although he was not there, he accepted Sekito as enlightened.

It is a very strange story. When Sekito came to him with a letter to deliver, they could not find any attunement with each other, and Sekito returned without delivering the letter. At that time he was not enlightened. This time, on the same mountain where Nangaku had his temple and monastery—and the emperor had given the name to the whole mountain, Nangaku Mountain—on a small hilltop, on a flat stone, Sekito had settled.

After Sekito's master died, Nangaku heard that Sekito was just sitting on a rock. He wanted to know whether Sekito had become enlightened or not. He must have seen that very day when Sekito had come as a disciple of Seigen — he must have seen the man, his strength and his power. He had asked a question and Nangaku had said, "Your question is very arrogant. You should ask in a humble way." And Sekito had said to him, "I might fall into eternal hellfire but I will not ask the question in any other way." And he had gone back directly, a man of steel.

Nangaku was a famous master. When he heard these answers brought by the monk, he folded his hands, and bowed down; he recognized that that fellow Sekito had become enlightened. These answers cannot be given by any scholar. They cannot be borrowed knowledge. They can only arise as an experience.

At that time, Kengo, Ran and Nangaku were thought to be the three masters
in the country, and all three of them said, "From the stone-head comes
the lion's roar to my ear."

Because he was sitting on a stone with a shaved head he became known as Stonehead Sekito. All three masters said, "From the stone-head comes the lion's roar to my ear. He is sitting far away, but I can hear the lion's roar."

The monk went back to Sekito and said that if there were anything the monk
could do for him, to let him know. A little later, the master, Nangaku, came
with the monks to see Sekito.

It is a strange phenomenon. Once, Sekito had gone as a disciple to Nangaku. Things have changed completely, now Nangaku comes to pay his respects to Sekito.

Sekito stood up to receive him, and the two greeted each other. Later, Nangaku
had a temple built for Sekito's convenience.

Zen gives a totally different taste—no competition. Nangaku made a temple for Sekito on his mountain for his convenience and took care of him. A monk would come regularly to ask him if he needed anything. But soon thousands of people started coming to Sekito. He became one of the greatest masters of Zen. He was a very straightforward man, not a philosopher or a theologian; his answers were very simple, but absolutely to the point. His sword was very sharp, and just in one blow he used to cut people's whole intellect, their whole mind. He helped many people to become enlightened. Very few masters can claim that they have made so many people enlightened as Sekito.

Chinejo wrote:

Suddenly light
suddenly dark –
I am a firefly too.

You have seen the firefly. It goes on…as it opens its wings, you see the light, as it closes its wings, there is darkness.

Suddenly light,
suddenly dark –
I am a firefly too.

Chinejo must have been meditating deep into the night. And the silence of the night and many fireflies moving around, sometimes dark, sometimes light, sometimes dark, sometimes light, suddenly he became so attuned to the fireflies that he said, *I am a firefly too.* Sometimes I am ignorant and sometimes I am awakened. Sometimes all is dark and sometimes everything becomes light."

Every buddha in his past was as ignorant as you are; and everybody who is ignorant has a future. Any day suddenly, light; and in that light all the past, maybe millions of years, disappear like dreams. Buddha used to measure people's age from the time they became enlightened. He did not count the previous age.

One day, a great emperor of those days, Prasenjita, was sitting by the side of Buddha asking him questions. And an old monk—he may have been seventy-five years old at least—asked Prasenjita, "Forgive me please. I have been waiting because I have to leave before sunset. I have to reach the other village"—a Buddhist monk cannot travel in the night—"so I am in a hurry. I have to disturb you just for a moment, just to touch Buddha's feet and ask if there is any message. I may not be seeing him again and who knows about tomorrow?" So he touched the Buddha's feet and Buddha asked, "How old are you?"

And the old man said, "Four years."

Prasenjita could not believe that and could not resist the temptation to interfere. He said, "What? Four years? You must be at least seventy-five."

Buddha said, "Prasenjita, you don't know. In my commune we count only those years which he has lived as an enlightened being. Before that was just darkness and dreams, nightmares, misery, not worth counting. You are right, he is seventy-five years old according to the ordinary world, but this is not an ordinary world. He is living in an extraordinary commune. As far as I am concerned he is four years old. I was just asking him whether he remembers or not. He remembers. He knows what is real life—only four years. The seventy-one years were just fake, they do not matter, have no meaning at all. There is no need to count them."

Buddha said, "With my blessings you can go because your remembrance is correct."

Friedrich Nietzsche wrote of himself—"One day there will be associated with me a crisis like no other before on earth, of the profoundest collision of conscience, of a decision evoked against everything that until then had been believed in, demanded, sacrificed. It is my fate to know myself in opposition to the mendaciousness of millennia....

"I am not a man, I am dynamite." This seems to be much more true of you than it was of Nietzsche.

Would you please comment?

There is no need to comment. I am not a man, I am dynamite. What Nietzsche was saying did not happen in his life; he ended up in a madhouse. No crowd gathered, no disciples, no friends.

His last phase of life was a tragedy. The woman he loved refused to marry him because she did not think he was in his senses. The man he respected, Wagner, a great musician, told him not to come to his house because it was Wagner's wife to whom he had proposed. All his friends deserted him, only his sister remained to take care of him. And finally she was also unable to take care and had to put him into a madhouse.

He was certainly a man of great insight, but all his insights were only intellectual. Those great insights drove him mad, because he could not manage to live with the crowd, and he could not manage to live alone. He was against everything, just the way I am.

But I am absolutely capable of living alone. My aloneness is absolute silence. I just come for the evening talk to be with you, then I am alone the whole day, the whole night. But my aloneness is not lonely, my aloneness is so full of existence, so full of ecstasy and divine drunkenness. My aloneness is my innermost depth, my highest consciousness.

Friedrich Nietzsche was poor in the sense that he never knew anything of meditation. So his dynamite turned against himself. He burned himself in his own intellectual, rational, logical arguments.

But I am certainly not a man, I am dynamite. And my people have come already and they are coming more and more. Millions more will be here. No boundaries of nations, no boundaries of any church can prevent them. And my whole work is to put dynamite in you to destroy you completely, so that you can enter into the cosmos with an easy heart, relaxed, at peace, finally at home.

You are right, your feeling is right. It does not need any commentary on it.

Now, after such a serious and difficult time, a little bit of laughter has come to help me.

Gilda and Gilbert Goldfish are swimming around in their fish bowl one day, having a deep philosophical discussion.

"So," gurgles Gilda, "you say that you do not believe in the existence of God?"

"That's right," bubbles Gilbert, throwing down his copy of *Thus Spoke Zarathustra*. "And Friedrich Nietzsche says that God is dead and fish are free!"

"Hah!" splutters Gilda. "Then who is that guy that changes our water?"

Chester, the obsessed golfer, is preparing one Sunday morning to go golfing at the local course.

"Golf! Golf! Golf!" nags Betty, his wife, standing with her hands on her hips and curlers in her hair. "That's all you ever think about. If you ever spent a week-end with me I think I would drop dead!"

"Look," replies Chester, putting on his golf hat. "There is no point in trying to bribe me!"

Chief Patrol Officer Kowalski and his partner, Officer Jablonski, are walking down Main Street in Warsaw late one night. Suddenly, Officer Kowalski stumbles over a dead body lying on the sidewalk with a huge knife in its back, just in front of the Philharmonic Hall.

"Ho!" shouts Kowalski with surprise. "What do we have here?"

"It is a dead body, chief!" exclaims Officer Jablonski, his eyes popping out.

"Right!" says Kowalski, and he pulls out his pad and paper and starts writing.

"Time!" shouts Kowalski.

"Er, one a.m." replies Jablonski, nervously looking at his watch.

"Okay," says Kowalski, writing furiously. "Now, date!"

"Er, March seventh," replies Jablonski, checking his calendar book.

"Good!" shouts Kowalski. "Description!"

"Er, knife stuck in back," cries Jablonski.

"Right!" exclaims Kowalski. "And location!"

Jablonski looks up at the huge building and says, "Er, *f-i-l-a-m-o-n-i-c*. Philharmonic Hall?" Kowalski scratches his head, and starts writing.

"*f-i-l*...no, that's not right," he says, and then he tries again.

"*p-i-l-l*...no, that's not it! Maybe it is *f-h-i-l*—oh, shit!" snaps Kowalski, breaking his pencil. "How the hell do you spell 'Philharmonic'?"

"Gee," replies Jablonski, "I don't know."

Then Kowalski bends over, picks up the bleeding body, throws it over his shoulder, and starts walking away.

"Hey! Chief!" cries Officer Jablonski. "Where are you going?"

Kowalski turns around and says, "Let's put him in front of the post office!"

Now the meditation:

Be silent, close your eyes and feel your body to be completely frozen.
This is the right moment to look inwards.

Gather your energy, your total consciousness, and with an urgency, as if this is going to be your last moment in life, rush towards your very center—faster and faster, deeper and deeper.

As you come closer to your center, a great silence descends over you. It is falling almost like soft rain, so tangible. A little closer, and a great peace arises from your very sources, surrounds you in a glory you have never known before, in a grace that is not of this world.

One step more and you are at the very center of your being.

For the first time you are seeing your original face. As a symbol in the East we have accepted the face of Buddha as the original face of everyone. You are facing your own hidden buddha.

This is your hidden splendor. This is your nature, your dharma.

The buddha has only one quality, witnessing.

Witness that you are not the body, witness that you are not the mind, witness that you are only a witness. And suddenly you have become one with the buddha.

As your witnessing deepens, a great ecstasy starts, starts arising in you just as if a lotus flower is opening in the morning sun, so fresh.

On its petals there are still cold dewdrops of the night, shining in the morning sun like pearls.

At this moment you are the most fortunate people on the earth. To be at your center, to be a buddha is the greatest experience of life.

To make this witnessing deeper…

Relax… Let go… But keep on witnessing.

Slowly slowly, you start melting like ice in the ocean, disappearing as a separate unit and becoming the oceanic vastness, eternity, infinity.

This is your ultimate nature. This is your birthright, to be a buddha; and you have gone beyond the mind and you have reached to the very source of your being from where you have come. And when the source and the goal become one, the circle is complete. This completion of the circle is enlightenment. Every day it will become deeper and deeper.

Collect all the experiences that are happening right now: the feeling of vastness, the oceanic feeling, the great peace, the strange silence, the great ecstasy and flowers of bliss showering on you.

Collect everything, you have to bring all these things to your ordinary day-to-day life—the same grace, the same peace, the same silence, the same joy, the same celebration.

If you can manage to bring all these things from the center to the circumference, the buddha is bound to follow.

But anyway, persuade him. Persuade the buddha to come a little closer, just following you so that he remains a continuous presence behind you.

In every act, in every gesture, in every word, in every silence, day, night, waking, walking, sleeping, whatever you are doing, his presence is always there following you like a shadow.

But the shadow is very solid and the shadow is very radiant; the shadow fills you with great joy. Your heart starts dancing.

Now come back…but come back very peacefully as if there is no one here, very silently, with great grace. You have to remember that you are a buddha.

Sit down just for a few seconds to remind yourself of the golden path that you followed, to remind yourself of all the experiences that open their doors at the center of your being.

The experience of the center is the only miracle there is.

Just by your honesty, just by your sincerity, you have made this evening a magic evening. Feel the presence of buddha behind you.

These are the three steps of meditation: first, you will find buddha as a presence behind you; second, you will find buddha as a presence in front of you, you will become a shadow; and third, your shadow will disappear into the buddha, you will become the buddha himself.

You will not be anymore, only the buddha is.

Buddha is just a symbol of pure existence, of ultimate liberation, of nirvana.

One day, these three steps will be fulfilled in you. When the third step is fulfilled, you are awakened, enlightened. Then there is no birth for you, no death for you. You have become part of the ultimate cosmos.

God is dead, and Zen is the only living truth.

CHAPTER 5
God is your insecurity

Sekito wrote:
The mind of the great sage of India was intimately communicated
from India to China. In human beings there are wise men and fools,
but on the way there is no northern or southern teacher. The mysterious
source is clear and bright, the branching streams flow through the darkness.
To be attached to the relative, this is illusion, but to take to oneself the absolute
is not enlightenment.
Each and all the elements of the subjective and objective spheres are related,
and at the same time independent; related, yet working differently, though
each keeps its own place.
Form makes the character and appearance different; sound, taste, smell,
distinguish comfort and discomfort.
The dark makes all things one; the brightness makes all things different.
The four elements return to their nature, as a child to its mother.
Fire is hot, wind moves, water is wet, earth hard. Eyes see, ears hear;
the nose smells, the tongue tastes, one salt, another sour.
Each is independent of the other, but the different leaves come from
the same root.

Friends, first the questions.

? **Could one summarize the difference between a God-oriented religion and the quality of religiousness as the difference between a judge external to us, a projected conscience, and a witness within our consciousness?**

The difference between God-oriented religions and the religions without God is immense. The God-oriented religions are simply fiction. But lies told again and again and again start appearing to be almost true. God as the ultimate lie creates many lies around itself, because no lie can stand alone. Because no lie is self-evident, it needs other lies to support it; hence, all God-oriented religions have created many lies to support God.

Truth can stand on its own legs, but not a lie. Truth needs no argument, but not a lie; a lie needs many arguments, many fabricated proofs, many imaginary evidences. Truth is utterly naked—either you know it or you don't.

God-oriented religions are a disease of the soul, a sickness of the mind, because God is only your fear, your dread, your anxiety, your insecurity. Then comes prayer, and then comes the priest, and then comes the organized religion, the church.

True religiousness cannot be God-oriented. True religiousness is your own interiority, your own inner space.

And you can see the differences between these two kinds of people. Those who follow a God-oriented religion don't show any compassion, don't show any ecstasy, don't show any blissfulness. On the contrary, they are very violent, they are very much against freedom. They are in constant fear that somebody will object to their lies and they will not be able to answer, because all they have is just a belief system. A belief system can help you to forget your ignorance but it does not destroy it. So the God-oriented man lives in ignorance and believes that he knows.

And mere words, theories, hypotheses, are not going to change your character. They can at the most make you a hypocrite. They can give you a beautiful mask but not the original face. They can create a very convenient personality, but they cannot create or discover your beautiful individuality. And the personality, however convenient, is a heavy weight on your chest, on your heart, because you are living a lie. Nobody can feel at ease when he is living a lie.

The man who has no belief system but has encountered truth itself, suddenly finds himself changing into a new man. There is no effort involved. Grace comes by itself, compassion comes by itself, violence disappears, fear disappears, death and birth disappear. One starts feeling at home with the universe. There is no tension, one is absolutely relaxed. This is our home. One stops searching and seeking, one starts living, dancing, loving. Knowing one's own interiormost center is also knowing the center of the universe itself. Doors of all the mysteries open—not that you start getting answers, you become more mysterious.

All answers are mind products. Questions arise out of the mind, and answers are also from the same mind. Neither the questions lead you towards the truth, nor the answers. Answers only repress your questions, but they will surface again and again.

A man without God finds himself in total aloneness. He has nowhere to go except withinwards. All roads leading out are meaningless; they don't lead you anywhere because there is nobody outside, no God, no paradise.

Removing God is a great rebellion, and an absolute necessity to be awakened, to be enlightened. God is holding millions of people prisoner outside their own consciousness. And, God being a fiction, your prayer is false and your religiousness is imposed. Hence, all these religions demand: "Do this, don't do that." Everything is imposed from the outside. And whenever something is imposed from the outside, your dignity is destroyed, your individuality is crushed. Your freedom turns into slavery, and the ugliest slavery is spiritual slavery.

With God you can only be a slave. With God you can never be liberated. Liberation begins with liberating yourself from God and all the lies that surround him.

Liberation brings you to your own very center, and there you find a totally different experience that is not of the mind; it is of pure silence, truth and beauty, of eternity, of life as a constant festival. And because you experience this festivity inside you, it starts overflowing you. In your actions you become graceful, your eyes start shining with love, with depth; your very movement shows a centered, balanced, harmonious being. Your words carry something of that which is beyond words. Your silence is no longer the silence of a cemetery, it is not dead. It is very alive, throbbing. It has a heartbeat, it is a silent dance of pure awareness. It is a silent song without any sounds, but it is immensely alive.

Anything imposed from outside destroys you, your freedom, your individuality. Your inner space is completely closed, and it is closed in such a beautiful way that you never think that your parents, your teachers, your priests, your leaders, politicians—all kinds of so-called wise people—are poisonous. With all good intentions they are poisoning every child. And God is the original sin, original sin because we created a great lie, the ultimate lie.

You will be surprised that Indian Christianity is the oldest Christianity in the world. One of Jesus Christ's closest disciples, Thomas, came to India directly. His gospel is not included in the Bible, because his gospel was written in India, but it is the most beautiful gospel. Those four gospels included in the New Testament are nothing compared to it.

Thomas became a transformed man here, because he started seeing the difference between God-oriented religion and a religion without a God. A religion without a God gives man dignity, because man becomes the most evolved consciousness in the whole of existence. It gives man freedom from a burden imposed by the priest in the name of God.

And you have asked, "Could one summarize the difference between a God-oriented religion and the quality of religiousness as the difference between a judge external to us…" There is no judge, and there is no religiousness in a God-oriented religion. It is mere theology, it is a mind-projection. It is not existential, it is not experiential. First remember: the God-oriented religion is only a name. God is fiction, so anything oriented in God cannot be anything else but a lie.

The God-oriented so-called religion has no religiousness in it. It has a certain morality, it has a certain discipline imposed against nature.

God is the enemy of nature, because nature is truth and God is a lie. But the lie is dominating millions of people and telling them to withdraw from nature, which is the only truth.

So there is no religiousness in a God-oriented person. What he has is morality, which is nothing but a social convenience. It differs from place to place, from country to country, from race to race. What seems to be religious to one fragment of humanity is not religious to another fragment of humanity, because every society has its own climate, its own heritage, its own past—which is different from other societies.

For example, the Hindu concept of heaven is that of a centrally air-conditioned place. Not that they have used the words "centrally air-conditioned", but they say, "The whole day a cool breeze blows, fragrant; it is never hot in heaven." Obviously, it shows that the people who have projected this lie are living in a hot country and they don't want to live eternally in a hot place.

The Tibetans have their heaven very warm, no snow at all; no winter ever happens in their heaven. They suffer from cold and winter and snow. They are projecting something which they can tolerate eternally. This life is small, but to suffer the same thing eternally would be too much. The human mind is too frail, too weak.

Just watch what each country thinks of as religious. In India, you have to take a morning bath before sunrise and do your prayer, and only then can you eat your breakfast—not before that. In the religious scriptures of Tibet it says you should take a bath at least once a year. But the trouble is that people go on carrying their concepts even though they move into different climates.

One of my friends, a very scholarly brahmin, wanted to go to Tibet. He was very interested in the Tibetan language and Tibetan scriptures.

I said to him, "All that literature is available. You don't have to go to Tibet. And you will not be able to remain there for more than two days."

He said, "Why not?"

I said, "How will you manage a bath before sunrise? And without a bath you cannot take your breakfast. You cannot eat anything unless you do your prayer, but the prayer needs as an absolute necessity that you take a bath."

But he didn't listen to me. He went to Tibet, and after just two days he was back. He could not even make it to Lhasa, he turned back from Ladakh, which is just in between Tibet and India. Even Ladakh gave him too much trouble. Taking an early morning bath in Ladakh can kill you. It is ice cold! So he came back, he did not go further.

I said, "What happened? It is just two days and you are back?"

He said, "You were right. I am a brahmin and I follow my religion. I cannot remain without a bath."

Tibetan lamas came with the Dalai Lama as he escaped from Tibet when China invaded it. So hundreds of lamas came with him. I was holding a meditation camp in Bodhgaya, the place where Gautam Buddha became enlightened. In the same campus, by the side of the same tree exactly, I was offering a meditation camp. A group of Tibetan lamas came to pay their respects to the tree under which Gautam Buddha had become enlightened.

You will not believe it … even from far away they stank. They were still following the idea that you should take one bath every year—in India! It was a hot summer and they were perspiring. And they were still wearing the same kind of clothes as they worn in Tibet—layer upon layer. In Tibet they wear many layers of clothes, and these were so dirty, so oily, and dust had gathered on the oily clothes. They were good in Tibet, they prevented the cold from reaching to the person's body, but in India…! They had not changed.

I asked them, "Do you understand that all kinds of so-called religious principles are just social conveniences? It was good in Tibet, but here you are being stupid. So many layers of clothes upon clothes, you are being insane!"

But they said, "Our religion says one bath a year is absolutely necessary. More than that is luxury. More than that is condemned, it is dangerous." And to make people afraid that if you go against the dictates of your scriptures you will fall into hell… They said, "It is better to stink than to fall into hell."

I said, "That's right. You are already in hell! I don't think the Devil is even going to allow you into hell, because in no scripture of the world is it said that the Devil stinks; he is a gentleman, a nice fellow." I said to those people, "You just keep these clothes on in India and they will save you from hell. As the Devil starts sniffing you, he will close the doors: 'Tibetan lamas no longer allowed! You go to the other place.'"

Jesus used to drink alcohol. Now in India, no religion can conceive that a man of understanding, a man who is enlightened, could drink alcohol. I don't see any problem, because if the body is illusory, the alcohol is going into the body, not into the soul. It is called "spirits," but don't think it is spiritual! It does not go into your spirit. It may affect your mind, and you may fall unconscious, but still it is not touching your consciousness at all, because the mind and brain are part of the body. Mind is the program and the brain is the computer that is programmed.

When a child is born, he has a brain but no mind. Mind is nothing but the whole collection of information, knowledge; it is the programming. So the brain will be affected by alcohol, but not your spirituality.

What is the problem? To me there is no problem. Even a buddha can once in a while have a little drink, enjoy a little party—Italian style. In Italy, "party" means something absolutely different to what you understand. It is a real party, with two partners. But why prohibit a buddha from enjoying a little party, a little spaghetti, a little wine? All these things are material, and they don't touch your spiritual being.

But in India nobody can conceive that a buddha would drink—even tea he will not drink. One cannot imagine Mahavira drinking alcohol. The reason is simple. In the hot climate of India, drinking alcohol is not needed. But in a cold climate, alcohol is absolutely necessary. It keeps you warm; it does not make you intoxicated, it only keeps you warm. And there is no harm in feeling warm when snow is falling all around you. So in a cold country the morality will be different. In a hot country the morality will be different. This is just an example. On every point, different climates will create different moralities.

Mohammed said to the Mohammedans, "You can marry four women." The reason was that in Saudi Arabia at that time, fourteen hundred years ago, the proportion of men to women was four women to one man. It happened because the men were continuously fighting. It was a tribal society, and every tribe was fighting with another tribe. Of course, the men were being killed and the women remained. The proportion became such that there were four women to one man. So I don't condemn Mohammed, he was making it convenient for the society. Otherwise, what will three women do? They will disturb the whole society. They will start having love affairs with married people, they will become prostitutes, and such a vast number of prostitutes will create so much ugliness and perversion. It was better that a man married four women.

Strangely enough…I have been in deep contact with a few Mohammedans who have been my friends. I was amazed. I used to think, theoretically, that one woman was enough to drive a man either insane or enlightened—the only two alternatives. What will four women do to a man? But my actual experience, when I came into contact with Mohammedans who had four wives, was totally different.

That's what I always say, that theoretically something may look logical, but life has no obligation to follow your logic.

I was surprised that the Mohammedan household has no quarrel as happens when one man and one woman are continuously nagging and fighting and jealous. The reason is, those four women are fighting amongst themselves; the man is simply out of it. They are not much concerned about the man, the whole question is about the four women. So the man is far happier than anybody who lives with one woman.

I asked those friends, "What is the matter? One woman drives people either insane or they renounce the world—really it is renouncing the woman—and they become enlightened." So now I understand why no Mohammedan has ever been enlightened. They are very normal people, they don't go insane either. It is because of those four women fighting amongst themselves, and the man is simply out of the game. He can watch the game but he is no longer part of it.

But nowadays the proportion is not the same as it was then. In a country like India, the proportion of men to women is exactly the same, and now even in Saudi Arabia the proportion is exactly the same. Now, to go on allowing one man to marry four women in Saudi Arabia will create problems and inconvenience for the society, because three men will be left without wives. Now these three men will create trouble. They will have love affairs with other people's wives… And always remember, the other person's wife is far more beautiful than your own wife, far greener—just as the lawn of the neighbor looks so green, you would like to eat it.

The French actually have an expression. When you are in deep love in France, tell the woman, "I want to eat you," and she will be immensely happy. But only the French do that much. If you say that in India—that I want to eat you—the woman will give such a scream. You will be arrested by the police: "What did you say to that woman that she was screaming so loudly?" And if you say, "I was just telling her I love her, and I told her, 'I want to eat you'…"

Even language changes — just as morals change, as religions change according to the climate, according to tradition, according to their past.

I have heard about a very great French warrior. In the Middle Ages, the warriors were always going on crusades. The Christians were going to kill Mohammedans, and they were going to kill Jews, or convert them into Christians. The only chance was, if you want to stay alive, be a Christian; otherwise be finished.

So the warrior was going on a crusade, but he had a very beautiful wife. In the Middle Ages in Europe, they used to have locks: when the husband went out for a few days, he would put a certain lock on the woman called a "chastity belt." It was a belt with a lock, and strange locks were developed so that nobody could make love to the woman. Some locks, which the richer people used, had a knife inside. Anything entering the lock, and the knife would simply fall on it. They are exhibited in the great museums of Europe, particularly in London.

So the warrior who was going away for months—and maybe it would take a year or two—locked his wife. But he was worried about taking the key with him, because it was war and if the key was lost it would be very difficult to open the lock. You would need to call some locksmith or somebody who could make another key. But it would be very embarrassing. So he called his best friend, and he told him, "I am going on a crusade, and I trust you; you are my best friend, so keep this key. When I come back I will take the key from you. This is the key for my wife's lock."

The friend said, "Don't be worried." And just five minutes after the warrior had gone on his horse, he saw his friend coming fast on his horse. The warrior stopped and asked, "What is the matter?" The friend said, "You have given me the wrong key." Just five minutes!

When the number of men and women are not in proportion, what Mohammed said is good; there is nothing wrong in it. But it belonged to his time and the situation. It has now become a rule amongst Mohammedans, and because they cannot find so many wives in their own religion, they go on abducting other people's wives.

In India it is a game. You just catch hold of somebody's wife…and Hindus are very fussy about it. Once the wife has stayed one night outside the house, she is finished. She cannot enter the husband's house again, the husband won't allow it. She cannot enter her parents' home again, the parents will throw her out because she has degraded their respectability, their prestige: "Just go and commit suicide, there is no other way." Rather than committing suicide the woman returns to the Mohammedan. That seems to be saner and more logical.

A woman has to be out of the house just for one night. It does not matter whether she has made love to anybody or not. This is how Indian Mohammedans go on increasing their population. Obviously, one man with four wives can create at least four children per year. The same is not possible when there are four husbands and one wife. They may not even produce one child—the four husbands may kill the child before it is born.

So remember, your God-oriented religions are only conveniences for the society. They should not be called religions, they are only moral precepts to keep the society together, and in the least inconvenient way. It is not religiousness. Religiousness arises only as a blossoming of your own consciousness.

God-oriented religions certainly create a *conscience*, but not *consciousness*. Many people have the false notion that conscience and consciousness are one. Their root is one, but they are two separate branches moving in diametrically opposite directions. Conscience is forced on you by others.

Consciousness is an evolution rising from your own depths to the ultimate heights. Conscience is just like a plastic flower.

Once I had a neighbor. I had a beautiful garden with all kinds of flowers and all kinds of trees. Of course, he was jealous. So what he did…I could see only one of his windows. I could not see his whole house from my house. Tall trees hid the house from my garden, but one window was available for me to see—he brought a pot and arranged plastic flowers in it. And just to deceive me, because plastic flowers don't need watering, he would water them every day just to show me that he also had flowers. But I saw that the flowers remained the same—six months passed and the same flowers. I said, "He has found a great flowering tree!"

Plastic flowers are permanent flowers. In fact, scientists are worried that plastic is one of the things the earth cannot absorb. And now so many plastic things are being thrown into the ocean, into the earth, that they are destroying the whole ecology. Plastic is something eternal.

A tree grows out of the earth, a man grows out of the earth; you put the tree back into the earth and it will disappear into its basic elements. But plastic is man-made. You can put it into the earth and after many years you can dig and find the plastic exactly the same, nothing has changed.

It is because of the American idea of using a thing once and throwing it away. It is cleaner, but it is dangerous. The whole bottom of the ocean around America is full of plastic things: plastic bags, plastic syringes, plastic containers, plastic toys. Everything is plastic. And those layers of plastic have created something strange. Millions of fish have died because the plastic has made the water poisonous. Its aliveness has gone, it has become dead. The fear is growing every day that more plastic thrown into the oceans, into the rivers, into the earth, will make everything dead; everything will be plastic.

I knocked on the neighbor's window. He came, and I said, "You have great flowers. I have very poor flowers; in the morning they blossom, by the evening they are gone. Although you have only one pot, it is better than my whole garden."

He was very embarrassed. I said, "You are such an intelligent man. You have been watering these flowers…." He had not a single word to say. His wife came behind him and said, "You are saying he is intelligent. He is an idiot! I have been telling him that plastic flowers don't need water."

I told his wife, "You don't know. He was not watering the plastic flowers, he was trying to deceive me. These plastic flowers have been there for six months, and they will remain forever. This man will die, you will die," I told his wife, "but these plastic flowers will remain. They are immortal beings. But they are dead, that's why they are immortal—already dead."

You cannot kill a dead man, can you? Once a man is dead he becomes immortal. You cannot kill him twice. Resurrection has happened only once, and that was also false. Once a man dies there is no more death.

This is the difference between imposed morality and religion, and an inner growth of consciousness. They are totally different. Perhaps only in the French language are conscience and consciousness equivalent. I am not certain, I don't know French. But I have a certain feeling that in French those two words are not different: conscience is used for both conscience and consciousness, but it is absolutely wrong. The French linguists have to change it.

Conscience is God-oriented; consciousness is your own innermost being flowering. Then you have a spontaneous response to situations. The God-oriented morality cannot have a spontaneity in it. It researches what the holy scripture is saying, what Moses is saying, what Jesus is saying; it has to consult its memory system. But spontaneity has not to consult anybody—Manu, Moses, Mohammed, anybody. Spontaneous action simply arises in you, and because it arises in you it has an authenticity, an honesty. Then you are functioning as an individual, not as a sheep. You are functioning as a human being with dignity and splendor and honor.

A God-oriented religion takes away everything that is beautiful in you and leaves behind just a dilapidated human being, crippled in every possible way, exploited by all kinds of parasites. God is the ultimate parasite. He goes on threatening you. Of course, because there is no God, the priest is the spokesman, and he goes on threatening you: "You will be thrown into hell if you don't listen to me. I represent God." It is a pure invention of the priesthood all over the world to dominate man, to exploit man. And what they are saying to the people, they themselves don't believe. How can they believe it? They know it is a fiction. But it is a good profession, it is a good business.

Just recently the archbishop of Jerusalem—which is a holy land for three religions, Jews, Christians, Mohammedans—the archbishop of this holy city was arrested in London because he was misbehaving in the railway station public toilet, exposing himself, exhibiting his sexual machinery to other people. The archbishop of Jerusalem! One cannot believe that these people go on teaching celibacy to others, and they themselves behave in such stupid ways.

I have heard that three bishops were going to Pittsburgh. But the woman at the window where they had to get their tickets had such beautiful breasts….

The youngest bishop was sent to purchase the tickets. When he saw the breasts of the woman, he forgot everything. He said, "Just give me three pickets for Tittsburgh." The woman was angry, and the bishop felt very ashamed, so he went back to the others. He said, "Forgive me, but I forgot myself completely."

The second bishop said, "Don't be worried. I will go." As he gave the money, he told the girl, "Give me the change in dimes and nipples."

The girl was furious. She said, "You are all idiots of the same type! Can't you behave like human beings?"

The second bishop ran from the window. And the oldest bishop said, "Don't be worried. I will take care." He went there, and he said, "Woman, you will be in trouble...If you go exhibiting your breasts like this, at the pearly gates Saint Finger will point his Peter at you!"

What to do with these people? Once you repress something it is bound to come up. You simply become a fool. Now all three bishops proved to be utterly foolish and absolute idiots.

But they are victims of a constant harassment by religion, by their abbots, by their popes— against nature.

All moralities are against nature, and in favor of a certain social structure. The social structure is man-made, it is not perfect, it needs to be changed. But all moralities, all God-oriented religions, are protective of the social structure. They are against any revolution. They don't have any consciousness. They have created in place of consciousness a bogus conscience that is plastic consciousness. What they call conscience is simply implanted, it is programmed in you. You have to act accordingly, but your inner being is not in favor of it. So when you want to say, "Pittsburgh," your inner being says, "Tittsburgh." When you want to say, "Saint Peter will point his finger," your nature says, "Saint Finger will point his Peter." This dichotomy is created by your God-oriented religions.

Man is suffering from schizophrenia, neurosis, psychosis—all kinds of mental diseases— because of one fiction that he cannot drop. Just drop God, and you will find yourself saner, natural, and a certain beauty will come to you which only comes to natural beings.

If you believe in a God, you are bound to be afraid of his judgment. But if there is no God, there is no judgment. You have only a witness, and a witness is not a judge. A witness is only a mirror. It shows you clearly the situation, and it gives you a spontaneous response. Then it has tremendous beauty and harmony, and your life is without any regret. You don't look back, you remain constantly in the present, just a witness, acting, responding to whatever encounters you according to your own consciousness.

And remember one thing: Even if you fall into hell, but you have lived spontaneously and according to your consciousness, you will not regret it. On the other hand, if you enter heaven because others forced you to act according to certain precepts, certain commandments, you will regret even in heaven that you have not lived your life according to your own nature.

There is only one blissfulness in the world, and that is to be in accordance with your nature, with your existence. Don't bother about any commandments, don't bother about any disciplines, don't bother about any morality. Just live according to your own consciousness, and go on growing your consciousness. Soon you will see the spring, and all the flowers will bring a clarity of vision, a certainty of action, a totality to every response. Your every response will be beautiful because it will be coming out of a growing consciousness.

Conscience is borrowed. Consciousness is your nature. The difference is vast.

It seems life is not the ultimate value, the mechanical man is expendable. God is nothing more than a sick fantasy, so obviously *that* cannot be the ultimate value. What then, does that leave us with?

With nothing — just yourself. Once God is no more, there you are, alone and responsible.

People are clinging to God for a certain reason. They are throwing all the responsibility on God; he will take care. All we have to do is to go to church every Sunday—that's enough—and God will take care. But you don't know: The moment you give your responsibility to God, you have also put your freedom into his hands; you have become a puppet.

Once you know God is just a sick fantasy, that very understanding will make you healthy and whole. And your wholeness, your aloneness, is such a beautiful experience that you don't need any value, any ultimate value. You are the ultimate value. Your very being, when discovered in its totality, is a Gautam Buddha. You don't need any other value as an incentive to make the journey towards the goal.

All that you need is to drop all sick fantasies. Then all your religions will disappear from the earth, and that will leave you absolutely healthy. Out of that health and aloneness, out of that freedom, you will find your ultimate peaks and ultimate depths. And this is what can be called the real meaning, the real significance, the ultimate value. You are the ultimate value. It is because of a sick fantasy that you are not looking at yourself, you are looking at the stars.

Primitive societies have always conceptualized God as parts of the environment, such as rivers, trees, and the sun and moon. As societies became more civilized, they began to conceptualize God as a separate individual. Why is this?

Primitive societies had no private property. Primitive societies had no families, they were tribal. Nobody knew who the father was, people only knew about "uncles" and the mother. Primitive societies were matriarchal; the mother was the only person they knew, the father had not yet come into being.

As societies started moving from hunting to cultivation, they stopped being gypsies; otherwise they had been continuously moving wherever there was the possibility of finding more animals to hunt. They could not remain in one place because soon the food was finished. As animals moved away from them, they had to follow the animals. Their whole concern was how to get food. There were no houses, there were no cities, there were only temporary camps. Private property had not yet arisen.

With cultivation, private property came into being. The people who were stronger managed to get as much land as they wanted. The people who were weaker only managed to live at the minimum—whatever was left over from the stronger gangsters they could have. Those strong criminals became finally your kings, and your lords, and your counts. These are basically criminal people, who have deprived humanity of much of their joys, forced them into a corner.

But once private property arose, the father had to be certain that his son was his son. With private property, the family came into being. And with private property the woman was transformed into a subhuman species. She became imprisoned. Now she was nothing but property, the property of a certain man, and her whole function was to be a factory to produce children.

Tribal people had no idea of a father, but the tribal people knew many things that we have forgotten: they felt life surging in the trees; they felt life moving in the rivers; they felt life in the tidal waves of the ocean shattering continuously, eternally, on the seashore. They were more sensitive. They were illiterate, uncivilized, but they were more sensitive and more receptive.

I have heard about the native Australians. Most of them have been killed by the white man, and killed in such an ugly way that the white man seems to be the most barbarous man on the earth. The native Australians were killed almost like animals. People used to go hunting the natives because they thought them to be not human beings, but a far lower species. Almost ninety percent of the natives of Australia were killed by the white people, even eaten, because it was just thought of as hunting. Just as you hunt tigers and lions and deer, you were hunting a different species from humanity. They were not white, their faces were different, their behavior was different.

But the natives of Australia had a very strange custom. They had no post office, they had no telephone system, no wireless. They used to hypnotize a tree, a particular type of tree. Their sensitivity must have found the right kind of tree that was ready to be hypnotized. In humanity, a third of people are immediately capable of being hypnotized, only thirty-three percent. But strangely enough, only thirty-three percent of people are intelligent; they are the same people. Only thirty-three percent of people are creative; they are the same people. The remaining ones are insensitive, unreceptive, unintelligent. The natives of Australia found out which tree was more hypnotizable, so each village had its own hypnotized tree. And through the tree they used to send messages to another tree in another village. For example, somebody's son had gone to another village, and the father wanted to send a message to him. When the son was leaving, the father would say, "If I have to send a message to you, I will send it exactly when the sun is rising. At that time, you listen to the hypnotized tree in that village." It may have been hundreds of miles away. And early, exactly when the sun was rising, the father would go to the tree in his village if he wanted to send a message to the son. He would tell the tree, "Please inform the tree in that village, where my son will be waiting for a message..." And then he would tell the tree the message, and it would be received, "You can stay two days more, but finish the work"—or any other kind of message.

For thousands of years they practiced it, but slowly they have forgotten, most of them have forgotten how to hypnotize trees because Christianity has been forcing them into schools to learn to read. Christianity is absolutely against hypnotism. It thinks it is something to do with the Devil. Hypnotism or mesmerism or anything is accounted dangerous. So they have destroyed, along with the natives, those trees, which had been hypnotized for centuries. They had become so sensitive that they immediately sent the message to the other tree hundreds of miles away, maybe thousands of miles away. The space did not matter, nor the distance.

Primitive man was very sensitive because he lived with trees, he lived with animals, he lived with rivers, he lived with oceans, he lived with mountains. He was part of nature. The primitive man had no religion, no organized church, no priesthood. Obviously, the primitive man was aware of a surging life all around. He lived amidst an ocean of life. And obviously, his love for trees, his love for rivers, his love for the ocean, his love for the high mountains, the stars, the sun and moon, was immense. He lived in a totally different world—very related. He was one of the members of the cosmos, just as every living thing is. As far as sensitivity is concerned, he was far more human than the so-called civilized man, who has become hard, has become more mechanical, more robot-like; he has lost much of his sensitivity.

You can watch, holding hands with different people. Some hands will feel almost as if you are holding the hand of a dead man: no energy, no warmth, no throbbing of life, no transfer of any loving, friendly energy but just closed, dead. And you will find hands that suck energy out of you. You find afterwards that you are feeling weaker. There are people with whom you don't want to be, because being with them you feel your energy sucked out, as if somebody has taken blood out of you. They are parasites of energy. They don't have any energy to give, but they are ready to take any energy possible. And you will find the opposite also: holding someone's hand you will feel healthier, fresher. Their hands will be flowing into your being, pouring some energy into you, some love, some warmth.

Just the other day, my secretary brought one very rich woman to see me. She owns some newspapers and magazines, a very beautiful woman. She wants to write an article about me, so she wanted a photograph of me with her. I took her hand in my hand, and it was a sad shock to me. The woman was smiling, but her heart was sad. I could feel in her hand immense sadness.

If you are sensitive, you will be able to feel whether a person is blissful, sad, feeling unworthy, feeling a sinner, or is standing on his own feet, feeling the dignity of being human, feeling rooted, centered; feeling that he has a place in existence of his own, that he is not accidental, that existence needs him otherwise he would not be here. "The very fact that I am here shows clearly that existence needs me. There is some tremendous purpose, some destiny that existence wants to be fulfilled by me. I am existence's ambition, just as you are." The moment you feel this, you have a great gratitude arising in you.

Out of that gratitude primitive man was bowing down to the trees, to the rivers, to the sun, to the moon. It was far more beautiful than going into a church and bowing down to a sad Jesus Christ. Obviously, Jesus has to be sad; he is crucified. You don't expect him to laugh; that would have been absolutely inappropriate. I would have laughed, but Jesus has a long face, utterly sad.

You will find all God-oriented people serious and sad, because deep down there is doubt. God is not their experience, it is just a belief. How can you make belief a truth? It will remain a belief. You can repress your doubt as much as possible in the unconscious, but it is there and very alive and kicking. It makes you sad because you are living a fictitious life, a life that is not your own, a life that others have imposed on you. God is more responsible than anyone for taking away your prestige, your dignity, your pride.

The primitive man loved existence. To me, he was more religious than the civilized man.

With private property the father came in. The father can protect you when you are a child, but when you become a youth, you get married; you have to live your own life. By that time perhaps your father will have died, or will have become sick and old. But you have lived from your very first breath under the protection of your father. He was the big man in your life, the first big man. When you are alone, you start feeling some vacuum within you that your father used to fill. Hence, God became the father, a father who is not going to die.

Your father betrayed you, he left you alone. You trusted him so much, and he cared so little about you that you will be left alone? You have lived with that program from the very first breath. So when the father leaves you and you are on your own, suddenly you feel a vacuum. That vacuum can be filled by another father, but that father cannot be a human being because a human being has already deceived you. You are feeling hurt, so you project a father that is eternal and immortal, and far away, and omnipotent—not like your father, whom you used to think in your childhood could do anything...

You can see it when small children are fighting: "My dad is the greatest man in the world!" "Your dad is just a chicken!" Every child thinks his dad is all-powerful; he can do anything, because as he looks around his dad is doing all kinds of things. He repairs the car, repairs the television, bullies his mother...the child knows the father is powerful.

But that powerful father...slowly, slowly, as you grow in intelligence, you start seeing his frailties, his weaknesses. Suddenly there is a gap. Even if the father is alive and with you, you know he is not invincible. He is becoming older, soon he will die. You know he is not all-powerful. Before his boss he starts wagging his tail, his invisible tail. There is a place in your backbone, just at the end, where some millions of years ago there used to be a tail connected. The place is still there. That was the greatest argument by Charles Darwin: if there was no tail connected to you, then why this space? This space would not have been here. The tail has dropped, leaving the connecting link, leaving the space where it used to be attached.

Why do you start smiling as you see your boss? You don't smile at your servant; the servant has to smile, not you. You don't take any notice, you go on reading your newspaper; you know he is passing by, smiling, but you don't even look at him. Your boss is doing the same with you. You smile, and he goes on writing. Perhaps he is not writing anything, but just seeing you coming in, he starts getting engaged in his files, turning pages, looking very occupied and busy.

I used to stay with one of the presidents of the ruling Congress Party, U.N. Dhebar. He was very much interested in me. He used to attend my meditation camps, even though all his political friends tried to prevent him, telling him, "Don't go to this man." But he was not a politician, not cunning. He was a very simple and very authentic man. It was just by chance, accidentally, that he had become the president.

It happens in many cases. He was chosen as the president because he was the most polite—a nice man who would never say no. And Pandit Jawaharlal Nehru needed a yes-man. Nehru was the prime minister and he wanted the Congress Party to be ruled either by himself—which would look dictatorial—or by a yes-man. U.N. Dhebar was such a simple man that he would say yes to whatever Jawaharlal wanted. So it was Jawaharlal who was dictating almost everything.

I was staying once in his house in New Delhi, and he was talking to me and gossiping about all the political leaders, what kind of people we had; all kinds of idiots he was telling me about. There was one Maulana Azad, a Mohammedan, who knew no English and knew no Hindustani. He was a scholar of Arabic and Persian, and he was the education minister of India. U.N. Dhebar was talking about this Maulana Azad.

Once Pandit Jawaharlal Nehru had gone to a conference in London, a conference of the commonwealth nations. At that time India was part of the commonwealth, now it is no more; and Maulana Azad was the second man in the cabinet. He had been given that second place because he was a Mohammedan, to satisfy the Mohammedans of India.

You will be surprised to know India is the biggest Mohammedan country. No other Mohammedan country has as many Mohammedans as India. Even after Pakistan was separated and Bangladesh was separated, still India has a greater population of Mohammedans than any other country in the world. To satisfy the Mohammedans, a Mohammedan had to be number two in the cabinet. And when Jawaharlal went to London, Maulana Azad thought, "Perhaps now I am the acting prime minister, because I am the second man."

Prime ministers are prime ministers wherever they are. There is no such thing as an "acting prime minister." If the president, who is the head of the government, goes out of the country, then the vice president becomes the acting president. But the prime minister is not the head of the government under a constitution like India or England has. The prime minister is not the head of anything, so there is no need for any acting prime minister. But Azad thought otherwise, and U.N. Dhebar was saying to me, "We all told him that this was absolutely unconstitutional. There is no place in the constitution for any acting prime minister; there is only a place for an acting president."

But Azad did not listen. He immediately phoned the Jawaharlal's chauffeur: "Bring his limousine to my house; while he is away I am the acting prime minister." And with the flag of the prime minister on the car, and two motorbikes ahead, two motorbikes by the side, and two motorbikes behind, he drove to the Parliament. Everybody laughed…

U.N. Dhebar was telling me, "Such idiots there are! Jawaharlal had to phone from London, 'Don't do this stupid thing. It is absolutely unconstitutional. There is no such thing as an acting prime minister.'" Then suddenly a phone call came. U.N. Dhebar took the phone and said, "I am very busy and I cannot give you any appointment for at least seven days," and put the phone down.

I said to him, "You are not busy, you are just gossiping with me."

He said, "This is the trouble in politics. You have to pretend that you are very busy, that you don't have any time—and you have all the time in the world. But you have to show the people that you are a very busy man, not approachable so easily. So I told him that after seven days he should phone again. If I have time, then I will see him. Although I am completely free…because you are here I have canceled all my programs. While you are here in my house, I don't want to waste my time with anybody else. I want to be with you. This is a rare chance, because in the meditation camps I cannot have much time with you. This is a great opportunity. And I have told everybody—the guards—not to allow anybody to disturb us.

I said, "This is strange. That man who just called you may have some important work."

He said, "Who cares? Nobody cares about anybody." Such a nice person, very cultured, educated, but … "Who cares?"

The moment he said it to me, I said, "This is very insensitive. And you pray every day to God." He had a small temple in his house with the statue of Krishna. He was a devotee of Krishna. "Your prayer is meaningless. It is better to go outside and pray to a rose bush. At least the rose bush is alive! This Krishna that you are praying to is man-made, just a stone, cut into a statue. Can't you see the deadness of your Krishna? Look outside, the whole world is alive. Birds are singing, flowers are blossoming, the sun is setting. Soon the whole sky will be full of stars."

The primitive man lived in the universe as an essential part of it, and he was grateful just to be alive. His gratitude was more authentic than the God-oriented religions' thankfulness to God. You are being thankful to a fiction.

One of the English writers, a well-known linguist, Dr. Johnson, had a strange habit, almost neurotic. Whenever he went for a morning walk he had to touch every lamppost. If he forgot to touch some lamppost, he would go back, touch it and then go ahead. Whoever was with him would ask, "What are you doing?"

He said, "What can I do? I feel such an urgency that it has to be done. I know it looks stupid, and I know there is something wrong with me, but what to do? If I leave one post, it creates so much upset, so many sentiments, emotions, feelings—'What are you doing? Just go back!' And I have to go back." A lamppost!

I used to go for a morning walk, and an old retired professor of was also always going for a morning walk. He became friendly with me and started walking with me. But he had the habit… In India you find temples everywhere. Just after a few houses, there is again a temple. If not a temple, then under the tree there is a red stone representing the monkey god. This man would bow down at every temple and stone.

I said, "This is torture to me. Either you leave me, or leave your gods. What nonsense! Every place… this whole city is full of temples of this god and that god, and you have to bow down… And I have to stand with you, and I look embarrassed: What kind of companion have I got? So either you stop following me—you can go on your own way—or you have to stop this stupid habit. All those stones are dead. If you want, then look at something living. I don't see you ever looking at the trees, looking at the flowers, or looking at the last star that is disappearing."

And it is such a quiet moment in the early morning: the sun has not risen yet, it is still dark and the last star is disappearing. At this moment, such a moment, Gautam Buddha became enlightened. The last star was disappearing, and as the last star disappeared, something in him also disappeared. Suddenly the sky was there, empty, and he looked inside. There was also utter emptiness: two skies—one outside, one inside—and a great silence. For the first time he bowed down, not to anybody in particular, but to the whole existence. This is gratitude, this is authentic sensitivity.

With private property, the father became important. And when the father was seen in his true reality — was found lacking in omnipotence, in omniscience, in omnipresence; he was not a god — you had to create God as a substitute for your father. So when Jesus falls down on the ground on his knees and calls, "Abba!" in the Aramaic language which Jesus spoke…

Jesus never spoke Hebrew; Hebrew was the language of the highly-cultured scholars, rich people, educated people. Aramaic was the language of the villagers, uneducated people; it is still Hebrew, but not sophisticated. *Abba* is father in Aramaic. But the way Jesus fell on the ground and looked at the sky and call "Abba!" ... it shows that he had not grown beyond his childhood. It is childish.

And remember the difference between childlike and childish. The awakened one becomes child*like*, he is not child*ish*. And the God-oriented person becomes childish. His behavior is just like a child who has lost his way in the fairgrounds and is searching for the father. "Abba!" he is crying. "Where is my father?" Without his father he is not safe, he is not secure.

All these prayers show your fear, all these prayers show your disappointment in your father. You have created a fantasy, and the fantasy is sick.

A little biographical note before we discuss the sutras:

Sekito's enlightenment was realized while he was reading the *Chaolun*, a work written by Sengchao in the year 400. Sengchao had composed this work while in prison awaiting execution. The passage which inspired Sekito's enlightenment was: "He who makes himself to be all things of the universe, is he not the real sage?"

One who makes himself the whole of existence, is not he a real sage? Just this statement, and there suddenly transpired in him a great revolution. From ignorance he took a quantum leap towards enlightenment.

This is just what I have been saying to you: religiousness without God simply means feeling yourself one with the whole universe. Just this statement: Sekito must have been just on the brink, just on the borderline. And as he read this sentence, "He who makes himself to be all things of the universe, is not he the real sage?"—just reading this sutra, a metamorphosis. He became a totally new man. The old personality dropped and he was for the first time an individual, in tune with existence.

And this man, Sengchao, was also a great master. But the greater a master is, the more the society goes against him. He was imprisoned just because he was talking against the old religion of Japan—which is not much of a religion. It is just as ordinary a religion as Hinduism, Mohammedanism, Christianity. It has no flavor of the genius and the giants.

But whenever a genius and a giant appears, the little man in the masses becomes angry, feels inferior, becomes enraged. He has killed Socrates, and he has killed Jesus, and he has killed Mansoor. He also killed Sengchao. Because the whole crowd was against him, the emperor had to arrest him. He was causing great turmoil in the country by his statements. And his statements are so beautiful that a single sentence made Sekito enlightened.

Sengchao's small book, *Chaolun*, consists of very condensed statements, because he wrote that book before he was sentenced to death. But what a man! — not bothering about death, but writing his last testament with no fear of death, no question of death. His book was written just before he was going to be sentenced. It is a small book. You will not find the shadow of the cross on it. If you didn't know, you would never dream or imagine that this book was written just before he was going to be sentenced to death. This shows the caliber of the man; this shows the depth and the height of his enlightenment; this shows his grandeur, his splendor.

A small statement in that book made Sekito enlightened. And, inspired by *Chaolun*, Sekito wrote a book called *Sandokai*. It is as beautiful as *Chaolun*.

Very rarely have such cases happened in the contemporary world. It was Friedrich Nietzsche's *Thus Spake Zarathustra* that inspired Kahlil Gibran to write *The Prophet*. He wrote *The Prophet* when he was only twenty-one, and in his whole life he must have written at least fifty books. In every book he was trying to go beyond *The Prophet* but could not, because *The Prophet* was an inspired book. He was so overflowing with Friedrich Nietzsche's insights that they triggered him also into new spaces.

The Prophet is a great work, but all his other books…He wrote *The Garden of the Prophet*, a desire to go beyond *The Prophet*, but failed. At least fifty books he has written: thirty in English; twenty in Lebanese, his mother tongue. But in no other book could he even come close to *The Prophet*—the other books *he* was writing. *The Prophet* was written under the vast shadow of Friedrich Nietzsche's insights. It is not to be compared with *Thus Spake Zarathustra*, but it comes very close.

The same thing happened with Sengchao's *Chaolun*, and Sekito's *Sandokai*. But the difference is that both were enlightened. *Sandokai* reaches the same height as *Chaolun*.

Neither was Friedrich Nietzsche enlightened, nor Kahlil Gibran, but Friedrich Nietzsche was a giant compared to Kahlil Gibran. Both were unenlightened, but Nietzsche reached the very boundary of the mind. Just one step more and he would have become enlightened. Kahlil Gibran could not reach even to the boundary, that's why he never went mad.

Nietzsche's madness is a symbol that he was almost ready to become enlightened, but he could not find the door. He had no idea that there is something beyond the mind, and he was rushing against the wall, trying to force his way beyond the mind. But you cannot force your way. There is a door, you have to know the door; meditation is the name of the door. Otherwise you will hurt yourself by rushing against the wall. That's how Nietzsche went mad.

Kahlil Gibran never went mad. He never even reached to the boundary of the mind; the question of no-mind does not arise. But just the shadow of Nietzsche's giant intellect triggered in him a tremendous inspiration, and he created *The Prophet*.

These two books, *Chaolun* and *Sandokai* stand on the same ground, on the same height. We are going into *Sandokai*; these sutras are from *Sandokai*. Each statement is magical.

The sutras:

The mind of the great sage of India was intimately communicated from India to China.

It was intimately communicated because a man of the same height as Gautam Buddha, Bodhidharma, went to China. He was full of the light, full of the joy, full of the ecstasy. His spring had come. He went to China as an awakened one. That's why the word "intimate" is used.

Before Bodhidharma reached China, thousands of Buddhist scholars had gone there. Hundreds of Buddhist scriptures were translated into Chinese. Almost the whole of China had already become Buddhist before Bodhidharma reached it. But none of those people were awakened ones. They were great scholars who had gone and translated scriptures. The scriptures were beautiful. China had nothing compared to it. It had only one book written by Lao Tzu on Tao, but that too does not come to the height of Gautam Buddha's sutras because it was a written book, and written under the threat of force, compulsion.

Lao Tzu had never written in his whole life, and he never spoke. People used to sit by his side in silence, and if something happened in the silence, good. If nothing happened… "What can I do?" That was his answer. A few people became enlightened, but very few. One Chuang Tzu, one Lieh Tzu—just two persons became enlightened sitting silently by the side of Lao Tzu. To understand silence is not easy; you have to reach that same depth. Otherwise you may be sitting by the side of Lao Tzu, but your mind will be going in circles, a continuous rush of thoughts. You may be silent from the outside, but inside there is too much talk going on.

When for the first time talking movies came into existence…before that there were silent movies. The first name that was given to the talking movies was "talkie." And in Indian villages the movies are still called "the talkies." In your mind that "talkie" is continuously going on. Whether you want it or not, that does not matter. In spite of you, it is continuously there.

So although thousands of Buddhist scholars had reached China and the whole country had been converted to Buddhism, the emperor of China had been converted to Buddhism, nobody had given the taste; it was not an intimate phenomenon. It became intimate only when Bodhidharma reached China.

Now a buddha himself had reached China — a different body than Gautam Buddha, but the same consciousness. A different body, but the same height and the same depth. It is perfectly right of Sekito to call it an intimate communication from India to China.

In human beings there are wise men and fools, but on the way there is no northern or southern teacher.

Neither teachers from India nor teachers from China are of any help on the way. You need a master; you need an intimate communion with the master, not a teaching. You don't need a teacher in the real religious world, you need a master. You need a buddha who has already arrived and who can provoke you, challenge you to come. A buddha is nothing but a clarion call to everybody: Whoever wants to know can come close. The master has arrived — the teacher has only heard, he has no individual intimate experience of the truth.

So in the ordinary world there are wise people and there are "otherwise" people, but on the path neither the wise are of any help, nor the otherwise. On the path you need someone who has gone beyond mind, beyond wisdom, beyond foolishness, who has gone beyond intellect and beyond retardedness, who has simply moved into the silence of the beyond. You need someone who has found the truth. Just in his finding the truth, he has become a radiation. Around him there is a field of energy which can penetrate you, which can wake you up.

The mysterious source is clear and bright, the branching streams flow through the darkness.

As far as the master is concerned, *The mysterious source is clear and bright, the branching streams flow through the darkness.* But the moment the master speaks, his words start moving towards darkness. By the time they reach to you, they are streams flowing in darkness, branches moving towards darkness. You have to come into deep intimacy with the master, so you can share his brightness, his clearness, his clarity, his transparency. If you only hear his words and note down those words, you are already going wrong. The master does not consist of words. He may use words to call you closer. The master consists only of absolute silence, pure silence.

To be attached to the relative, this is illusion...

The whole world is relative. Albert Einstein was not the only one to bring the word "relativity" into the world. Long before him mystics in different lands had found that everything outside is relative.

That has created a problem for the philosophers, but not for the mystics. Philosophers have heard the mystics say that everything outside is relative, and whatever is relative is illusory. Why is it illusory? It is a little bit subtle, but you have to understand it.

You think yourself homely when you see a beautiful woman; you see a tall man and you feel small. But your smallness is relative. Until the tall man came, you were perfectly okay, there was no problem. You were not worried about your smallness.

In India there is a saying that the camels never like to go to the mountains. They love deserts where *they* are the mountains. They live in the desert, they don't like mountains at all, because a mountain makes them feel very inferior.

It is very psychological. Why do you feel that you are small, unworthy, that you don't deserve any respect, that you are a sinner? These are all relative things. That you are beautiful, that you are very educated…these are all relative. Anything relative is illusory, illusory in the sense that if you don't compare, you are yourself and somebody else is himself. What does it matter if he is tall? What does it matter if you are small? Both of your feet reach the earth, just as the tall man's feet reach the earth. It is not that you are small and dangling in the air. What is the problem? Comparison creates relative illusions.

Trees are not worried. The rose bush is small, and the cedar goes two hundred feet high. Neither is the rose bush worried why the cedar is so tall, nor is the cedar worried why the rose bush has such beautiful flowers. A rose bush is a rose bush, a cedar is a cedar.

One Zen master was asked, "Why are we miserable?" He said, "Look at the cypress tree in the courtyard."

The questioner looked at the courtyard and the cypress tree. He said, "But I don't understand."

The master said, "Look again. By the side of the cypress there is a rose bush. I have never heard the rose bush complaining, 'Why am I small?' And I have never heard the cypress tree complain, 'Why do no roses blossom? I have gone so far up in search of the roses—two hundred feet—and no roses — what kind of justice is this?'

"No, there is no quarrel. I go every day in the morning—sometimes at dusk, sometimes in the night—just to see whether they are quarreling or having a dialogue and discussion. There is absolute silence. Both are satisfied as they are, because no comparison is arising; no relative idea of inferiority or superiority is arising."

The relative is called illusory because it is your creation, it does not exist anywhere. Otherwise you would go mad. You are passing by the side of beautiful trees, and you could start thinking, "Why am I not green?"

You don't do it, because you are not that neurotic yet. Because you don't compare, there is no problem. But you pass by a woman who is beautiful, and if you are a woman, immediately the comparison arises, anger, jealousy. But what is the problem? She has just a little longer nose. And what will you do with a long nose? In the dark every woman is the same. Just put the light off! That is why people make love in the dark. First they put the light off, then every woman is a Sophia Loren. What is the difference? The same skeleton, the same bones, the same blood, the same mucus, the same deodorant, the same perspiration, the same huffing and puffing…

Darkness has a great quality. It makes everybody equal. Who cares? In darkness you can make love to the ugliest woman, thinking she is Cleopatra.

Whenever you compare, the very comparison brings you into an illusory space.

… but to take to oneself the absolute is not enlightenment.

That's what philosophers have been moving into. They think the world is illusory, so God is the absolute, the non-relative. God is beyond relativeness. The world is relative, changing moment-to-moment; nothing is permanent, nothing is stable, it is flux. God is absolute. The absolute is another name for God. He never changes, he is the same, always the same, from eternity to eternity. This is the philosopher's idea: because of an illusory world he creates the extreme opposite of an absolute God.

One of my professors, S.S. Roy — who is now retired, an old man — loved me very much. It was because of him that I entered the university where he was a professor. He was continuously trying to persuade me…I was in another university, but I used to go for debates, discussions, eloquence competitions, to the university where S.S. Roy was a professor. The very first time, at first sight, he fell in love with me. He was a judge—there were three judges—and he gave me ninety-nine points out of a hundred. I came first; I won the shield and as I was leaving with the shield, he came up to me and he said, "Wait. I have to apologize to you."

I said, "For what?"

He said, "I wanted to give you a hundred percent, but feeling that people would think I was showing favoritism to you, I cut one point. I gave you ninety-nine percent. Please forgive me. I wanted to give you a hundred percent, but I could not be that strong. I knew that the other professors would say that I was being too favorable."

I said, "There is no harm. I won the shield anyway, and others have also given me good marks. Somebody has given eighty percent, somebody else has given eighty-five percent. So there is no problem. The other competitors were far below me in their scores, so your not giving me one point makes no difference."

He said, "It does not make any difference to you, but it makes a difference to me because I went against myself. I wanted to give you a hundred percent."

I said, "Next time. I will be coming again and again," because I was going to all the universities, to all the colleges, wherever there was any competition for eloquence or for debate.

There was only one time that I got the second prize; otherwise I had hundreds of prizes, always first. The day I got the second prize, the whole audience of the university could not believe it. I had to stand up. I told the vice chancellor, who was presiding, "I know why I have got the second prize, and you must be puzzling yourself also." A girl had got the first prize. So I said, "I have to be absolutely clear about the matter, because I know what happened.

"One of the professors, who is the judge, is in love with the girl, and he has given too many points to her. The other two judges had no idea. They both gave me the highest marks, but that man has given her so many points that she has come just one mark ahead." I said, "You have to ask the professor because I know they have both been walking in the park together at night.

"The park is in front of my house, so I know perfectly well. And I can produce witnesses, because all the gardeners in the park know that these two people come late at night when the park is closed. They bribe the gardeners and enter the park, because that is the safest place in the night."

The girl and the professor both started perspiring. I said, "Look at their perspiration! Nobody in this whole hall"—there were at least a thousand people—"is perspiring. Only these two people. Why are they perspiring?" I said, "Stand up!" I said it so loudly that even the professor stood up.

And the vice-chancellor said, "You are creating such trouble, but I can understand."

I said, "You have to cancel this whole debate; it has to be done again, and this man has not to be a judge."

He felt so ashamed that he resigned from the college that very night and escaped from the town. After twenty years I came across him in a train. I said, "Hello."

He said, "My God! I wanted never to see you again."

I said, "Life is mysterious. Where is the girl?"

He said, "You have not forgotten yet?"

I said, "I have neither forgotten, nor have I forgiven. Where is the girl?"

He said, "That girl, because of you, deserted me! She became so ashamed that she stopped meeting me."

I said, "That's great! Now I forgive you and I will forget you. I wanted to finish that relationship because you were doing an injustice to me. You thought I would remain silent."

And from that day every judge was aware not to do anything, because, "This man seems to be strange." Everybody felt that it was an absolute injustice. The girl was not even worth being fourth!

And S.S. Roy became interested in me, because I had spoken up. He loved it, and he said, "I will arrange every facility for you, a scholarship, whatever you want I will arrange; you just change university. I want you to be my student." He was a professor of philosophy. So

I changed. He was a very well-known scholar, and an expert on Shankara, whose whole philosophy is that the world is illusion and God is the absolute truth. And on Bradley, an English philosopher, whose philosophy is the same: the world is illusory and God is the absolute truth. He had written his doctoral thesis on Shankara and Bradley.

The very first day I entered his class...He had invited me, but he had not been aware that he was inviting trouble. He was talking about illusion and the absolute, the world and God. I told him, "If God is unchanging, he must be dead. Any living thing cannot be unchanging. You show me any living thing in the whole world—every living thing is moving, growing, going. It is a constant flux. Life is a flux. If God is alive, it is not possible that he can remain stable, the same forever. Then how will you differentiate between a dead god and a living god?

"Just tell me. Both are sitting in front of you, the living god, the dead god. Neither the dead god changes nor the living god changes. How will you find out who is the living God?"

He said, "My God! I have earned a doctoral degree on the basis of my thesis, but I never thought about this."

I said, "The very word "absolute" is a reaction. First you call the world illusory, which it is not. You know perfectly well that you don't enter into just anybody's house. If it is illusory, what does it matter? Why do you go on entering your own house every day? What does it matter? You can enter somebody else's house."

He said, "Your philosophical discussion is dangerous. I have discussed problems, but you are telling me to enter somebody else's house?"

I said, "Yes, because if it is illusory, all dream, what does it matter whether it is your wife or somebody else's wife? Whether they are your children or somebody else's children, all is illusory. And your God is only a philosophical concept: you say that because the world is changing, God has to be unchanging. But it is only logic, not reality. If there is a God he *has* to be changing, otherwise he will be dead."

I told him that day, the first day of my encountering his class, "Your God is certainly dead, that's why he is not changing."

This absolute idea of God is only a philosophical concept, that's why Sekito says: *"To be attached to the relative, this is illusion…"*

He is not saying that the *world* is illusion: *to be attached to* this world is illusion. Remain unattached, the world is perfectly real. Attachment is illusion, not the world; not the woman but the attachment, not the money but the attachment, not the body but the attachment.

Sekito is making a tremendously significant statement. No philosopher has said that. They say the world is illusory. Sekito is making a distinction: not the world, but the attachment to the world, to the relative, is illusory. And because of this, philosophers have moved to the other extreme: God is not illusory, he is the most real, the absolutely real.

And Sekito immediately counters these philosophers. He says,

"...but to take to oneself the absolute is not enlightenment."

Don't think in terms of absolute. There is nothing absolute, everything is always becoming absolute, but it is becoming and becoming and becoming, and it never comes to a full stop, because a full stop will be dead. The day existence comes to perfection, there is nowhere to go, a full stop. Perfection is death. To be absolute is to be dead.

Sekito is saying something which only a mystic, only a buddha can say, "Even the experience of buddhahood goes on growing. There are no limits to its growth. It is not that once you have become a buddha you have come to the full point. No, the path is endless, the journey is infinite, the pilgrimage goes on and on and on. And that is the beauty of existence, that nothing comes to an end. Everything goes on moving eternally."

So the concept of the absolute is the concept of the philosophers, not of those who are enlightened.

> *Each and all the elements of the subjective and objective spheres are related,*
> *and at the same time independent...*

He is saying, the outer world and the inner world are both independent but related, because their functions are different. They are related because they cannot exist separately. The outer cannot exist without the inner, the inner cannot exist without the outer, so they are related. But their functions are different: the outer is moving towards the objects, and the inner is moving towards subjectivity. Their directions are different, their realizations are different, but they are related at a point.

He is making immensely significant statements which will be clear to you only when you stand at your very center—absolutely clear, no dust in your eyes—and you see the objective world has a beauty of its own, a reality of its own, a life of its own, a hidden consciousness of its own, just as the inner has its own stars, its own sky, its own expanse, its own universe. Outside you there is an infinite universe, inside you also there is an infinite universe. Both are related, both are dependent on each other, but their functions are different.

If you move on the outer line, you will find yourself becoming more and more scientific. If you move on the inner line, you will find yourself becoming more and more a mystic.

> *Related yet working differently, though each keeps its own place.*
> *Form makes the character and appearance different; sound, taste, smell,*
> *distinguish comfort and discomfort.*
> *The dark makes all things one; the brightness makes all things different.*

But it is only appearance. In darkness you cannot see, hence everything seems to be one. In light you can see, hence everything seems to be separate. But these separate things in their deepest roots are joined. We are all joined to one center of the universe. As branches, as leaves, we are separate, but as we go deeper into the roots, all the branches, all the leaves, all the flowers are getting the nourishment from the same roots. Existence nourishes you and the trees and the mountains and the birds equally.

So it is a mystery that one existence manifests in so many ways. This variety of expression makes life beautiful. This variety makes life unboring. The variety is a richness, but this oneness makes life equal. Nobody is inferior, nobody is superior, hence there is no need of any comparison.

The four elements return to their nature, as a child to its mother.

That's what I have been telling you. When the source of life also becomes the goal of life, the circle is complete. And whenever the circle is complete, you don't have to move unnecessarily into birth and death, and again birth, and again death. You have been moving into this wheel of birth and death for millions of years. It is time to jump out of the circle. This very jumping out of the circle is enlightenment.

Fire is hot, wind moves, water is wet, earth hard. Eyes see, ears hear; the nose smells, the tongue tastes, one salt, another sour. Each is independent of the other, but the different leaves come from the same root.

You taste from your tongue, you see from your eyes, you touch from your hand. All your senses are different: you cannot see with your hand, and you cannot taste through your eyes, and you cannot smell with your ears. They are all separate, but they are all joined in one brain from where they come like separate branches. They all feed the same brain, and the same brain nourishes them.

Whatever the hands bring from touch reaches the same brain. Whatever the nose brings from a fragrance reaches the same brain. Eyes bring their survey of the world to the same brain. These senses are just branches spreading in different directions, to collect different experiences, and to make the brain richer. But they are all rooted in one brain.

Sekito is just giving an example. We are all separate, independent, but we are rooted in the same existence. We should be independent, we should be individuals, but we should not forget that finally we are one, waves of the same ocean.

Basho wrote:
What happiness,
crossing this summer river,
sandals in hand!

A man who is enlightened, everything to him becomes a mystery. Now such a small thing! You will say, "What is there?"

What happiness,
crossing this summer river,
sandals in hand!

You will say, "There is nothing in it. Sandals in hand? The summer river must have become very shallow. What is there to be happy about?"

But that is the very point of Zen: you don't have to have any reason to be happy. Even this, crossing the summer river, sandals in hand… what happiness!

Any act or no act, doing or no doing, becomes utterly blissful. It does not have to be caused by something. When your happiness is caused, you become attached to the cause because you are afraid that if you lose the cause your happiness will disappear. If you are happy with a woman or with a man, you become attached; not only attached, you start creating prisons for each other, because without this woman, without this man, you cannot be happy. So your happiness turns into misery for both.

Meditation brings you a great experience that happiness need not be caused, and when you have found a happiness that is not caused by anything, you are simply happy—just to be is to be happy—then you don't create any prisons for anybody. Then you don't possess anybody, and you don't destroy anybody's dignity as a human being. You don't enslave people. You love, you share, just because of your abundance — not that you want anything in return. Without your asking, much comes to you. The moment you start asking, you have lost the very ground of being happy.

Hence, I have been contradicting Jesus' statement. He says, "Seek and ye shall find," and I say unto you, "*Don't* seek and ye shall find." Jesus says, "Ask, and ye shall be answered," and I say unto you, "Don't ask, and you *are* the answer." Jesus says, "Knock, and the doors shall be opened unto you." I say to you, "There is no need to knock, the doors are already open. They have always been open; just open your eyes!"

? **Friedrich Nietzsche condemns man for his lack of creativity in not being able to produce a better concept of God than the Christian one—which he regards as the sickest, the most decrepit, which he calls "this pitiable God of Christian monotono-theism."**
Do you agree that the Christian version of God is the most ugly?

All concepts of God are fiction, so there is no question of any God being ugly or beautiful. God does not exist. Nietzsche has forgotten that God is dead.

That's what happens to people who are not enlightened. He has been writing, "God is dead," and suddenly starts saying that man is not very creative because he has not been able to produce a better concept of God. That would be a better fiction only, a better lie. But he has forgotten completely that he has declared that God is dead. Even if it were a better fiction it would still have been dead. Fiction is fiction, a lie is a lie; however polished, however refined, you cannot make it true.

So whether it is a Christian god, a Hindu god, or a Mohammedan god, it does not matter. God is a fiction, and the fiction arises out of the sickness of the mind. Nietzsche had no idea of Eastern gods, he only had the idea of the Jewish god and the Christian god. If he had known the Hindu gods, he would not have written this sentence.

The Christian god is not the only ugly god; all gods are ugly in different ways. But in the first place they are lies, so there is no need to refine them. Man certainly is not very creative, but that does not mean that he should create a better god! A better god will be a better prison. A better god will be a far stronger chain. A better god will destroy you more efficiently than the ordinary gods are doing. Do you want a better god, a better prison, a better poison?

Nietzsche has completely forgotten that lies are lies. There are no good lies and there are no bad lies. Lies are simply lies, there is no distinction. Truth is truth. There is no "better" truth, you cannot refine it. Lies are lies. You can refine them, but still they will be lies, they cannot become truth.

So I cannot agree with Nietzsche; he has forgotten. That is the trouble with philosophers. He is a great philosopher, but he is not beyond the mind. He cannot have the clarity of the enlightened person.

Man is certainly not creative, but his creativity should not be concerned with God. His creativity should be concerned with making a better world, a better society, better literature, better poetry, better paintings, better sculpture, better human beings. A better god is not needed, a better god will be more dangerous.

I hate the very word "God". And I would hate it more if somebody refined the concept of God, because lies have to be destroyed! And you cannot destroy them unless you hate them. All your love for God has to be completely demolished.

Dilly is the manager of the Last Resort Old People's Home. One morning, he is going from house to house collecting.

He walks up to one household and rings the doorbell. When the head of the household answers the door, Dilly says, "Good morning, sir. Would you like to make a contribution to the Last Resort Old People's Home?"

"Okay," replies the man. Then he turns around and calls back to the house, "Hey, Grandma! Get your hat and coat on!"

The psychiatrist is sitting in his chair and looking intently at his patient,. He closes his notebook, smiles and says, "Now, sir, I am pleased to pronounce you a hundred percent cured!"

"Rats!" sighs the man, looking depressed. "What happened?"

"I don't understand," replies the shrink. "Are you not happy? I have cured you!"

"Happy?" asks the patient. "Why should I be happy? Last week I was Jesus Christ. And now I am nobody!"

Now the meditation:

Be silent…

Close your eyes, and feel your body to be completely frozen.

This is the right moment to go inwards. Gather your energies, your total consciousness, and rush towards your center with a great urgency, as if this is going to be your last moment. Only with such urgency can one reach to the center immediately!

Faster and faster…

Deeper and deeper…

As you come closer to the center, a great silence descends over you, just like soft rain, very tangible, very cool.

A little closer, and you find a tremendous peacefulness surrounding your inner space. Flowers of the beyond start raining on you.

One step more and you are at the center. For the first time you see your original face. For the first time you encounter your eternity. The East calls this original face the face of the buddha, the awakened one.

It has nothing to do with Gautam Buddha personally, it is everybody's original face: peaceful, graceful, with a grandeur, with tremendous clarity, transparency, majesty. Your splendor is great, your treasure is great.

Just one quality of the buddha has to be remembered. He consists only of one quality: witnessing.

This small word "witnessing" contains the whole of spirituality.

Witness that you are not the body.

Witness that you are not the mind.

Witness that you are only a witness.

As the witnessing deepens, you start becoming drunk with the divine. This is what is called ecstasy.

To make the witnessing deeper, relax...

Let go of the body and the mind.

Just remember only one thing: you are a buddha, a witness, a pure eternal awareness. And by and by you will start feeling a certain melting; separations disappear. This oceanic consciousness is the very essence of Zen, the very essence of authentic religiousness.

Gather as much as you can of all the ecstasy, of all the divine drunkenness, all the flowers that are showering on you, the grace, the beauty, the truth, the godliness. You have to bring them with you, and you have to express them in their utter beautifulness in your day-to-day activity.

Chopping the wood, you are a buddha. Be graceful with the tree, it is also a potential buddha. Carrying water from the well, be a buddha.

Every act has to turn into grace, into gratitude. Only then will the buddha be coming closer and closer to you.

Before you come back, persuade the buddha to come behind you as a great presence. Persuade him to remain with you twenty-four hours a day.

His presence is going to become the alchemy of your transformation.

These are the three steps: on the first step buddha comes behind you, you feel his warmth, his love, his compassion, his beatitude; on the second step, you become the shadow, buddha comes in front of you; in the third step, your shadow disappears into the buddha, you are no more, only buddha is. You are no more, only existence is.

God is dead, and Zen is the only living truth.

Come back, but come back as a buddha.

Even your movements should be graceful and beautiful, blissful, radiating your consciousness and awareness.

Sit for a few moments to remind yourself of the golden path that you have traveled, and the inner space that you have touched, tasted, the fragrance of the beyond that is still surrounding you, and the presence of the buddha who is just behind you, almost touching you.

Let buddha become your very reality, and you dissolve yourself, you disappear completely.

You are the disease; the buddha is the cure.

You are birth and death; buddha is transcendence from the circle of birth and death.

You are momentary, just a soap bubble; buddha is your eternity.

CHAPTER 6
God is the original sinner

Sekito wrote:
Cause and effect both necessarily derive from the great reality.
The words 'high' and 'low' are used relatively. Within the light
there is darkness, but do not be attached to this darkness.
Within the darkness there is light, but do not look for that light.
Light and darkness are a pair, like the foot before and the foot behind
in walking.
Each thing has its own intrinsic value, and is related to everything else
in function
and position. The relative fits the absolute as a box and its lid;
the absolute works
together with the relative like two arrows meeting in mid-air.
Reading the above lines you should have grasped the great reality.
Do not judge by any standards. If you do not see the way, you do not see it,
though you are actually walking on it. When you walk the way, it is not near,
it is not far. If you are deluded, you are mountains and rivers away from it.
I say respectfully to those who wish to be enlightened, do not waste your time
in vain.

Friends,

It seems that for those who worship God, the opposite to God is not that which is "evil," but that which is natural. What has made man such easy prey for the priests with their concept of a God who is hostile to life?

The questioner is very clear and very right. On the surface, Christian theology seems to be saying that God is opposed to evil, but if you look deeper you see that it is not actually opposed to evil, it is opposed to the natural.

All religions are against nature, it is not only Christianity. Why are they against nature? There is a great psychological strategy. The strategy is that if you are programmed to be against nature, you will live a miserable life, you will live in anxiety, anguish, perversion, guilt.

This whole phenomenon can be created only if you are programmed to be against nature. If you are natural, then you will be just as happy as all the birds, and all the trees, and all the animals. They don't worship God, they don't go to any church, they don't have any theology. They don't have any feeling of guilt, they are simply natural.

The priests found out very early in human history that man can be forced to be God-oriented only if he is forced to be against nature. Once you are against nature you are schizophrenic. Your whole being is part of nature; just your mind is against nature, because only the mind can be programmed, not your body.

So you may take a vow of celibacy, but that does not change your biology; it does not change your physiology. It is just a mind concept, just words. Your blood will go on creating sexual energy, your body will go on creating sexual hormones.

Have you seen the statues of Buddha, of Mahavira and the twenty-three other *tirthankaras* of the Jainas? You will be surprised. They don't have any beard, any mustache. Do you think these people had no beard, no mustache? But it is the cunning priests who made these statues, to make it clear to you that these people are not sexual, because mustaches and beards come because of certain hormones. Men have those hormones, women do not. To show that their physiology has also changed, their beards and their mustaches have been removed. No photographs exist and the statues were made after they had died—three hundred years after—so nobody had any idea, nobody has seen these people. But the desire you can figure out.

Krishna has no beard, no mustache. Rama has no beard, no mustache. What is happening to these people? You can see your celibate monks, and they continue to grow beards and mustaches. Their celibacy has failed. The beard and mustache show that your manhood is still the same in spite of your promise in front of the statue of Jesus or any other god that you are going to follow celibacy. Celibacy remains in your mind only, but your whole body, your whole structure is in favor of nature. So you are split into two parts, and a house divided is going to fall any moment.

These religions have created insanity and nothing else. That is their only contribution to humanity: insanity, split consciousness, split personality. One part — which is very impotent, the mind; it has no power over the body, it cannot change anything in the body—this mind is programmed according to a certain ideology. And when this mind finds that your body is acting against the program, it feels guilty, it feels miserable. It feels worried that there is going to be some great punishment after death and you will be thrown into hellfire for eternity.

Your body wants — just naturally, it wants food, it wants nourishment, it wants love. Love is also a form of nourishment. If nobody loves you, you will shrink and die. There are experiments done by the scientists on monkeys. In one experiment, which has been repeated and found to be completely certain, the small baby monkey is brought to the lab and two mother monkeys are provided. Both mothers are artificial. One is just wires, but it has pipes from which the baby monkey can drink milk. But he cannot hug the wires, and he cannot feel while drinking from a pipe the feelings of the mother, the love, the warmth.

Another baby monkey is given a version of an artificial mother just a little different. The wires are covered with woolen clothes and with fur. It is artificial, just made-up, and warm like the mother's blood. It is kept warm through electricity, so the baby feels the warm body because of the warm clothing. Inside there are tubes carrying milk, kept continuously warm by the electricity. It has breasts for the baby monkey, not just like pipes, but looking almost like real breasts—plastic, but warm and so the milk comes out warm. And the baby monkey can hug the mother.

Strangely, all these experiments proved that the child who gets the warmth and a certain idea that he is with a living mother, lives; the other child dies. Within three months the other child dies, although he is being nourished, taken care of. Only one thing is missing: the warm breasts of the mother. Only one thing is missing: some feeling of love. Even deceptive, artificial warmth is helping the child to grow.

In America, the Red Indians have almost all been killed. A few remained who live on reservations and they are given pensions, because America is using their land—the whole country belongs to them. But they are very few, so it is not much of a problem. It was felt that it was better to provide pensions, money, than to create the possibility of any revolt from them.

Money is very destructive when no work is given. Work makes you feel that you are doing something, you are worthy, you are contributing to life, to existence, you are taking care of people whom you love. But no work is given to the Red Indians. That gives a feeling that they are not needed at all. If they die, the government will be happy, the nation will be happy, because that much pension money will be saved.

And what is a person going to do with money if he has no work? He will drink alcohol, he will gamble, he will go to the prostitutes. And in his drunkenness he will fight, and sometimes he will rape and murder. And when they commit crimes, then immediately the American government forces them into jail.

What I am leading you to is the strange fact that the Red Indians who have been forced into jail, almost all of them were declared to have committed suicide. But I know the American jail—I have been in five jails—and there is nothing that can help you to commit suicide. You cannot carry even your watch into the cell. It is absolutely empty in the cell, there is not a rod that you can hit your head with, there is nothing. Absolute care has been taken that the person cannot do anything as far as suicide is concerned. But I can understand why those people must have died. Either they were killed or most probably they simply shrank. They died from shrinking—life is useless. It was useless before, now it is even more useless. And they had been sentenced for thirty years, forty years, or for their whole life. To live in this cell where there is no love—although they are given food—where nobody accepts them as human beings, their dignity is taken.

My feeling is that a person can die out of shrinking; there was nothing that he could commit suicide with. It is possible that the police and the jail officers thought he had committed suicide. He has not committed suicide. You have forced him into a space where he is not needed, neither loved, nor respected—no pride. He shrinks. There was no meaning, no significance… Why go on living in this slavery, in this indignity, humiliation?

The whole of humanity has shrunk because of the religions continuously teaching you to be against nature. And you cannot be against nature, so all that you can do is become a dual personality. On the front gate of the house you are a Christian, you are a Hindu, you are a Mohammedan, and you are showing a mask to the people, a false face. And from the back door you are natural. So you start feeling a struggle within your own heart.

This struggle is the root of how the priests can exploit you; because you are feeling so miserable, you are in need of somebody wise to advise you, to give you some way of getting out of this anxiety.

So first religions create anxiety, anguish, misery, suffering. And the way they create it is by turning your mind against nature—that is the simplest method. Just be against nature and you will be very sad, empty, not needed, you will lose your whole desire to be alive. Then naturally one wants some advice, and these priests have been bragging that they know the way to get out of misery: prayer. "God will take care of you if you believe in him."

This is the whole strategy of all the religions. First create misery, anguish, guilt, and then people are bound to come to you, to the priests, because all priests for centuries have been keeping their holy scriptures—which are not very holy at all—their monopolies.

For example, in India, only after the British Empire came into existence were Hindu scriptures printed for the first time. And Hindus were very much against printing them, because once you print them they become available to everybody.

They kept handwritten scriptures; particular families had the monopoly—from father to son it passed like a heritage—it was their property. And the public was never allowed to know what was in their holy scriptures. So they were the wise men.

Half of humanity, women, were not allowed to read holy scriptures. In India, half of humanity, the women, and one fourth of the population, the untouchables, were not allowed even to enter a temple, or to hear a Brahmin chanting mantras from the Vedas. The punishment was death.

What was this secrecy? The reason was that if everybody comes to know, then two things are going to happen. First he will know that there is nothing holy in it. Ninety-eight percent of it is sheer nonsense. In perhaps two percent can you find some beauty, some inspired sayings. So it will be a great exposure: "You have been hiding these scriptures, and there is nothing in them." And secondly, the monopoly will be lost. People will be able to look into the holy scriptures for their own consolation.

The priests were very much against publishing their books. Finally they agreed because under British rule they had to agree; they had no power. They agreed, but they agreed that the books should be published in Sanskrit, which is not a living language. Only the priests know it, only the Brahmins know it. It has never been a living language of the common people. Buddha had to speak in Pali, not in Sanskrit. Mahavira had to speak in Prakrit, not in Sanskrit, because the public had no idea of Sanskrit.

Not only have they kept the Vedas secret, they have kept the language also as a monopoly of the Brahmins, of the priests. And this has been the case all over the world in different ways. So you are forced finally to go to the priests. When you are feeling so miserable and you don't see anywhere any light, and the night is so dark and goes on becoming darker and there seems to be no hope for the dawn, where are you going to look? The priest is there, who claims he knows God, who claims that he has the sole monopoly on God's message for humanity.

Man easily became a prey because he listened to all these people, and they managed to convince him. They were more educated; they were the only educated people. They knew how to argue, how to convince—the masses had been kept in darkness—so they argued against nature, and they convinced people. And it is very convincing. For example, everybody is suffering because of marriage, and marriage is a creation of the priests. It is a good device to keep people miserable.

You should live as individuals in freedom. Out of your freedom you love, but not against your freedom. If you sell your freedom for love, you are going to be in despair. So marriage was one of the devices to keep people harassing each other, fighting with each other, because they cannot separate. No divorce was allowed by any religion, and it is human nature to get fed up. Nobody can eat the same food every day—except me. My cooks, the people who take care of my body, *they* get fed up. I eat, and they get fed up, because they have to bring the same food.

But unless you are enlightened, you are going to be fed up with everything. It is good when it is new. You have to change your car every year. It does not mean that the new car is better than the old, most probably it is not. The older was stronger, had a sturdier body, a stronger engine. The newer cars are becoming more and more like toys. And because you are going to change in one year, there is no need to make a very strong car. What are you going to do with a strong car? Strong cars were made to serve you for your whole life.

The newest car will be even more fragile, and in fact it is for the benefit of the manufacturers that you change your car every year; otherwise how is he going to produce new cars? The factories will close. So there is great propaganda for the new cars, and what changes is just the bonnet, a little design change, new colors, different colors. But the reason why people change their cars is that they get fed up.

One gets fed up with relationships also. In the beginning everything seems to be just great. But how long is it going to be great? Soon you become acquainted with each other's geography. Once you have seen a woman naked, it is the beginning of the end.

Only in India do marriages go on being happy, for the simple reason that the husband and wife cannot see each other in the daylight. They cannot talk to each other in front of their elders. Families are joint families, so one family may be forty persons all living together. And there are many elders.

My mother has told me that not only can the husband not see the wife in daylight, but he cannot even play with his own child in front of his elders. This is a program, centuries old. And when you see your wife in the darkness of the night…you cannot even talk, because all around is the joint family. Your elders are sleeping; if you start talking somebody may wake up. Silently, under the blankets, without even saying, "I love you," just make love and reproduce and get out of the bed to your own bed so that nobody is disturbed. But you don't know your wife, you have never seen her, so the interest remains. It is the darkness that keeps the interest alive.

But otherwise, it is very difficult to remain interested in the same woman for your whole life. After the honeymoon the marriage is finished. I think the honeymoon is the only time you are happy, and then begins a long journey of misery and unhappiness. Now the same is happening in India, because now India is becoming civilized, entering into the twenty-first century.

So people get fed up, but they cannot say the truth, that they are fed up with you. So anger comes, violence comes. They both become sad. It is better to spend a little less time with each other. Twenty-four hours hanging around each other's neck, nobody is going to be happy, neither you nor the person you are hanging with.

Religions have been using all these devices to create misery in people. And they have been telling people not to look at anybody's wife, or anybody's husband. And it is very natural. When you are tired of your woman, you start looking all around for some way out. But all religions are saying that adultery is the most sinful act. I don't see it…

When you become adult, you are bound to commit adultery. I see it as simple human nature, and once in a while it is good. It helps you keep your love relationship fresh if some other woman comes at the weekend. It is not against marriage. It can keep the marriage floating forever, because during those two days of the weekend you realize again that the old woman was better.

Five days a week it is good to be married. Two days at the weekend it is good to be free. And it is perfectly human. You want to explore new experiences, you want to love as many people as possible.

It is one of the characters of Jean-Paul Sartre who says, "I would like to love *all* the women of the earth." It is not possible, but the desire is there: "I would like to love *all* the women of the earth." Every woman is a unique individual; every woman is a different experience. Every woman has her own whims, every man his own insanities. So when two new people meet, it is a meeting of different kinds of cuckoos. It is good, because it gives you an opportunity to see that the old one was better. You were settled with the old one; this new one is an unnecessary trouble. But in five days you will again forget it; that is also natural to the mind, to go on forgetting. After five days living with the old woman you will again think that it is getting to be too much.

Whenever I see any marriage, I cannot resist the temptation to corrupt it, because I only see that unless you corrupt it, people are going to be sad and then they will be prey to the priests.

The question is important. "What has made man such easy prey for the priests…?" His misery. So it is very much a con game. Religion is a con game. The priest first destroys your happiness in every possible way, forces your mind to be against nature: "Nature is a sin." And once you have become miserable the priest has his shop open, you can come for advice.

A doctor's son returned from the medical college. He had become an M.D. The son said to the old father, "Now I am here, you need not work. You have worked hard your whole life. I will take over your work, you just rest."

After three days he told the father, "That old rich woman you have been treating for almost thirty years, I have cured in three days."

The father said, "You idiot! That woman has been supporting our family. It is because of that woman you are an M.D. It is because of that woman your other brothers are becoming educated — and you cured her? Do you think I was not able to cure her? Of course I could, but to cure her was to destroy your education. She was half my income!"

A doctor cures poor people quickly; with rich people he takes his time. It is natural, there is nothing wrong in it. The rich man can afford it; the poor man is unnecessarily wasting the doctor's time. And not only time, but the poor man may start asking for medicine to be given to him free, because he has no money. The rich man has to be kept. If he gets tired of one sickness, give him another sickness. Just put the idea in his mind—"I feel you are going to have a heart attack." Just the idea, and his heart will start pulsating and in the middle of the night he will want to check his heart, to see whether it is failing or it is still there. Just give the idea, and then he remains your patient. Tell him, "You need a checkup every week. Your body is in very fragile condition."

Doctors are living a very contradictory life. They are supposed to cure people, but if they cure all the people then what will happen to them? If a society is completely healthy, and nobody is sick, the doctors will start getting sick, starving, dying. They will become beggars.

It was only in China, under Lao Tzu's influence, that for the first time a new method was introduced. It was out of Lao Tzu's great compassion that he went to the emperor and said, "The whole medical profession is basically wrong, because the doctor lives on the diseases of the people, and he is supposed to cure them. You are putting the man in a contradictory position."

The emperor asked, "What do you suggest?"

He said, "I suggest that the doctor should be paid by the emperor for keeping people healthy. When people feel they are losing their health, when they become sick, the doctor's money has to be cut. He is not taking care well enough. It should be just the opposite of now: he will be paid to keep people healthy and if somebody falls sick, his pay will be cut. That will bring a totally different perspective to the whole medical profession."

That's how enlightened people have been giving new perspectives to people, which the people don't understand in the beginning. People would not understand that you have to pay for health. Health is yours, what has the doctor to do with it? And the doctor has to lose money if you fall sick? That was absolutely right, though it looked strange.

The same is the situation with the priests. If everybody was without guilt…That's what they think about me—that I am a dangerous man, because my whole effort is to make you free of guilt, free of sin, free of the idea of morality. I want you to learn only one thing, and that is clarity beyond mind. Then, out of that clarity, let everything happen: your love, your morality, your behavior. But this will destroy the priests absolutely. This will destroy religions and churches, and this will destroy God. Who is going to pray to God if you are blissful? If your life is just a dance, who is going to pray to God? For what?

If you can be kept healthy, if you can be kept well nourished…If you can live a long life, a hundred and fifty years old and still young…These are possibilities. You should remember the arithmetic. It is at seventy-five that the majority of people die. At eighty-five fewer people die. At ninety-five very few people die. Beyond hundred, very rarely does someone die. And beyond one hundred and eighty, there is every possibility you may not die. A simple arithmetic! Who has ever heard of somebody dying after one hundred and eighty? There is no precedent.

Scientists say man has the capacity within his body to live for at least three hundred years if everything remains natural. It is the unnaturalness of life that makes people's life not only miserable, but cuts their life from three hundred to seventy-five. Even at the age of sixty people start feeling, "It is better to die, what is the point of living?"

One old man married a young girl. He was ninety and the girl was only nineteen. His sons—one was seventy, another was sixty—all told him, "This is not the time for you to marry. Don't make us all ashamed. Everybody will laugh."

He said, "It is not your business. I have fallen in love, I am going to marry." And he married, and the doctor who used to look after the old man said to him, "You're getting married…It is very dangerous at your age. It would be better to have a boarder in your house." He meant him to keep some young man in the house who would take care of his wife, but that was understood.

After nine months the doctor saw the old man in the market, and he said, "How are things going?"

He said, "Great! My wife is pregnant."

The doctor said, "And what about the boarder?"

He said, "She is also pregnant."

Now *this* is life!

Live totally, and live naturally, and there will be no religion for you, there will be no priest for you, and there will be no God for you. And there will be nobody who can exploit you and destroy your intelligence, your life, and make you pathological and sick.

…Now do you see why I am dangerous?

? Why is the lie of God so successful?

Because you are a failure. It is your failure that makes the lie of God so successful. In your life you have not loved totally, you have not lived totally. You have never done anything totally; this is your failure.

I don't mean by failure what you understand. You understand you are a failure if you are not super-rich. You are a failure if you are not a great politician, a prime minister, a president. You are a failure if you are not world famous. That is not failure, that is simply the competitive, egoistic life.

And that kind of life is the most miserable, because you are continuously fighting, fighting, pulling others back by the legs, rising over people's heads, making them as if they are steps for you to climb higher. Your life is violent, and a violent life cannot be beautiful. You are merciless; only then can you become super-rich. You don't have any compassion; otherwise how can you exploit millions of people to such a stage that they are starving, and you are simply accumulating money which you cannot use? There is no point in accumulating more; it has just become a habit to go on accumulating.

The richest man in the world now is in Japan; he has twenty-six billion dollars. What are you going to do with twenty-six billion dollars? There is nothing that you can do with twenty-six billion dollars, but he is still running for more.

The people you think are successful are continuously running for more. Deep down they are not successful.

I have heard about a man whose seventy-fifth birthday was celebrated by his friends. But while they were singing and dancing and drinking and enjoying, suddenly they found that the man was missing. So one of his best friends, a great successful attorney, went out in the garden to look for the man. He was sitting under a tree, very sad.

The attorney went to him and said, "This is strange. We are all enjoying your birthday.

For you we have arranged this whole ceremony, and you are sitting here under a dark tree in darkness. What is the matter?"

He says, "You are the matter!"

The attorney said, "I am the matter. What have I done to you?"

He said, "Remember, fifty years ago I came to you saying that I wanted to kill my wife, and what would be the punishment? You told me it would be at least fifty years in jail. And now I am feeling, if I had murdered my wife I would have been a free man today. Fifty years have passed. Because of you I suffered. I would have at least rested in the jail for fifty years and today I would have been free, and there would have been a real celebration. It is you who destroyed my whole life!"

A man is successful if he follows his own natural way and lives it as totally and intensely as possible. If you want to be a musician, you will not be a very rich man. If you want to be a flutist, you are not going to be a great politician but you will be utterly happy. Maybe there is only just enough to eat, but playing on the flute, who cares? You simply disappear in your music. Your flute becomes your meditation. Your song, your dance becomes your meditation.

Anything that is *totally* lived is equal to meditation. You don't need meditation. And a man who is living moment-to-moment, absolutely naturally, according to himself, has nothing to regret, is not a failure. Hence, a happy man, a blissful man, needs no God. It is your misery, your failure to be natural, that makes the life of God so successful. God fills your vacuum. But a man who lives totally has no vacuum.

I don't have a God—not because I am philosophically an atheist, no. I simply don't need a God. I am so fulfilled in myself that I don't need any religion and I don't need any prayer, and I don't need any meditation. Every moment is so exquisite, so immensely ecstatic, who cares about all these stupid questions of God, heaven and hell? These are questions of an insane humanity, and the insane humanity is bound to be exploited by the priests in the name of God.

So first they drive you nuts, and then you have to bring offerings to them. It is a strange game. The priest is playing the ugliest game in the world. His whole success depends on your failure, and your failure depends on being unnatural.

If you understand, my approach is so clean and clear: just be natural and God will not matter at all, nor heaven and hell, nor any priest. Every moment you will be so much in tune with existence that you will blossom like flowers, you will dance like peacocks, you will sing like nightingales. Your life will have a totally different flavor. It will have the fragrance of a man who is utterly contented with himself and existence as it is, with no desire to change, no desire to make this existence better, no desire to bother about what will happen after death.

Socrates' statement is very significant at this point. When he was facing death somebody asked, "Are you afraid that you are going to be poisoned this evening as the sun sets?"

He said, "Why should I be afraid? There are only two possibilities: either I will die, then there is nobody there to be worried, or I will not die — then what is the worry? Only two alternatives, simple: I will be completely gone, and when I am gone, there is nobody left; who is going to worry? Who is going to suffer? Or I will not die. If I don't die, why should I worry? I know how to live. I have lived my whole life so joyously. If there is any life after death, I will continue to live, I know the art. If there is no life, I will rest. I know how to rest totally, eternally. There is no problem. Either I will be dancing or I will be resting, but I know both are beautiful. Rest has its own beauty—eternal rest, no worry, no despair, no anxiety, no anguish. Or I will be dancing, I know the art. My dance can go on eternally."

A man who is really successful will have the same approach as Socrates. Who cares about death? Only people who have not lived are worried about death.

It is a very strange phenomenon. People who have not lived, who have simply hoped to live someday, tomorrow or the day after tomorrow, or maybe after death, in paradise—those who have been postponing life are the only people who are afraid of death because they don't know the art of living.

The art of living is simple. Be natural. Don't be bothered by Manu, Moses, Mahavira, Mohammed—don't be bothered at all by anybody. They lived their life, they never bothered about anybody.

Just learn that secret. Buddha lived his life, not according to any scripture, not according to any Vedas, not according to any discipline. He lived according to his own insight. That is his greatness. That's what makes him a beautiful flower, a lotus, perfectly open to the sun, to the rain, to the wind, dancing, enjoying. Mahavira lived his own life. All the people who have lived their life totally, without any guilt, without any priest interfering, are successful people.

I know only of one success, and that is that your life should be *your* life, your natural existence. But if you fail to be your authentic nature, then the lie of God is going to be successful. Then you have to look for somebody to take care of you. Then you are worried what will happen after death. Perhaps there is a God; how will you face him if you don't worship him? It is better to worship: if there is no God, there is no harm; if there is God, you can always say, "I was worshipping you." These people are chickens; they are not to be called human beings.

Be authentic, be natural, be honest in every act you are doing. And this is possible only if you enter into your being and find the center. That is the only success in the world: to find your center and then let the center guide you. The light will come from the center, radiating from you, and you will be a natural human being. The natural human being is the buddha.

The unnatural human being is pathological, sick. Then he is bound to be exploited by the priests, or by the psychoanalysts—who are the new priests. They don't have anything to offer. Their psychoanalysis is as bogus as the religions. They are the new rabbis, new bishops, new popes. They don't give anything, they simply exploit you. And the priests have not contributed anything to humanity, they have simply exploited. They are the greatest parasites in existence.

? It seems the thought of God arises from the feeling that there is something greater than ourselves. Is this "greater" the no-mind or something else?

There is nothing greater than you. There is nothing greater than yourself, because you are the universe. You are existence, there is nothing greater than you. This idea is also implanted in you, that the saints are holier than you. And what are they doing that they have become holier? Because they eat only one time a day? But look at their bellies. One time they eat, but how many calories?

I don't think any saint has eaten sixteen hundred calories—that is what I am eating, only sixteen hundred calories. Even your breakfast could be two thousand calories! In twenty-four hours I eat only sixteen hundred calories. In twenty-four hours your calories must go beyond four or five thousand—if you are not an American. If you are an American, then a thousand more.

And they condemn me, that I am a hedonist. Food with sixteen hundred calories and a hedonist! Each time, just two small slices of bread and a cup of soup. The same breakfast, the same lunch, the same supper, the same dinner—those two slices of bread and one cup of soup.

No saint of yours has ever lived on sixteen hundred calories. But I am a hedonist, I am a materialist, I am characterless! And only *you* know my character. People who have never seen me, people who have never been here, who don't have the intelligence or the courage or the guts to enter the gates of this campus, they think I am characterless because I am not living according to their scriptures.

I am living according to my own consciousness. And my understanding is that all the great people of the world—Socrates, or Buddha, or Lao Tzu, or Chuang Tzu, or Rinzai, or Sekito—lived according to their own light. That's what makes them great and brings a great splendor to their life. Their contemporaries were as much against them as my contemporaries are against me.

But I have more enemies than anybody else, because they were very local people. Sekito was not known outside Japan. Buddha was not known outside Bihar, a small state of India. Mahavira was not known outside Bihar. I am a world-notorious buddha—for the first time. And I live in my room the whole day. I just come to see you in the evening.

But I can understand what the problem is for these people. It is the same old problem: they cannot accept a lion; they are sheep, they are poor little men, hungry for money, power, prestige. They cannot tolerate a man who lives according to his own insight, according to his own awareness, who does not follow anybody, who has no scriptures and no religion. Such a man creates a great inferiority complex in millions of people. Otherwise, what harm am I doing to anybody?

But because I have been known around the world—I am not a local person, a local buddha—I have enemies all over the earth. I have friends also, all over the earth. Obviously, the friends are going to be very few chosen ones who can understand my insight and who are ready to live on their own, without looking for any God, and without looking for any scripture, without looking for any leader, who have guts and courage to go alone, dancing joyously.

But there is nothing greater than you. Your religions are teaching that you are sinners, saints are holier, and God is greater, and you are just small creatures crawling on the earth. Religions have given you an inferiority complex. That inferiority complex is always looking for somebody who must be greater. But it is not a natural thing, it is implanted, programmed, conditioned. You have been reduced to a subhuman species. Your whole pride, your dignity, your honor, has been taken away. You are left without honor, without self-respect, without dignity. Naturally you think that somebody must be greater.

And then you have all kinds of frauds. You know only their outside, you don't know their inside. On the outside they behave as unnaturally as possible, which gives you the idea that all these saints are very superior—because religions have been teaching you, "Unless you go beyond nature you cannot realize God."

All they are doing is self-torture. To me they are masochists who need psychiatric help. But religions have been praising them as saints. They are in the middle between you and God, but God is the highest, of course; he lives above you in the skies. Have you ever thought that the earth is round? When I was in America, God used to live just above my head. But now, America is just exactly below my feet.

God is above, but the earth is round, so what is above and what is below? People who live on the other side of the earth, their god is below your feet, and your god is below their feet. So when you raise your hands in prayer, just think—you are living on a round earth. Don't be stupid. There is nobody higher, nobody lower, it is one existence.

That's what triggered the enlightenment of Sekito—reading the sutra of an ancient master, that one who feels oneness, one life in all things, one who is in tune with existence is absolutely one with existence. No one is higher than you, no one is lower than you. There is only one existence, one life. We are different expressions of one life, and it is good that there are so many different expressions. It makes existence beautiful, it gives variety, it gives color. It makes it a rainbow. It is not monotonous, it is immensely interesting.

Go on exploring and you will always find something new coming up. Outside, science comes every day upon some new truth. Inside, those who have been exploring, they come every moment as they go deeper, into new bliss, into new ecstasies. Doors upon doors, doors upon doors, and there is no end to this mystery.

I love this mysterious universe, and I love all that has come out of this mystery. It is unfathomable, hence it is inexpressible.

The sutra, the *Sandokai*, second part:

Sekito wrote: Cause and effect both necessarily derive from the great reality.

Everything derives from the great reality. There is no other reality; there is only one reality, the great reality. Outside and inside are just two aspects of this great reality. Every cause, every effect, necessarily comes from this great reality.

The words 'high' and 'low' are used relatively.

Don't take any notice of those words. They are relative.

But even your so-called great people suffer from strange ideas. Napoleon Bonaparte, whom you will think a great, successful man, always suffered because he was only five feet five inches tall. Even his guards were nearly seven feet tall. One day he was trying to fix a picture on the wall, but he could not reach. His guard, his bodyguard said, "I am higher than you, I can do it."

He said, "Shut up! Don't use the word "higher". Just say you are taller than me, not higher." Some vulnerable wound was touched that he had been carrying his whole life.

The man who created the Russian Revolution, Vladimir Ilyich Lenin, suffered his whole life from an inferiority complex. The greatest revolutionary in the world, he was always hiding behind a desk because his legs, being smaller than his upper body, were dangling, they never reached to the earth. He could not sit on a smaller chair because that would look odd: "Why are you sitting on a small chair?" So he used to have a big chair, but in front of him a desk always covered his legs. He was so self-conscious about his legs, he never allowed anybody to come very close. You had to sit just opposite him on the other side of the desk so you could not see his legs. Just feeling unnecessarily inferior…

All your ideas of high and low are relative—your imagination—because you continuously compare. Everybody is unique, hence all comparison is wrong.

Within the light there is darkness—because there is no difference between darkness and light. The difference is only relative. Darkness can be defined as less light, and light can be defined as less darkness—just as the same thermometer can be used for cold water and for hot water. The hot water is a little less cold, the cold water is a little less hot; but these are degrees, and all degrees are relative. They are the same.

Light and darkness are one complete whole, two extremes of one reality. There are animals who see in the night. You know the owl, whose night begins when your day begins. He goes to sleep as the sun rises, because his eyes are very sensitive. He cannot open them in the light, it hurts his eyes. His eyes are so sensitive that he can see only in darkness, but in darkness it is all light to the owl, it is all light in darkness. So it is only a question of the capacity of your eyes. With certain instruments your eyes can see in darkness, your eyes can be brought to the same level of sensitivity as the owl's eyes.

You don't hear radio waves passing by, but they must be passing because once you turn your radio on, it immediately picks them up. So when you are feeling that there are no radio waves around, there are—it is just that your ears are not capable of picking them up.

It happened in Switzerland in the Second World War that a man got a bullet in his ear. The bullet was taken out and the ear healed, but something strange followed: the man started hearing the nearest radio station the whole day—nothing could turn it off.

He reported it to the nurses. They wouldn't believe him. "You must be imagining. It can't be. How can you hear the radio station?"

He said, "Call the doctors." And the doctors wouldn't believe him. He said, "Then make some experiment if you don't believe me. I am going crazy! There is no way to shut it off!"

So they finally decided—because the man seemed to be absolutely sane, although what he was saying was insane—to make an experiment to satisfy him. They brought a radio into an adjoining room and told the man, "You go on writing down whatever you are hearing." There was another doctor sitting in that room with the radio, writing down whatever was playing on the nearest radio station. When the notes were compared, they were exactly the same! The man's ear had to be operated on so he could become normal.

But that opened the possibility that one day you will not have radios anymore. You will just have small buttons you fix in the ear, and on the button will be all the stations. Just push the part you want to hear and your ear will be able to hear directly. There will be no need for a big radio or any other instrument.

That leads to another idea which has not happened yet. Just as radio waves pass by, in the same way television waves are passing. So someday there is the absolute possibility you will just have to change your glasses, that's all. Your eyes are sensitive to certain waves, and on your glasses will be all the television stations. So you set up the television on the glasses, put the glasses on, and enjoy it silently without troubling anybody else.

We are not aware of many things that are happening around us. We are not aware even of our own being, things that are happening within us.

Sekito is right.

Within the light there is darkness, but do not be attached to this darkness.
Within the darkness there is light, but do not look for that light. Light and
darkness are a pair, like the foot before and the foot behind in walking—
two legs of the same man, of the same reality. Each thing has its own intrinsic
value, and is related to everything else in function and position. The relative
fits the absolute as a box and its lid; the absolute works together with the rela-
tive like two arrows meeting in mid-air.

The whole existence is functioning together with you. This is your success: if you come together with existence and meet like two arrows in the air. This is your failure: if you don't come from your side, and existence stands there while you are going sideways. You can go anywhere but you will not be satisfied unless you come to existence, meet, and then your heartbeat becomes the heartbeat of the whole universe. That is success, and that is enlightenment.

Reading the above lines you should have grasped the great reality.
Do not judge by any standards. If you do not see the way, you do not see it,
though you are actually walking on it.

You may not be aware that you are a buddha, but you are carrying the buddha all the time. You may not know that you are reaching to the ultimate, but you are walking on the way without knowing. The whole difference is between knowing and not-knowing. Not-knowing, you are miserable; knowing, you are dancing with joy and celebration.

When you walk the way, it is not near, it is not far. If you are deluded, you are
mountains and rivers away from it.

Only in your delusion — in your mind fictions, hallucinations — is it far away, mountains and rivers away. But if you are not deluded, if you are simply silent without thoughts, you are *in* it. There is no distance between you and the truth, there is no distance between you and existence. This very moment, just a little awareness, and suddenly you will find yourself merging with this vast splendor, this great miracle of existence.

I say respectfully, says Sekito, To those who wish to be enlightened,
do not waste your time in vain.

That is his last statement: "If you want to become enlightened, don't waste your time. Don't postpone until tomorrow."

Now and here put in your total energy, and you will be enlightened. Enlightenment is your nature, so you are not to find it somewhere else. You don't have to go on any pilgrimage. You don't have to go to any holy place. You don't have to believe in any theology, in any religion. You just have to dig deeper into yourself, in the present moment, and suddenly the whole of life springs up.

And you are in for a great surprise—the buddha was hidden within you, not in any temple. You have always been on the right path, you have always been carrying buddha in your womb as your nature. It is just that you never looked at it.

All I teach you is to look inwards to find your center. That is the center of the whole existence.

Buson wrote:

I grow old –
sweet bird,
you vanish
into autumn twilight.

He is saying, "I grow old, just as a sweet bird vanishes into the autumn twilight far away; you see it to a certain point and then it goes into the blue sky…" He is saying, "I am also growing old, sweet bird, my autumn twilight is going to come soon. I will also disappear into the blueness of existence." These are the words of someone who knows.

Death is a door to the divine, death is a door to the deepest mystery of existence. You just have to disappear. You are the only problem, you are the only barrier. Just drop that problem, drop that barrier, and all is just ecstasy and pure bliss.

Another question:

Friedrich Nietzsche saw man's energy in terms of a lake that up to now has "flowed out into God." He looked forward to that day when the lake would cease to leak outwards, when a dam would be created so man's energies could rise higher and higher.
It seems he was on the right track in assessing the need for one to go in, but the damming up of energies sounds dangerously like the idea of the ascetics. Would you please comment?

Friedrich Nietzsche is a thinker, a philosopher of tremendous genius. But whatever he is saying is only a logical, rational, philosophical statement. It is not existential. So try to understand that a man who has not gone beyond the mind can still make certain statements that come very close to the truth. But even to be close is to be at a distance.

He is saying that up to now human energies have been just like a lake that has been flowing out into God, outwards. "He looked forward to that day when the lake would cease to leak outwards; when a dam would be created so man's energies could rise higher and higher." He is coming very close to the point of meditation.

Your energies are going outward to objects, to money, to power—and finally, if you become religious, to paradise, to God, but they are all out. So your energies are leaking out and the ultimate result is a feeling of utter emptiness, hollowness, unworthiness, failure. He is only thinking that the day must come when people will start creating a dam to prevent the leakage, so the whole energy gathers inwards. Rather than spreading outwards in thin layers, it starts rising upwards like a pillar.

He is perfectly right, but it is not his experience. He is just imagining—"someday."

I am offering you that day that he was imagining. What is your meditation? Just taking all your energies from outside to the interiormost space. And as energies go on gathering, not only do they go higher, they also go deeper, simultaneously, just like the roots of a big tree. Roots go on going deeper and deeper, and the tree goes on higher and higher.

Exactly like that, your consciousness, your life energy, moves higher and lower simultaneously. It touches the very depth of the earth—that is materialism. And it touches the stars—that is your spirituality. Just as a tree cannot be without roots, any spirituality without roots in the earth is bound to fail.

The East knows perfectly that its spirituality has failed, and still they go on insisting that materialism is against spirituality. Because of this idea the whole East has suffered poverty, starvation. No science has been developed, no technology developed that can help people. And the West has suffered because they think only the roots are enough, there is no need for the tree and the flowers and the fruits. What will you do with the roots?

The West has roots very deep in the earth in technology, in science, in objective research, but it is feeling utterly empty inside. The East has huge trees and all the branches rising towards the stars, but they go on falling, because without roots you cannot keep the tree standing. Both need a great meeting point. East and West, materialism and spirituality, the inner and the outer, the higher and the deeper—both have to come to a certain synchronicity, then man will be whole.

And your worry is unnecessary. You say, "It seems he was on the right track in assessing the need for one to go in, but the damming up of energies sounds dangerously like the idea of the ascetics."

He was not aware at all about meditation, so he used the word "damming". But his word "dam" should be taken symbolically from a philosopher who is still within the mind. The mind of Nietzsche must have been one of the greatest minds that has ever lived on the earth, because he could conceive something beyond the mind while living in the mind. Living in a dark cell with no opening, he can still visualize, in his dreams, the sunrise. He has not seen it. He can visualize in his dreams beautiful flowers — he has never seen them. His capacity to visualize is great and should be appreciated.

No, he is not an ascetic. He was absolutely against ascetics, so he cannot mean what you are worrying about. It sounds as if holding all your energies inwards is creating a prison for the energies so that they cannot flow outward. He could not use the right symbols because he had no experience.

When you have energies rising like a pillar and going deeper into the ultimate depth, you will have both the worlds together—the inner world and the outer world, because the inner and the outer are two aspects of the same energy. Of course you will not be flowing towards God, which is a fiction. You will be flowing towards a real ocean of consciousness; you disappear into it.

It is not ascetic. Certainly he was not an ascetic, so he cannot mean it. But a man without eyes who is talking about the light—and he comes so close to it!—is worth praising. He has no eyes to see, so he has no idea what light is, but just thinking about it, he comes very close. Also he cannot make exactly the right statement, it is only approximately right, but no other philosopher has come even that close. His beauty is great.

It is time for laughter.

Late one afternoon at the Pearly Gates of Heaven, Saint Peter is inspecting twenty married women who have just arrived for judgment.

"Now, girls," says Saint Peter. "If any of you was ever unfaithful to your husband on earth, please take one step forward! And remember, no lying, and no cheating! I have ways of checking up on you!"

Immediately, nineteen of the wives move forward, but one woman remains standing alone. Saint Peter nods quietly to himself and walks over to the telephone. He dials up Hell.

"Hello! Satan!" exclaims Saint Peter. "I am sending down twenty unfaithful wives to you— but be careful. One of them is completely deaf!"

One morning the phone rings in the office of Doctor Shelby. "Good morning," says Doctor Shelby, cheerfully.

"It may be a good morning for you," snaps Brenda Chubbs, at the other end. "But ever since you have been treating my husband, I have not had a single good morning!"

"I am sorry to hear that, Mrs. Chubbs," says the doctor. "What seems to be the problem?"

"Well," grumbles Brenda, "before he came to you, he was a perfect husband and father. But now he has become a rat. He used to tell me how pretty I am—now he calls me an ugly old witch! He used to love our family life, but now he is critical about my housekeeping, hates the kids, and chases after any loose woman who happens to walk by! I think you have been giving him hormone injections which have completely altered his personality!"

"Hmm," says Doctor Shelby, "I want you to know that I have not been giving your husband injections of any kind. All I did was fit him with a pair of contact lenses!"

The meditation:

Be silent...

Close your eyes, and feel your body to be completely frozen.

This is the right moment to go inwards. Gather all your energies, gather your total consciousness and rush towards your center of being with an urgency, as if this is the last moment of your life.

Only with such urgency have people become enlightened.

Faster and faster…

Deeper and deeper…

As you come closer to your center, a great silence descends over you. It is falling almost like soft rain, cool, very tangible, and very mysterious.

Gautama the Buddha Auditorium has become absolutely silent, as if there is no one here at all.

A little deeper, closer to your being. And suddenly you are surprised, great fountains of peace burst all around you.

A little closer, and there arises for the first time a divine drunkenness, a deep ecstasy, a blissfulness you have never known before.

One step more, and you are at the very center. Suddenly you see you are no more.

At the center is your hidden nature, your original face.

We have used Gautam Buddha's face as a symbol for everybody's original face. So let me say, you have disappeared, only buddha is. In other words, you are no more, only existence is. And this is the greatest experience, the highest peak of consciousness and the greatest depth, simultaneously.

The only thing you have to remember at this point is buddha consists of only one element, consciousness, awareness, witnessing—different names of witnessing.

Just witness the way a mirror mirrors—no judgment, no appreciation, no identification.

Witness you are not the body.

Witness you are not the mind.

And witness you are only a witness.

Relax…but go on keeping the witness as clear as possible.

Buddha used to call this witness, *sammasati*, right remembering. You have remembered you are a buddha. You are not the body, you are not the mind. You are only a pure consciousness.

And as your witnessing deepens, you start melting like ice in the ocean. Gautam the Buddha Auditorium is turning into an ocean, and you are disappearing into it just like ice melting. No waves, no ripples—such silence!

You are at the very center of existence. You can now feel your heartbeat to be in tune with the universal heartbeat.

Absolutely unknown, unacquainted, flowers are showering over you.

The whole existence is rejoicing with your entry into the beyond. Going beyond the mind is going into the very cosmos.

Mind is your prison. To go beyond it is your freedom.

Collect as many experiences as you can: all the flowers, all the fragrances, the silence, the serenity, the tranquillity, the calmness, the peace that passeth understanding, and the divine ecstasy, the great splendor that you are a buddha, that you are one with the cosmos.

At this moment you are the most fortunate people in the whole world. The whole world is concerned with trivia. I am calling you the most blessed ones because you are concerned with the ultimate, with the essential, with the eternal.

God is dead, and the only living truth is Zen.

Zen simply means what you are experiencing at this moment: a pure mirrorlike innocence.

One thing you have to remember: don't forget to persuade the buddha to come along with you. He has to come, it is your nature, and he has been hiding at the center for centuries, perhaps for millennia. And he has been waiting for you to invite him. Invite! Welcome! Request!

Unless the buddha comes into your day-to-day life, in your actions, in your gestures, in your words, in your silences…His grace, his presence has to be felt.

Unless you are completely possessed by the buddha, and all these experiences of silence and beatitude, and blissfulness and divine ecstasy start overflowing you in all your actions…

In your very presence an energy field is created around you; you for the first time become a mystery unto yourself, a shrine, a holy land; the place where buddha grows comes to its full flowering.

This very body is the buddha, and this very earth is the lotus paradise.

Come back…but come back as a buddha, with the same peace, with the same serenity, with the same silence.

Sit down for a few seconds just to remember the golden path that you have traveled, the experiences that you have encountered.

Some fragrance must have come with you.

Some silence must be hanging around you.

Some peace will be overflowing you.

Some drunkenness you will still be feeling.

And remember that just behind you there is a new presence standing, the presence of the buddha, the awakened one.

There have been thousands of buddhas. The buddha is no one's monopoly, it is everybody's birthright.

These are the three steps to become a buddha.

The first step: the buddha comes because you have invited him, following you like a shadow just behind you.

The second step: as you become more and more attuned with the buddha, he comes in front of you. You become the shadow behind the buddha. And as you become a shadow you are starting to disappear. The shadow has no existence.

The third step: you have disappeared completely, you don't exist even as a shadow. You are absorbed into the buddha. You have merged into that ultimate consciousness. You have become one with the universe.

This is the only existential truth.

I don't teach any philosophy. I teach you existence, truth, beauty, and grandeur. It all happens at the third step without any effort—the metamorphosis from a man into a new man.

The new man is the superman of Friedrich Nietzsche, and it is the awakened one, the buddha of the Eastern mystics.

My effort is to bring East and West into a meeting, not only a meeting but into a merger, a deep synchronicity between materialism and spirituality, between Zorba and the Buddha. When you are both—the zorba as far as the outside world is concerned, and a buddha, as far as the inner world is concerned—you are a whole man. And the whole man is the only holy man. There is no other possibility.

Chapter 7
God is the business of the priest

When Impo took leave of Ma Tzu, Ma Tzu asked, "Where are you going?"
Impo replied, "I'm going to Sekito."
Ma Tzu warned, "The path on the stone-head is slippery!"
Impo said, "I have the pole of an acrobat with me—I can make a show with it
whenever I want," and with that he left.
When he got to Sekito, Impo went around Sekito's Zen stool one time,
swung his stick with a shout and asked, "What is the dharma of this?"
Sekito said, "How sad! How sad!"
Impo didn't have anything to say, but he went back to Ma Tzu and told him
the story. Ma Tzu said, "You go again, and when Sekito says, 'How sad,'
you start crying."
So Impo went to Sekito again and asked in the same manner, "What is
the dharma of this?"
At that, Sekito started crying.
Impo again was left without any word, and returned to Ma Tzu. Ma Tzu
commented, "I told you—the path on the stone-head is slippery!"

Friends, first the questions.

**We humans seem to like to be told what to do. If we don't have a "God,"
we have someone else to tell us what is right or wrong and what is good or bad.
Why such a resistance to thinking for ourselves?**

It is not a question of thinking. In fact you think too much. It is a question of how to stop thinking and see directly into every situation that you are facing. If there is no thought, there is no barrier, there is no dust in your eyes; you can see clearly. And when this clarity is there, you don't have alternatives of good and bad. With this clarity, there is a choiceless consciousness. You simply do what is good—not that you make any effort to do it. It comes effortlessly to the man of awareness, consciousness, alertness. He simply cannot imagine the bad, the evil. His whole awareness simply points him towards the good.

So your problem is not why there is such a resistance to thinking for yourselves. You cannot think for yourself, because the vision of good is not part of the mind. And you know only the mind, hence the whole problem arises. Because you know only the mind, you don't have clarity. You have hundreds of thoughts moving continuously in your mind. It is a rush hour twenty-four hours; a crowd of thoughts goes on, clouds go on moving so fast that you are completely hidden behind the clouds. Your eyes are almost blind. Your inner sensitivity is completely covered by your thoughts.

Through the mind you cannot know what is good and what is bad. You have to depend on others. This dependence is absolutely natural because mind is a dependent phenomenon; it depends on others; its whole knowledge is borrowed.

All that your mind knows has come either from the parents, or from the priest, or from the teachers, or from the society. Just watch, and you will not be able to find a single thought that is original to you.

All is borrowed; mind lives on borrowed knowledge. In every situation it wants somebody to guide it. Your whole life is being guided by others. From the very beginning you are told what is right and what is wrong by your parents. Then your teachers, then your priests, then your neighbors…not that they know, they too have borrowed from others.

This borrowing goes on century after century, generation after generation. Every disease goes on being inherited by the new generation. It is just a replica of the older generation, a reflection, a shadow, but it does not have its own originality. It is because of this you need a god, an ultimate guide. You cannot depend on your parents, because as you grow older you start seeing their falsities, their lies. You start seeing that their advice is not perfect; they are fallible human beings. But the small child has believed in them as if they were infallible.

It was not their fault, it was the small child's innocence; the child trusted the father, the mother, who loved him. But finally he comes to know as he grows towards a little maturity that what these people say is not necessarily true.

One day I was playing—I must have been five or six years old… A man used to come to see my father, an utterly boring man, and my father was growing tired of him. So he called me and told me, "I see that man is coming; he will waste my time unnecessarily and it is very difficult to get rid of him. I always have to go out, and say to him, 'Now I have some appointment'– unnecessarily I have to go out, just to get rid of him. And sometimes it happens that he says, 'I am coming with you so that on the way we can have a good talk.' And there is no talk, it is a monologue. He talks, and tortures people."

So my father said, "I am going inside. You just keep playing outside, and when he comes, you simply tell him that your father is out."

My father used to tell me continually, "Never speak an untruth." So I was shocked. This was contradictory.

When the man came and asked me, "Where is your father?" I said, "He is in, but he says that he is out."

My father heard this from inside, and the man came into the house with me, so he could not say anything to me in front of him. When the man had gone, after two or three hours, my father was really angry with me, not with the man.

He said, "I told you to tell him, 'My father is out.'"

I said, "Exactly, I repeated the same thing. I told him the same thing: 'My father says to tell you that he is out. But he is in, the truth is he is in.' You have been teaching me to be truthful whatever the consequence. So I am ready for the consequence. If you want to give me any punishment, give it. But remember, if truth is punished, truth is destroyed. Truth has to be rewarded. Give me some reward, so I can go on speaking the truth whatever happens."

He looked at me and he said, "You are clever."

I said, "That you know already. Just give me some reward. I have spoken the truth."

He had to give me a reward; he gave me a one-rupee note. At that time you could live with a one-rupee note for almost half a month. And he said, "Go and enjoy whatever you want to purchase."

I said, "You have to remember it. If you tell me to speak a lie, I am going to tell the person that you have told me to. I am not telling a lie. And each time you contradict yourself, you will have to reward me. So stop lying. If you don't want that man to visit you, you should tell him directly that you don't have any time and don't like his boring talk because he says the same things again and again. Why are you afraid? Why do you have to tell a lie?"

He said, "The difficulty is, he is my best customer."

My father had a beautiful clothes shop, and this man was rich. He used to purchase a huge lot for his family, relatives, friends. He was a very generous man—just being boring was his problem.

So my father said, "I have to suffer all the boredom because he is my best customer and I cannot lose him."

I said, "That is your problem, it is not my problem. You are lying because he is your best customer, and I am going to say this to him."

He said, "Wait!"

I said, "I cannot wait because he must be told immediately that you go on suffering all his boring talk just because he is a good customer—and you will have to give me a reward."

He said, "You are so difficult. You are destroying my best customer and I will have to give you a reward too? Just don't do it."

But I did it. And I got two rewards — one from that boring man because I told him, "Truth should always be rewarded, so give me a reward because I am destroying one of the best customers of my father."

He hugged me and he gave me two rupees. I said, "Remember, don't stop buying from my father's shop, but don't bore him either. If you want to talk, you can talk to the walls, to the trees. The whole world is available. You can just close your room and talk to yourself. Then *you* will be bored."

And I told my father, "Don't be worried. Look, one rupee I have from you, two rupees I have from your customer. Now one more rupee I am owed; you have to give it me because I have told the truth. But don't be worried. I have made him a better customer and he will never bore you again. He has promised me."

My father said, "You have done a miracle!" Since that day that man never came, or even if he did come he would stay just for one or two minutes to say hello and he would go away. And he continued to purchase from my father's shop.

He said to my father, "It is because of your son that I continue. Otherwise I would have felt wounded, but that little boy managed both things. He stopped me boring you and he asked me, requested me, 'Don't stop shopping from my father's shop. He depends on you.' He got two rupees from me— and he was saying such a shocking thing to me. Nobody has ever dared tell me that I am a boring man."

He was the richest man in the village. Everybody was in some way connected with him. People borrowed money from him, people borrowed lands from him to work on. He was the richest man and the biggest landowner in that village. Everybody was somehow or other obliged to him, so nobody was able to tell him that he was boring. So he said, "It was a very great shock, but it was true. I know I am boring. I bore myself with my thoughts. That's why I go to others to bore them, just to get rid of my thoughts. If I am bored with my thoughts, I know perfectly well the other person will be bored, but everybody is under an obligation to me. Only this boy has no obligation and is not afraid of the consequences. And he is daring! He asked for a reward. He said to me, 'If you don't reward truth, you are rewarding lies.'"

This is why this society is in such a mad space. Everybody is teaching you to be truthful, and nobody is rewarding you for being truthful, so they create a schizophrenia. The Indian Government has the motto *Satyameva jayate*—"Truth is always victorious." That is their motto. But every politician goes on lying to the people, giving promises they know they cannot fulfill. In every court is written *satyameva jayate*, truth is always victorious. But in every court it is not the truth that is victorious, it is the more efficient, more argumentative lawyer who wins the case. It does not matter whether he is in favor of the criminal or against the criminal.

I used to have a vice-chancellor who was one of the biggest legal experts in the world. He had three offices, one in London, one in New Delhi, and one in Beijing. He was continuously running from one country to another country, and he never lost a single case. All the great cases in which millions of dollars were involved…all the maharajas of India were his clients; but he was a drunkard.

He was fighting a case in the privy council in London, the highest appeals court for India under the British empire. The supreme court was in India but if you wanted to go against the supreme court, the privy council was in London. And he was a privy council man; he was continuously fighting cases in the privy council.

One night he was at a party and drank too much. Next day he had a hangover, and was still a little drunk, but he had to go to the court. The case involved two districts of Rajasthan, Udaipur and Jaipur. Both the maharajas were fighting for a certain bit of land—to which district did it belong? It was thousands of acres of land. And under the influence his hangover he forgot which party he was fighting for, Udaipur or Jaipur.

So he went on criticizing the maharaja of Jaipur; all his arguments were against that maharaja. Many times his secretary pulled on his coat, but he simply wouldn't listen. When it was lunchtime, the court stopped for an hour. Then the secretary said, "You have spoilt the whole case. You are *for* the maharaja of Jaipur and you are arguing against him. And you have created such a problem because the man who is against the maharaja of Jaipur, who is fighting you, another great expert, is at a loss what to do. All the arguments that he has prepared, you have already put against the maharaja of Jaipur."

Now he was getting over his hangover; he said, "Don't be worried. There is still time."

After lunchtime he said to the court, "Before lunch I gave all the arguments that the opposite party can give. Now I am going to criticize the opposite party, argument by argument, because I am standing here for the maharaja of Jaipur." And he criticized his own arguments so cleverly.

When he told me this…I used to go often to visit him. He loved me very much. He always told me: "You should join the law department, not philosophy."

I said, "That is not my field." But he loved my arguments.

He said, "It is a loss to the world of law and the constitution. You have such arguments that you would become a world-famous legal expert."

I said, "I am going to become a world-notorious illegal expert. Don't be worried about me."

But he loved me, so he told me that incident.

It is not a question of truth at all, it is only a question of who is a better arguer. On the one hand the government and all the religions and all the preachers go on saying, "You should tell the truth." But society does not reward the truth.

Just recently I received a threatening letter from a law firm in Madras saying that I have offended the religious feelings of their clients. I have told my legal secretary to write to them that in the first place there are no religious feelings. A religion is beyond feelings and beyond thoughts and beyond mind. There are only religious superstitions. A man of religion cannot be hurt. He knows the truth. It is the lies that you are living in that are hurt. Truth always hurts lies. So you should tell your clients to be really religious. Go beyond the mind, go beyond feelings, sentiments, emotions, thoughts, and you will not be hurt. But if you want to come to the court, you can. My whole life I have been fighting in courts around the same point that people's religious feelings are hurt. I have been telling the judges, "If I am right, and somebody's feelings are hurt, do you think I have to be punished for it? That man needs psychological treatment. If his religious feelings are so weak, that shows that they are only beliefs. He does not know what religion is. And if truth hurts people, what do you suggest? Should I start lying?" The judges would look all around—what to do? They cannot say I should start lying, so they are at a loss.

In my first court case they gave me a choice of the Bible, the Koran or Bhagavad Gita, whichever religion I belonged to. I was asked to take the book—all the books were on the table—and take the oath that I would speak only the truth and nothing else.

I said, "I cannot do that for one reason: all these three books are full of lies. To take an oath on a book which is full of lies is absolutely absurd; you are an intelligent man. Secondly, I cannot take the oath because I always speak the truth. Taking the oath will mean that I won't speak the truth unless I take the oath. The implication is clear. You are telling me that I am an untruthful man. You are insulting me in your court. If I insult you, you will say that the court has been insulted. But you are insulting me by telling me to take the oath. I cannot take the oath because I simply speak the truth. There is no question of an oath."

He looked at me and he said, "I can understand, but this creates a problem. Without taking the oath, the case cannot start."

I said, "That is not my problem. Who wants to start it? It is the other party that is starting it. I can go home right now."

He said, "I will make an exception for you because you are saying you will speak the truth."

I said, "I am not saying that, I am saying I only speak the truth. And that's the problem. These people are hurt by the truth. I have said that there is no God, and they are believers of God. Now they should prove that there is a God. That is their problem, not my problem. I simply repeat again, there is no God. Now they should prove the existence of God with evidence, with witnesses."

"What do you think?" I asked the judge. "Do you believe in God? Do you have any evidence, any witness who has seen God? Can you say that you have seen God?"

He said, "It seems you are the judge here and I am the criminal."

I said, "Truth is always victorious. It is just behind you. Read it."

The case was dismissed. Hundreds of cases have been dismissed. But the society goes on rewarding a person who consoles you. It does not matter that he is consoling you by a lie.

Once it happened that a man died and his wife was really in despair, crying and crying. And one of my neighbors went to her and said, "Don't be worried, the soul is immortal. Your husband has not died, it is just the body; his soul is immortal and cannot die. So don't unnecessarily be in despair, be sad and cry, there is no need."

I was listening, standing by his side. I thought, "Let me wait. When somebody dies in this fellow's house, then I will go." Two years later his father died. So I went immediately.

My father said, "Where are you going?" I said, "The same place you are going," because he was going to participate in the funeral procession; a neighbor has died and he was an old friend. He said, "He was my old friend. But why are you going?"

I said, "I am going to take care of his son, because that idiot was telling a woman whose husband had died, 'Don't cry, the soul is immortal.' Now I have to see whether he is crying or not."

And he *was* crying. I said, "Stop crying. You were telling that poor woman that the soul is immortal. What happened? Your father's soul is not immortal? Stop crying."

He said, "You are a strange person. I am in a deep sadness."

I said, "What happened two years ago? When somebody else's husband died, you told her great and beautiful things. All lies! Your tears prove you were lying. If you were true, there would be no tears. Your father's soul is immortal."

He said, "I know it. But what to do? I feel sad."

I said to him, "That woman also knew it."

All knowledge is borrowed; hence all knowledge that is borrowed is a lie. Deep down you are not in agreement with it. Deep down there is doubt.

So what you are asking is: If we don't have a God, suddenly the problem arises, to whom do we have to look for guidance about what is good and what is bad? And you feel, you think it is because there is a certain resistance to thinking. No, it is not as you think. It is not a question of resistance to thinking. Thinking cannot solve the problem.

For example, a man has fallen into a well. Now is it good or bad to pull him out? Can you decide that by thinking? You may think it is good to save the man; but if you save the man and tomorrow he commits a murder, then you will be responsible, at least fifty percent responsible for the murder. If you had not saved the man, there would have been no murder.

There is a religious sect, Terapanth, in India, which says: Don't interfere in anybody's life. If somebody is drowning, you simply move on; don't listen. He is shouting for help, "Save me!" Don't listen, because he is suffering from his past evil acts. If you interfere, you are committing two crimes. First, you are interfering in his personal life. He was suffering because of his personal evil acts. He has to suffer; you are preventing him. He will have to fall again some day. It is better to let him finish with the past evil acts. And secondly, by saving him you are taking an immense responsibility. He may rape a woman, he may kill somebody. He may turn out to be a thief or anything, and you will be responsible. So you have unnecessarily taken a responsibility on yourself which will disturb your own spiritual growth.

So the followers of Terapanth say, "Don't give any food to a beggar. He is a beggar because he is suffering from his past life's karmas." They don't believe in charity, they don't believe in compassion, they don't believe that you should help anybody who is in trouble. You should keep aloof, otherwise you are taking on responsibilities that will become too burdensome for you. The first task is to get rid of your own evil acts and now you are taking on other people's responsibilities? You will never become enlightened. So the people following this sect have become absolutely inhuman; nothing matters.

Thinking cannot decide anything, because something may be good in one situation and the same thing may be bad in a different situation. Sometimes even poison can be medicine, and sometimes even medicine can be poison—you have to understand the changing flux of life.

So by thinking you cannot decide. It is not a question of deciding as a logical conclusion, it is a question of choiceless awareness. You need a mind without thoughts. In other words, you need a no-mind, just a pure silence, so you can see directly into things. And out of that clarity will come the choice on its own; you are not choosing. You will act just as a buddha acts. Your action will have beauty, your action will have truth, your action will have the fragrance of the divine. There is no need for you to choose.

You have to look for guidance because you don't know your inner guide is hidden inside you. You have to find the inner guide, and that's what I call your witness. That's what I call your *dharma*, that's what I call your intrinsic buddha. You have to awaken that buddha and your life will shower blessings, benediction. Your life will become so radiant with good, with godliness, more than you can possibly conceive.

It is almost like light. Your room is dark, just bring light in. Even a small candle will do, and the whole darkness disappears. And once you have a candle you know where the door is. You don't have to think about it: "Where is the door?" Only blind people think about where the door is. People who have eyes and the light is there, they don't think. Have you ever thought, "Where is the door?" You simply get up and go out. You never give a single thought to where the door is. You don't start groping for the door or hitting your head against the wall. You simply see, and there is not even a flicker of thought. You simply go out.

Exactly the same is the situation when you are beyond mind. When there are no clouds and the sun is bright in the sky, you don't have to think, "Where is the sun?" When there are clouds covering the sun, you have to think about it.

Your own being is covered with thoughts, emotions, feelings, and they are all mind-products. Just put them aside, and then whatever you do is good—not that you follow certain scriptures, not that you follow certain commandments, not that you follow certain spiritual leaders. You are in your own right the guide of your life. And that is the dignity of man, to be the guide of his own life. That makes man a lion, transforms him from a sheep which is always looking for somebody else to defend it.

But this is not only your problem, this is the problem of almost the whole of humanity. You have been programmed by others as to what is right and what is wrong.

So when there is no God, there is no holy scripture and there is no son of God like Jesus Christ to save you, and there is no meaning in the pope who represents Jesus Christ who is the son of God who does not exist! Can you be a son of someone who does not exist? To be a son of someone who does not exist simply means you are a crackpot—and the pope is representing the crackpot, Jesus Christ.

He goes on saying that he is infallible, and each pope has contradicted other popes. In these twenty centuries there have been many instances when one pope acted in a certain way and another pope demolished that and changed the rule. Both cannot be right. Both cannot be infallible. Both can be fallible, but both cannot be infallible. One has to be fallible — but if one pope is fallible, then what is the guarantee that other popes will not be fallible, too?

And the pope is elected. Do you elect a buddha? By election you decide who is a buddha? Then your politicians will become buddhas, and your buddhas will not have any votes, because your buddhas will not go begging for them. A buddha is unconcerned whether you think him a buddha or not.

The pope is elected. And you will be surprised to know that even Jesus Christ, three hundred years after his death, was elected as a divine being by a conference under the Emperor Constantine. The conference is known as the Nicene Council. It was by election, by voting, that it was decided that Jesus is holy.

You cannot decide by election that Jesus is holy. You cannot decide by election whether Albert Einstein is right or wrong—by election, by people who don't know any mathematics, who don't know any physics. People who don't have any experience of the holy are voting for or against Jesus, whether he is holy or not. After three hundred years, people who have not known Jesus and people who have no idea and no experience of holiness, they are deciding by election!

It was just because of the power of Emperor Constantine; he forced people to vote for Jesus Christ as a holy man. Because they could not go against the emperor, they had to vote. And then the second thing he wanted them to vote on was that although Jesus Christ was holy and was a messiah, he failed in his mission. "I am the *real* messiah," Constantine said to the conference, "you now vote for me. I am the real messiah and a successful one." He turned the whole Roman Empire to Christianity. That's why the Vatican exists in Italy. Italy was the center of the Roman Empire, and under Constantine the whole of the Roman empire was converted to Christianity. Of course he was far more successful than Jesus.

You can't think Jesus was a success. He was crucified, poor fellow, do you call that success? Crucifixion? On either side were two criminals...even they were laughing. They were crucified but they had committed crimes, so there was no question; they knew that this punishment was justified.

Jesus told those two…first, to one he said, "Don't be worried, you will be coming with me to paradise. I am the son of God so I will help you to enter paradise." Then he told the other the same thing, and both started laughing. They said, "You cannot even save yourself! And you are not a criminal, we know. You have not committed any crime, and you are being crucified. You cannot save yourself and you are promising us that you will save us?"

But Constantine forced the council of Nicene to accept him as the real messiah—and certainly Constantine was successful; he converted the whole of the Roman Empire to Christianity.

Jesus had only twelve apostles, uneducated, carpenters, fishermen, uncultured—not a single rabbi, not a single learned man was ever his follower. No educated, cultured people ever gathered around him.

But Pontius Pilate, the viceroy of the Roman Empire—Judea was under the Roman Empire at the time—heard about Jesus from his wife. Just by chance she was passing by when Jesus was preaching to a crowd, so she stopped her chariot. From her chariot she heard Jesus and she loved what he was saying. Those sayings were beautiful. She told her husband, "This man has something, some quality. I have never heard any man speaking with such authority, such beautiful sayings. And he is uneducated and very young,"—he was only thirty years old at that time. By thirty-three he was crucified. Pontius Pilate, as a viceroy, could not go to listen to him, but in disguise as a soldier he just passed that way and stood under a tree far away, listening to what this man was saying. And his wife was right.

Pilate was a very educated man, but he had never heard anybody speaking with such authority; such beautiful words from an uneducated man! So he was very favorable to Jesus and wanted somehow to save him from crucifixion, but the Jews were too much against him—not that he had committed any crime, but because he was claiming something the Jews could not accept. He was claiming, "I am your last prophet for whom you have been waiting for centuries. I have come."

But he was just a carpenter's son, and there was even a difficulty believing that he was his own father's son because he was born just four months after the marriage. That is how the whole story begins about the Virgin Mary and the Holy Ghost. The whole thing was that the girl was already pregnant when she married Joseph the carpenter. It was not the Holy Ghost, it was some unholy neighbor. Jesus was not God's son; he was not even the son of his own father!

But if you tell the truth, if you call him "the bastard" then Christians are going to be hurt in their religious feelings. And I am simply telling the truth! They have to prove where the Holy Ghost is, and what is the logic behind calling him holy if he is raping virgin girls? But people feel hurt because they don't know what authentic religiousness is. You are living with ideas, borrowed, so when God is no longer there, Jesus is no longer there, popes are no longer there, who is going to guide you?

If God is not there, then all your Hindu incarnations of God are phony. When God himself is not there, how can he be incarnated in Krishna, in Ram…? These are just arch-egoists proclaiming something they cannot prove. Not a single incarnation of God has been able to prove on what grounds he is calling himself an incarnation. Self-styled, so-called incarnations of God, self-styled prophets and messiahs, they have all created your morality, your religion, and you have been depending on them. Do you think the truth can come from these people?

Truth can only arise within you. Nobody else can give it to you. And with truth comes beauty, followed by good. This is the authentic trinity of a truly religious man: truth, beauty, good. These three experiences happen when you enter into your own subjectivity, when you explore the interiority of your being.

You have been living on the porch outside your being; you have never gone in. Once you go in you will find your buddhahood, your awareness, your choiceless consciousness. Then you don't have to decide what is good and what is wrong. That choiceless consciousness takes you towards the good without any effort. It is effortless. And because it is effortless it brings you great joy.

When there is effort...have you ever thought about it? Effort simply means repression. Otherwise there is no need of any effort. Do you make any effort to feel hungry? Or do you make any effort to feel thirsty? When you are thirsty you know you are thirsty, when you are hungry you know you are hungry. But you have to make an effort to be celibate. All efforts are futile, against nature. I declare unto you there has never been a single man who was celibate, unless he was impotent. But the impotents don't count. I say it on the grounds that nobody can go against nature.

Those who try to go against nature have to make an effort. All effort is against nature, and all relaxation is in tune with nature. To be in tune is to be religious, to be in tune with the universe. And you don't have to look for any guide. That very tuning turns you into a beautiful flower, fragrant. It is not an effort on your part; it is simply a natural growth.

But all your religions are against nature. It is very strange—and you have never thought about it—but all these religions say God created nature. Yet, if God created nature, then to be against nature means to be against God. It is such a simple argument, it does not need much intelligence. If God has created existence, then to be in tune with existence is the only way of being religious—to be in tune with God's existence.

But, strangely, all religions teach you to be against nature. They tell you to fast — but fasting is not natural. Perhaps once in a while, but that too is needed only if you have been unnatural with your stomach. If you have been stuffing unnecessary things in your stomach, once in a while you may need to fast. But if you have been natural, eating only that amount which is needed by your body and not a single thing more, you will never need to fast in your whole life.

All religions teach you not to sleep for eight hours, which is natural. They are teaching you to cut your sleep. Saints sleep only three hours, two hours; the greater the saint, the less the sleep.

One day a woman came to me, the wife of a sardar, a Sikh. She said, "My husband is going bananas."

I said, "What happened to your husband?"

She said, "He has been following a so-called saint who teaches him stupid things, and he follows..."

The saint had told her husband, "First you should start living on pure food."

And what is pure food according to the Hindu mind? The only *pure* food is milk. In fact it is against nature. Have you seen any grown-up animal living on the milk of the mother? Just in the beginning, when the children of most animals cannot digest solid food—it is only a question of weeks—he has to depend on the mother's milk. Once he starts eating solid food, he completely forgets about the mother's milk. It is a temporary phenomenon. It is only man who goes on drinking milk even when he can digest solid food. And the milk is not from his mother, because the mother cannot manage to give you milk for your whole life. Just four or five years are enough to destroy her breasts. A whole life? You are seventy years old and drinking mother's milk... you will kill the poor woman! So you are not able to do that, and no other woman will allow you. Even your own wife will not allow it.

You are drinking milk from other animals—cows and sheep and goats—and you don't understand the chemistry. The cow's milk is for her children, not for you. So that poor woman told me, "That saint told him to live only on milk, and to be celibate. So his whole sexuality went into his head; the whole day he is just thinking about sex and nothing else."

That is the situation of all your saints' minds. You just need to open a little window in their head and inside you will see Marilyn Monroe standing naked, Sophia Loren standing naked, queues of women...I hope someday we will be able to create windows in the head so people can look.

When you are repressing sex it is going to become cerebral. It will go into the head, because the actual sex center is in the brain. It will create fantasies, sexual imagination...now you will go to the saint for another bit of advice: "What to do? My whole mind is just whirling with one thought: women." The saint then says you have to cut down your sleep.

So this saint told the poor woman's husband, "Cut your sleep." He was sleeping for only two hours, so now the whole day he felt sleepy. He could not go to work, because the work he was doing was dangerous. He was working in a gun manufacturing plant, so if he was sleepy he might get killed by the machines all around. He might do something wrong and explode the whole factory, so even his superiors told him, "First you get cured of whatever is wrong with you. The whole day you look sleepy. We won't allow you to operate the machinery."

He again went to the saint — that's how you keep on going to the guides and the rabbis and the bishops and the priests and the saints. They go on giving you advice which is not a cure, which is really creating more and more diseases. The saint said to him, "If you are feeling sleepy the whole day it means *tamas* is coming up..." In Hindu philosophy it is called *tamas* — your past lives have been of pure darkness; they are surfacing. The darkness is surfacing. *Tamas* is coming up. So you have to continue the whole day repeating the name of Rama—that is the Hindu God.

So now this sardar was continuously repeating, "Rama, Rama, Rama." Even walking on the street he had to repeat it. Now the repetition had become so automatic that he did not hear the horns of the trucks or the buses or the cars. He was so full of his own "Rama, Rama, Rama..." The wife was afraid that he would be killed. People had reported to her that he was walking straight in front of a truck, and the truck was honking the horn but he wouldn't listen. So she said, "I have come to you. You have to help. And he does not allow anybody else to sleep, so we are all getting sick. He gets up at three o'clock in the morning. He goes to bed at one o'clock in the night, so up to one o'clock he is chanting, 'Rama, Rama, Rama…' through the whole house. The children are crying, 'Our examinations are coming close and this man won't let us sleep.' And by three o'clock in the morning he's back. Even the neighbors are coming to say, 'This is too much, we cannot tolerate it. From three o'clock, "Rama, Rama"—and he shouts!'" So she said, "Something has to be done."

I said, "Certainly. You bring him to me."

But he wouldn't listen, because he was continuously repeating, "Rama, Rama," in front of me! I said, "Shut up!"

He said, "But it is the name of God."

I said, "Who told you?"

He said, "My saint."

I said, "He knows exactly that Rama is the name of God?"

He said, "His own master has told him."

I said, "It is just a tale told from one idiot to another idiot…and you are the last in the line. There is nothing holy in it, there is nothing divine in it; it is an ordinary name. There are millions of people in India who have *Ram* in their name—do you think they are all gods?"

He said, "No."

I said, "What is your name?" And by chance his name was Sardar Ram Singh. "You are an idiot! You are just repeating your own name."

He said, "I never thought about it."

I said, "You have never thought about anything! What else is your master telling you? Because you are not sleeping well, that's why the whole day you are feeling sleepy. And because you are trying to be celibate, the mind is continuously thinking of sex. Because you are thinking of sex, your master says to you that your food must be impure, so drink cow's milk. That will make you more sexual; you become a bull! Soon, Sardar Ram Singh, you will become a bull!"

He said, "My God! So what am I to do?"

I said, "First, stop drinking milk. Just be a normal human being. Yes, you can drink a little bit in your tea in the morning, but not the whole day. How much milk are you drinking? Your body seems so fat."

The wife said, "The whole day he is drinking, to make himself celibate. His job has gone, and whatever small balance he had in an account is wasted in purchasing two cows, and he drinks all the milk of two cows!"

I said, "You brought him at the right time. Soon he would have turned into a bull. He is just on the verge." So I said to him, "Sell those cows and start eating like a human being. Sleep like a human being. And there is no need to repeat 'Ram, Ram…'

"You can do one thing. In the morning, say 'Ram' and then say, 'Ditto—applicable for twenty-four hours.' It is just a small thing. You can write it on a page: 'Ditto,' applied to the twenty-four hours. Next day again you say one time, 'Ram,' and 'Ditto.'"

He said, "This is a great secret! I was getting bored and tired, and I was getting deaf because I was continuously repeating, repeating, repeating. Even those two hours in sleep I was continuously repeating inside, 'Ram, Ram…'" Because if you are repeating for twenty-two hours then you cannot leave it just for two hours in sleep; it will go on in an undercurrent.

I said, "You will be okay within two weeks. Not much is needed, just be normal and natural. And stop going to that stupid man you think is a saint."

He said, "Then can I come to you?"

I said, "No. You don't need anybody outside; you have to go within yourself. First, for two weeks get saner; then you can come to me and I will tell you how to meditate. You don't have to meditate the whole day; just one hour before sunrise. And there is no need to shout, because you are not praying for the benefit of the neighbors, and there is no God to listen howsoever loud you shout. No God is there to listen to it. Have you ever received any answer?"

He said, "No, I have never received any answer, only condemnation from everybody. My children are against me, my wife is against me, all the neighborhood is against me. My boss is against me. I have got into such trouble with this religion…"

Everybody is in the same situation, more or less.

All religions are driving people bananas.

And they give you advice that seems to be very significant because all the scriptures have been repeating it down the ages. It is so ancient, you cannot doubt it.

You don't need anybody to tell you what is good and what is wrong. All that you need is an awakening within you of a consciousness, which makes you see things as they are. Then there is no question of choice.

Nobody chooses the bad consciously. It is the unconscious, the darkness within you that chooses the evil.

Consciousness brings light to your whole being; you become full of luminosity. You cannot do anything that is harmful to anybody. You cannot do anything that is harmful to your own body. You become suddenly aware that you are one with this whole universe.

So your actions become good, beautiful, graceful; your words start having a certain poetry, your silence becomes so deep, so blissful, that your bliss starts overflowing to others.

This overflowing of bliss is the only significant sign of a man who is awakened. Just being with that man, just his presence, is enough to give you a taste of the beyond. But it is not according to anybody else, only according to your own awareness.

And when I say God is dead, all that is left for you is your own consciousness. And your consciousness is part of an oceanic consciousness that surrounds you. Once you become aware of your inside, you will become aware that, all over, that same consciousness is throbbing, dancing. In the trees, in the rivers, in the mountains, in the oceans, in people's eyes, in their hearts, it is the same song, it is the same dance—and you participate in it. Your participation is good. Your non-participation is bad.

Who invented God? Was it man simply not wanting to take responsibility for his own life? Is not the priest as much a victim of his own fear of looking inside as anyone else?

Fear invented God.

The priest is as much a victim as you are. But he is more cunning than you are.

Man's fear of darkness, his fear of sickness, his fear of old age... man's fear of death needed somebody to protect him. He could not find any protection anywhere. When you can't find any protection anywhere you have to invent one, as a consolation.

Just today I was listening to a song of one of the great Urdu poets, Mirza Ghalib. A sentence says:

Hamko maloom hai jannat ki hakikat lekin dil ke bahlane ko ghalib khayal achchha hai. "We know perfectly well the truth about your paradise, but it is good as a consolation."

We know it is not there, we know it is a lie, but to console yourself that after death angels will be there waiting, playing on their harps, that Saint Peter will be receiving you at the pearly gates and God will be waiting for you...Ghalib is right...*dil ke bahlane*...just as a consolation it is a good idea.

The priests know perfectly well, perhaps better than you, that there is no God. But the priest is in the most cunning profession in the world—the worst and the ugliest profession, far worse than prostitution. Prostitution is the product of the priest; it is number two. First comes the priest, then comes the prostitute, and then come all kinds of pathologies in the world.

The priests saw that everybody was afraid and wanted some protection.

So the fear created God as a security, as insurance after you die. Otherwise, it seems that after death all is darkness for eternity. What will happen? Where you will be? All your friends will be left behind, your family will be left behind, nobody will come with you. You can carry no money beyond death. Utterly a beggar, naked, just as a skeleton you will be moving into death. And then, for eternity...? It creates a great anxiety—what kind of life will there be after death?

So our fear, our dread, our death created God. The priest immediately saw a good excuse to exploit people. He became the middle agent. You can't see God, so there is every possibility that if there was no priest to continuously insist that there is a God—philosophizing, creating theologies, scriptures, temples, statues, rituals, prayers, the whole drama...He stands between you and God, and he says to you, "I have a direct line to God. You don't have a direct line. You tell me, you confess to me your sins, and I will tell God to forgive you."

You cannot see God, obviously. You feel it a great relief that somebody knows, somebody is there who has a direct connection. And you feel it is cheap. You commit a sin, and you are afraid you will have to suffer in hell. But the priest is there; you just go and confess your sin and the priest says to you, "Put five dollars into the charity box and I will pray for you."

And God is very compassionate; he always forgives. So your sin is forgiven for five dollars—those five dollars are pocketed by the priest; they never reach anywhere else because there is no God to whom he can give those five dollars.

What will God do with five dollars? He is alone, there is no shopping mall, what will he do with five dollars? And up to now he must have collected billions and trillions of dollars—all useless junk. What will he do with those dollars, notes and bills? He does not come to the world to purchase things, and I have never come across in any scripture that there are shopping markets in paradise. Saints don't need anything. In paradise you don't need food, in paradise you don't need anything. Everything is fulfilled; you simply live an eternal life. You are no longer a body, you are just a spirit. And spirits don't need food, don't need water, don't need medicine. The spirit never becomes sick, it never becomes old, it never dies. So what will God do with those five dollars?

But every Sunday the Catholic priest collects a good amount, and all other priests have their own ways. The Hindu priest catches hold of you from the very beginning. Even before the child is born, he is caught hold of by the priest. The Hindu priest even used to tell you in the past on what day, on what night you should make love to your wife, at what time, so you get a really intelligent, holy, saintly child. And the whole of India is proof that the priest was wrong. I don't see those holy children anywhere. The child has been caught from the very beginning, even from *before* the beginning. The child has not yet been received by the mother's womb, and the priest is telling you on what night, at what time…!

I used to stay with one of the oldest MP's in India. He was an MP for sixty years without a gap. He used to be called "Father of the Indian Parliament." There are only two persons who remained MP's for sixty years. One was my friend, Dr. Seth Govind Das, and the other was Winston Churchill in England, both continuously chosen, without any discontinuity, for sixty years. Dr. Govind Das was a very devout Hindu, so I had to suffer from his fanaticism continuously.

I used to stay with him in New Delhi. Whenever I was talking and giving lectures in New Delhi I stayed with him. And he was so fanatic…in India there are many people of that kind, he was not alone. He would ask his priest, when he was going back to his constituency, at what time he should leave the house. He asked the priest, who, consulting all kinds of charts and his birth chart through the scriptures and astrology, would find the *right* moment to leave the house.

Now, the trains don't run according to astrology. The train was leaving at twelve o'clock in the night, and his astrologer said, "You have to leave the house at three o'clock in the afternoon." I had to sit with him at the railway station from three to twelve.

I told him, "This is stupid, if we have to wait here. The best would have been you could have gone out of the house at three o'clock, and come back in through the back door. Unnecessary torture…"

But he said, "No, I had to *leave*."

I said, "There are millions of Hindus who go on asking the same thing, but still accidents happen in trains. There may be many Hindus who have consulted the priest and were told, 'This is the right time, a good time for you to travel'– and the train gets drowned in a river, the whole bridge collapses!"

In India the bridges collapse all the time, because it is a very religious country, a very spiritual country! It trusts in God, not in cement. So bridges are made with as little cement as possible; the larger part is just sand. It is good, the bridge is good for the inauguration ceremony by the prime minister. That's enough. The first time the train comes, both the train and the bridge go into the river. And all the Hindus in the train must have consulted their astrologers, their priests, "What is the right time?" In India there should not be any accidents.

I said to Dr. Seth Govind Das, "Why are there accidents? In India there should not be."

He himself was in a car accident. When I went to see him, I said, "What happened to your astrology?"

He said, "At least at this time when I am suffering from multiple fractures you should not start any argument with me."

I said, "This is the right time to make you clear that you have been stupid your whole life. Did you ask the astrologer or not?"

He said, "I asked."

"Then why this accident?"

But people don't have the guts and courage to go against the past, though it may be a completely rotten past. Marriages in India are made by the astrologers, and every marriage is a failure. I have never come across any marriage that was not a failure.

I used to live in a place called Raipur. I was a professor in Raipur, just for six months I lived there. The city was so out of date that I got tired living with those people. You would find everywhere written on the walls: "If you are suffering from ghosts, then come to me," and the address. "If you are suffering from witches, come to me. If you are suffering from black magic, I am the right man to cure you." The whole city was full of black magic, witches, ghosts.

Just in my neighborhood used to live a very famous astrologer, and he used to set up marriages by looking at birth charts. He became friendly with me. I told him that this was not working. "It is not working even in your case." His wife used to beat him. I said, "What happened? You are such a great astrologer. You are arranging hundreds of marriages. Without your confirmation people cannot get married because their stars do not meet." There has to be a certain synchronicity between the stars of both the charts. "What happened? Did you not consult the birth chart of your wife?"

He said, "I did."

"Then what went wrong?"

He said, "Don't harass me. I am already too harassed by my wife, and now you have come into my neighborhood to harass me?"

I said, "I will not harass you. I just want to know if you believe in your own astrology."

He was certainly a sincere man. He told me, "Don't tell anybody. It is my profession, but I don't believe in it at all. In fact sometimes it happens that the birth charts do not meet. But the man is rich and he is going to give me at least a hundred rupees if I give him the go-ahead that this marriage is going to be successful. So sometimes I change the charts. I put in a new chart for the girl which mixes with the boy's chart."

The priest knows perfectly there is no God. He is the only person who knows it perfectly. But it is his profession; he lives by exploiting people. So he goes on persisting that there is a God. God is his business. And when it is a question of business, it is his very livelihood.

And there are millions of priests belonging to different religions. There may be in every country different kinds of priests, but all they do is to exploit people by giving them consolation: "This marriage is going to be great." And every marriage is a tragedy. I have never come across any comedy.

People can only be happy if they are not married. Then you have a freedom. Then it is out of freedom you are together, not out of any contract, not out of some business deal, not because of society's enforcement. Not because of law but because of love — just out of love you are together, and when the love fails…

And everything fails, remember. It is a fiction created by the poets that love is eternal. No, the love that you know is not eternal and the love that poets know is not eternal; it fades away. It remains if lovers don't meet.

There have been only three or four couples in the whole history of man who are great lovers—because they never met. So there was no quarrel, there was no question of their love being disappointing. The society did not allow them to meet, their parents did not allow them.

In India we have the stories of Laila and Majnu, Shiri and Farhad. The lovers never met because society was against them. They belonged to different castes, different societies, different religions, so there was no possibility of their marriage. They are thought to be great lovers, their love never faded—because it never began! Once it begins the end is not far away.

Every beginning has an end. Even when you are born, death is not far away. Every day it comes closer.

And once you are married, the problem becomes more difficult. Out of freedom you can live together because you know you are living in freedom; you can move any moment. In great friendliness, with thankfulness to each other: "You gave us such beautiful moments, such beautiful days and nights. We lived in poetry, in music, in songs. These few days and nights were all golden, but now the season is gone, the spring is over, the honeymoon finished. It is better for both of us to separate." With great gratitude…there is no revenge, there is no hate, there is no reason for anger. Both gave whatever they could to each other; they are richer than they were before. The experience has made them more rich.

But marriage does not allow you to move away. Love finishes, but you have to pretend that you are still loving. And whenever you have to pretend it is a heaviness on the heart. Whenever you pretend, you are phony—you know it, your partner knows it.

When love fades there is no possibility of deceiving each other. Maybe for a few days you can deceive by bringing ice cream every day, but for how long? In fact the moment you start bringing ice cream that is a signal that the old warmth of love is finished, now the coldness is coming!

It is only people like Dale Carnegie…and they can be effective only in America, nowhere else. Dale Carnegie is America's only philosopher. He has sold his book in a quantity second only to the Holy Bible. The book is *How to Win Friends and Influence People*. Everything is phony in that book. He says, "Every husband, when he is going to the office, should kiss his wife." Whether he loves her or not is not material, but he should kiss her and say, "I love you, honey." When he comes home he should again hug her, bring a few roses, and say, "Sweetheart, I have been thinking of you the whole day." At least three times a day and three times in the night he should make her aware that he loves her. And the same is true for the wife. Both are following Dale Carnegie; there is no love. And you simply go on saying…

The word "phony" applies to America more than to any other country. It comes from 'telephone', because on the telephone your voice becomes different, it becomes *phoney*.

The husband calls the wife once or twice in the day, just to assure her that he loves her. And while he is calling, his secretary is sitting in his lap! This is happening in every office,

without exception. Secretaries are chosen not because they are more efficient than others…
When they are brought to the boss for their interview…

I have heard about one. A secretary came in and said that she was very experienced, she
had all the certificates and her speed was very good on the typewriter. Another came; she was
fresh, younger, but had no experience. Then the third came, then the fourth came; there were
at least a dozen. Finally, when the manager asked, "Which one have you chosen?" the boss
said, "The one who has the biggest tits."

Secretaries are chosen because of tits? But that's how things are.

Once you start feeling encaged in anything you immediately feel to get out of it, it is a
prison. Your God, your priests, are all your imprisoners. They go on creating new prisons for
you — of morality, of marriage, of responsibility for the children, all kinds of entanglements and
chains for you. The whole purpose is to keep you miserable, because unless you are miserable
you do not go to the church. Unless you are miserable you are not going to pray. Only in
misery you remember God—you know it! Only when you are suffering you remember God, you
think about the Holy Bible, you think about the Bhagavadgita, you go to the temple—but only
when you are in misery.

Bertrand Russell is absolutely right when he says, "If we can make the whole of humanity
happy, religions will disappear." I absolutely agree with him, but he does not know how to make
the whole world happy. I know how to make the whole world happy.

Out of deep meditation bliss arises, and then you are so happy the whole day, the whole
night…without any cause. It is just bubbling inside you. It is your very nature, your *dharma*.
Then you don't need any God and you don't need any priest, and you don't live in any kind of
misery or imprisonment. The moment you feel that something has become phony, something
has become pseudo, something has become just a mask, you simply drop it. You remain
truthful to your own consciousness—that is your only responsibility. And all else will follow, and
your life will be a life of rejoicing.

Not only will your life be a rejoicing, your death also will be a rejoicing. Death does not
destroy anything. The five elements of the body fall back into their original sources and for
the consciousness there are two possibilities: if it has not tasted meditation it will move into
another womb; if it has tasted meditation, if it has known its eternity, its immortality, it will move
into the cosmos and disappear into this vast existence. And that disappearance is the greatest
moment of life. You have become one with the source from where you had arisen. You have
gone back and disappeared into it.

Authentic religion does not need any God, does not need any priest, does not need any
prayer. All that it needs is an exploration of your inner world.

That exploration I call Zen. In Sanskrit it is *dhyan*; in Chinese it is *ch'an*; in Japanese it is *zen*.
But it is the same word. Going inwards, reaching to the very point from where you can look, a
door opens into the divine cosmos. Standing on that point, you are a buddha. And your whole
life changes; it is a metamorphosis. You have become a new man.

We need this new man urgently. It has never been so urgent as it is today. The new man is
the only hope for a whole humanity. If the new man does not arrive soon, the old man is ready
to commit suicide, global suicide.

Once, I heard a fundamentalist Christian say: "Do you realize that a slave is more free than the master? This is because the master has all the responsibility and the slave has no cares in the world. We are lucky to have God as our master!" Would you care to comment?

The statement is absolutely right in the sense that if you make somebody a slave, you also become dependent on him. You have to take care of him, you have to take care of his health. You have taken on a great responsibility.

But if the slave has lost his responsibility, he has also lost his freedom; he has also lost his dignity, his humanity. He has become a beast of burden; he is just like a machine. You take care of the machine also. You wash your car, you clean your car, you are always aware if something is wrong that it has to be replaced. Just as you take care of your machines, you take care of your slaves.

So it is true that the master also becomes in a certain way dependent on the slave. But the Christian who told you does not realize the implication of his statement. If God is his master, that means God is his slave. It is his statement; he is saying, "Do you realize that a slave is more free than the master?" So God is less free than you are!

But a less free God becomes inferior to you, a less free God cannot bring freedom to you. He himself is less free. So why bother about a God who is not even equally as free as you, to say nothing about his superiority in freedom—he is less free than you.

But fanatics don't understand logic, don't understand argument. Fanatics are just blind people. Otherwise, this one would not have said, "This is because the master has all the responsibility and the slave has no cares in the world. We are lucky to have God as our master!" He should have said, "We are lucky to have God as our slave, because he takes all the cares and all the responsibilities; he creates the world and he creates the sin and he creates all kinds of troubles and he creates all kinds of solutions, and he sends his own son to save the world."

And he sends prophets upon prophets to fight amongst each other and kill people — he has such a great involvement and business, he is so occupied! And what does he get in return? Just these fanatics!

If there is a God, man is not only a slave, man does not exist. Man is a puppet. If, the way the Christians believe, God made man out of mud and then breathed life into him, then man is just a created puppet. All the strings are in the hands of God. Any moment, just as at a certain moment that whimsical God created man... What was he doing before? One simply has to ask it, because according to Christians he created the world only six thousand years ago. It is absolute nonsense, because in India we have found cities of great culture and civilization—Mohenjo Daro and Harappa, which Christian explorers were excavating. They could not believe it—God destroyed those cities seven thousand years ago...before God created the world! And in China, the skeleton of a man has been found called the Peking Man, which is eighty thousand years old.

Certainly the world is far more ancient than your God. Perhaps man created God six thousand years ago—that may be right. But idiots are idiots....

One great scholarly bishop was very much puzzled about the Peking Man, about Harappa and Mohenjo Daro, and about the claim of a man who lived in Pune, a famous scholar, Lokmanya Tilak, that the Hindu Vedas are ninety thousand years old. And his evidence is such that it cannot be contradicted. His evidence is not logical but scientific, astronomical. In the Rig Veda, a certain constellation of stars is described in absolute detail; this happened, according to scientists, ninety thousand years ago. Unless Rig Veda was written by people who had seen that constellation they could not have described it in detail, and since then that constellation has not happened again. Perhaps sometime in the future it may happen, but for ninety thousand years it has not happened. The description is a solid proof that Rig Veda was written by people who had seen the constellation; without seeing that constellation there is no way for them to have described which star was in which position. And they have described it so scientifically that there is no possibility of making any improvement on it. When this bishop became aware of all these things...

And in the Himalayas, on top of the highest peaks of the Himalayas, sea animals' skeletons have been found. That simply means that at a certain time—perhaps a hundred million years ago—there was an ocean in place of the Himalayas. Otherwise, sea animals cannot move from the ocean, pass through the whole of India and go on top of the Himalayas to die there. The only possibility is—and this is now a scientific fact—the Himalayas arose out of the ocean. And as they arose out of the ocean, many animal fossils must have remained on these tops. The Himalayas went on being forced up and these fossils were covered in snow. And as this vast range of mountains called the Himalayas rose, the ocean receded.

The Hind Mahasagar, the great Indian Ocean, used to be where the Himalayas are—one hundred million years ago. Those animals prove it, because they are one hundred million years old. There are ways to judge how old a skeleton is, and now those methods are absolutely accurate.

The bishop was mad, because it was all going against the Bible. So he invented a theory—this is why I say a fanatic will not see the truth; he will try to continue his belief in a lie, will make all kinds of excuses. This excuse is certainly worth understanding. The bishop invented a theory that God created the world six thousand years ago as it is told in the Bible, but, as he is all-powerful, he created sea animals and put them on top of the Himalayas. He created them so that they would appear to be one hundred million years old. He created the Harappa and Mohenjo Daro ruins, making them appear seven thousand years old; he created the Peking Man as if it were eighty thousand yeas old...just to test the Christians' faith!

What great logic! God seems to be a con man: "It is just a question of your faith." But the fact is, this earth is four billion years old according to science. And man is at least a million years old, passing through many different stages up to Gautam Buddha, the highest peak of consciousness, the Everest.

This Christian fundamentalist is saying, "We are lucky to have God as our master." What about God himself? Is he lucky to have you as his responsibility? If God is responsible for everything... and he should be; if he created the world then he is responsible for Adolf Hitler, the second world war, Hiroshima and Nagasaki. Who else? If he is taking care of the world and pulling the strings of people, he pulls the strings of President Truman to drop the atom bombs on Hiroshima and Nagasaki. Now, Truman is not responsible—God pulled his strings;

what could he do? When the puppeteer pulls the strings of the puppet, the puppet dances. When the puppeteer pulls differently, the puppet fights. When the puppeteer drops the puppet, it goes down and sleeps. And whenever the puppeteer pulls the strings again, the puppet is back, ready to do anything. If God has created the world, then we are all puppets; we don't have any spirituality and we are just dust unto dust.

Is God happy to have all these puppets creating a mess of the world? And he is responsible! But fanatics don't look at any logic. His argument proves that God is a slave of his own slaves; he is not a master. You are the master; he is taking care of you.

Rather than seeing exactly into the reality of things, people go on creating hypotheses, lies, fictions—imagination, hallucination. Mind has all these capacities.

Unless you are beyond mind, you cannot be certain that what you are seeing is real. Once you are beyond mind, only then are you aware of that which is real. And in that reality no God is found.

Buddha could not find any God. In his ultimate state of enlightenment, he could not find any God and he could not find any beginning of the universe. Mahavira in his ultimate enlightenment could not find any God, and he could not find any creation either. The world, existence, is beginningless and endless. Twenty-three other tirthankaras of the Jainas could not find any God when they were in samadhi. When they were beyond mind, there was no fear, no dread, no death; there was no need of the hypothesis of God. God simply disappeared like a shadow of the mind.

As dreams disappear when you wake up…enlightenment is nothing but waking up and all dreams disappear. And God has been proved a dream by thousands of enlightened people.

God is believed in only by the ignorant. God is believed in only by those who don't have any sense of dignity. The people who have attained to the fulfillment of their potential, who have blossomed like lotus flowers, have all denied the existence of God.

There are three religions in the world: one that arose out of Gautam Buddha's inspiration, another that arose out of Adinatha's inspiration, and a third that arose out of Lao Tzu's inspiration, Tao. These three are the highest peaks ever reached, and all three have no God.

Compared to these three, Mohammedanism, Christianity, Hinduism, Judaism are just very childish. They are good as toys, as consolation, but they don't solve any problem and they don't give you any liberation. They don't take you beyond birth and death. They only make you slaves.

I hate slavery, and my whole effort is to liberate you from all that binds you. Only when you are liberated from all bindings will you have a tremendous beauty, a splendor that even emperors will be jealous of.

The sutra:

When Impo took leave of Ma Tzu, Ma Tzu asked, "Where are you going?"

Ma Tzu is one of the great enlightened masters; and not just great, but also very strange. There is no comparison to Ma Tzu anywhere. His whole behavior is just absolutely unique. It is said that he walked on all fours, just like an animal. Because he was so much in tune with nature, he dropped the idea of standing on two feet. He said, "Standing on two feet has created the mind." That's why animals don't have any religion, don't have any God. Animals are far better off; they don't go to any church, they don't bow down to any stone cut into the image of God. Animals simply pass by; donkeys don't care. It is only man who seems to be stupid.

If animals had languages—and there is a suspicion amongst scientists they have; they have symbols, they have certain languages, different kinds, not exactly like human beings—then they must be laughing. In secrecy they must be winking at each other: "Look at that fellow who is bowing down before a monkey god!"

Ma Tzu's idea was that the brain developed because man stood on two feet. And there is great understanding in it. The brain cannot develop—science is in agreement with Ma Tzu — the brain cannot develop if you go on moving on all fours, because when you are horizontal, moving like an animal, the brain gets so much blood flow that the small, delicate nerves cannot grow in the brain. The flood of blood destroys them. As man stood on two feet, the blood reaching to the head became less, because it is going against gravitation. Everything is pulled down and your heart has to pump blood upstairs. It is a difficult task. That's why only man has heart attacks—not animals. Only man is continuously sick and ill, because he is fighting with gravitation all the time. The earth is pulling everything down and you are taking everything up, against gravitation. So it is a struggle.

Ma Tzu moved on all fours just to go beyond mind and be in tune with nature. Everybody laughed. They said, "This is strange!"

And he looked like a tiger. He had such shiny eyes that he would look at you like a tiger. The disciples who gathered around Ma Tzu were men of great courage, because he used to jump on people, beat them. Ma Tzu devised beating and slapping and jumping on people as methods of meditation! You won't believe it, but he managed to make more people enlightened than even Gautam Buddha, because he had found a secret in it. When he jumped on you, suddenly your mind stopped. You could not think, "What is happening?" You could not figure it out, it had never happened before.

Mind knows only what has happened; mind knows only what you have learned. Nobody has jumped on you; you have seen nobody walking on all fours. When you first see Ma Tzu walking on all fours, your brain is in shock: What is the matter? And then he looks at you as if he is a tiger—that gives you another shock—and then suddenly he grabs you, and he was a very strong man, of course, just like any gorilla, and he sits on your chest and asks you, "Got it?"

One has to say, "Got it!" because if you don't, he may do something else. He may beat you, slap you, he can do anything. But his very jumping on you stopped your mind functioning. Something absolutely absurd is happening, mind cannot function. Mind is a rational and logical mechanism. With absurdity it cannot function.

So when Impo told Ma Tzu that he wanted to go, Ma Tzu asked, "Where are you going?"

Impo replied, "I am going to Sekito."

Sekito had become very famous by that time, and many people were going to him.

Ma Tzu warned, "The path on the stone-head is slippery!"

You can go, but remember that fellow Sekito Stonehead…Because he remained always on a rock, sitting on a rock, and he had a shaved head which looked also like rock, he was called "Sekito Stonehead." He was in his own right a unique master. Even Ma Tzu recognized his uniqueness, and when Ma Tzu recognizes someone, it is really a recognition.

Ma Tzu said, "Be careful. The path on the stone-head is very slippery."

Impo said, "I have the pole of an acrobat with me…"

You must have seen people walking on a tightrope. Whenever anybody walks on the tightrope he has to keep a pole in his hand, just to balance. He has to continuously balance otherwise he will fall down from the rope. The whole trick is balancing, and that balancing needs assistance…sometimes you feel you are going more towards the left, then just put the pole towards the right so it balances you. When you feel you are going towards the right, then turn your pole towards the left. That pole is just a help to keep you balancing between right and left, so you just remain in the middle. Without a pole no acrobat can walk on a tightrope. The pole is the whole secret. It is his support; otherwise, if he moves towards the left and he has nothing to support him and make the weight balanced, he will fall.

This man Impo said, *I have the pole of an acrobat with me.*" He said, "Don't be worried. Howsoever slippery the way of Stonehead Sekito, I have the pole with me, I have walked on tightropes. Don't be worried; I will keep my balance impeccably."

"I can make a show with it whenever I want," and with that he left.
When he got to Sekito, Impo went around Sekito's Zen stool one time,
swung his stick with a shout and asked, "What is the dharma of this?"

This is an important question. He is asking, "What is the truth of this?" By striking the stick on the stone where Sekito is sitting, he is asking, "What is the nature of thisness?" In Gautam Buddha's language, what is the meaning of tathata, suchness? Buddha's whole teaching can be brought to this one word: suchness, thisness, isness, the present moment. What is the meaning of this present moment?

When he asked, *"What is the dharma of this?"* Sekito said, *"How sad! How sad!"*

Why did he say that? He is saying it because, if you know *this*, you will not ask the question. And you cannot ask the question if you don't know *this*.

You see the problem: if you know this—this moment, this suchness, this silence—if you know *this*, you will not ask the question. And if you don't know *this*… how can you ask the question without knowing it?

That's why he said: *"How sad! How sad!"* You know the question only, but you don't understand what you are asking. This question cannot be asked, it can only be experienced. It seems you are a knowledgeable person, you must have read scriptures where it is described. Again and again, Buddha says, "This very moment is all." If you can understand the secret of this moment, you have understood everything of existence, because existence is always in the present. It is never in the past, never in the future. The past is your memory; the future is your imagination. Existence remains always in the present. It has no past, no future.

So if you understand isness, the presence of the present moment, you have understood all the secrets and all the mysteries. There is nothing beyond it.

But he is asking the question as a scholar, not as a meditator. That's why Sekito said, "How sad! How sad! You know the right question but you don't know the right experience. And without the experience the question becomes meaningless. If you had the experience you would not have asked it, you would have just sat by my side and experienced thisness. It surrounds this mountain. This silence, this immense tranquility and calmness…you disturbed it by striking your stick on my stone. That was the only disturbance in the silence of the mountain. Otherwise it was so quiet. And I feel so sad for you that you are only a man of the mind, that you don't know the secret of no-mind."

Mind cannot know anything about existence, it can only know through scriptures, statements of others. All its knowledge is borrowed. It cannot know any direct experience, and only direct experience liberates you.

"How sad…" Impo did not have anything to say, he could not figure out what to say. He had never expected that this man would say, "How sad! How sad!" This is not the answer to his question! And now he is feeling embarrassed.

Impo didn't have anything to say, but he went back to Ma Tzu and
told him the story. Ma Tzu said, "You go again, and when Sekito says,
'How sad,' you start crying."

Ma Tzu is playing a game, just as Sekito is playing a game. Between both of them they are trying to make him aware of this moment. Now Ma Tzu is saying, "You got into trouble. I had told you from the very beginning that Sekito's path is very slippery. Now you know. You have come back immediately. Just one question and you forgot your pole! Now go again and ask the same question." This is the strategy of Ma Tzu. He is putting him again into difficulty. He is telling him, "Go and ask the same question, and when Sekito says, 'How sad,' you start crying."

So Impo went to Sekito again and asked in the same manner, "What is the
dharma of this?"
At that, Sekito started crying.

This was a great device between two masters, who have not talked to each other, who don't know each other, they have never met! But both are enlightened.

This monk does not understand the language of enlightenment. When Ma Tzu sent him back with an answer, he knew perfectly well that Sekito is not going to repeat again, "How sad! How sad!" because no enlightened man ever repeats anything. He responds always freshly to the new situation.

Now, this is a new situation. The first time Impo came without knowing what he was going to say; now he comes knowing perfectly well what he is going to say. This has changed the whole situation. This man comes now, knowing his old response. But the old response is no longer applicable. And somebody else's answer cannot be your answer.

So Ma Tzu gave him the answer, "You go again. He will say, 'How sad, how sad.'" He knew he would not say that!—"And when he says that, you start crying." He supplied the answer.

But any answer supplied by anyone is of no use, because every moment the enlightened person responds afresh. So when Sekito was asked again, "What is the dharma of this?"...

At that, Sekito started crying.

Now he is saying, "This is too much! I was already sad; now sadness seems not to have affected you. You are still asking the same question! It makes me cry!"

Again the poor Impo is left without any answer, because he was given the answer, "You should cry." Now Sekito himself is crying, what to do?

Impo again was left without any word, and returned to Ma Tzu. Ma Tzu commented, "I told you—the path on the stone-head is slippery!"

"Where is your pole? You slipped twice! You make me ashamed!"—that's what Ma Tzu is saying—"Being *my* disciple, you slipped twice, and you could not answer."

That reminds me about a small story that will help you to understand.

There were two temples in Japan, both antagonistic to each other. One belonged to Shinto, another belonged to Zen. And for centuries they had been quarreling, arguing against each other. Both had masters, and they both had young boys, because the masters were old and they needed somebody to help them, to bring vegetables or cook food. Those small boys helped them.

Both told the small boys, "Don't talk to the other boy of the other temple—never! We have been enemies for centuries, we are not on talking terms."

But boys are boys, and because both were prevented, both were anxious…So one day, going to the market to fetch some vegetables, they met on the road. And one boy asked the other—this was the Shinto boy, coming from the Shinto temple. He asked the Zen boy, "Where are you going?"

And the Zen boy said, "Wherever the wind takes me." He had been listening to his master, all kinds of things, so he had also got the taste of Zen. He said, "Wherever the wind takes me."

The Shinto boy was shocked at this. What to answer? He wanted to make friends, but this boy seemed to be completely uninterested; he had completely cut him short. There was no way for conversation—now what to say? He is saying, "Wherever the wind takes me…"

Very sad, he came to his master and told him, "I did not obey you, I am sorry. I was just inquisitive, curious to know about the other boy. I was feeling alone, and I thought he must be also feeling alone. And your temples may have been for centuries antagonistic, but we are just boys. We can be friends.

"But you were right; it was not good to ask. Certainly those people are dangerous. I asked the boy, 'Where are you going?' and he said, 'Wherever the wind takes me.'"

The master said, "I had warned you. Now tomorrow, you go again and stand at the same place, and when that Zen boy comes, you ask him again: 'Where are you going?' And when he says, 'Wherever the wind takes me,' just ask him, 'If the wind is not blowing, then…?'"

The boy went. He stood at the same place, watched. The Zen boy was coming. He asked him, "Where are you going?" And the boy said, "Wherever the legs take me."

Now he could not answer what the master said, "If the wind is not blowing…" It would be absurd to answer that. He came very sad to the Shinto master and said, "Those people are very strange! That boy changed his whole approach! I asked the same question, but he said, 'Wherever the legs take me.'"

The master said, "I have been warning you. Now you are unnecessarily getting defeated and that means a defeat for our temple. This is not good. You go again! And tomorrow you stand in the same place, and when the boy comes you ask, 'Where are you going?' and when he says 'Wherever the legs take me,' ask him: 'If you were crippled, then would you go anywhere or not?'"

So, utterly happy, the boy went again, stood in the same place, watched. The boy came out of the temple. He asked, "Where are you going?" utterly happy that now he knows the answer.

And the boy said, "I am going to fetch some vegetables." Now the situation again becomes absolutely different. He cannot say, "If you were crippled…" he cannot say, "If the wind is not blowing…" So he returned, very angry, and said to the master, "Those people are strange! Even the boy is strange."

The master said, "I have been telling you, but you won't understand."

The story is exactly the same. The significance is that each moment is so new and so fresh that nothing old is to be repeated. That Zen boy has understood from his master and his constant dialogue with the disciples that nothing can be repeated, because the situation is never the same.

So every moment you have to respond freshly—out of your consciousness, just like a mirror. If a mirror is there and you look into it, you will see your face. And if a monkey looks at it, then the monkey will see his face. If a donkey looks at it, then the donkey will see his face. The mirror is the reflecting medium, it has no opinion. You cannot say that the mirror is very self-contradictory, that it is not consistent: sometimes it shows the face of a man, sometimes the monkey, sometimes the donkey, what kind of mirror is this? One should be consistent! Zen is not consistent with the past, but absolutely consistent with the present. Its consistency is a totally different phenomenon to anything that has happened anywhere in the world. It is unique.

Philosophers are consistent with their past statements. Whatever they have said before, they will continue to be consistent with their answers their whole life, but such a consistency is dead. The day he first made the statement, it died. And he goes on repeating the same statement although the situation goes on changing.

Zen has a consistency not in time, but with existence. It simply watches existence and whatever comes up. It is not made up. When the boy the first time said, "Wherever the wind takes me," that was his response in that moment. Of course next time he cannot repeat it, because the boy must have come with a ready-made answer, and ready-made answers are not applicable in the world of Zen.

Although he is just a boy, he has lived in a Zen atmosphere where he has understood one thing: never repeat, because existence never repeats. You will not find two persons similar in the whole world. You will not find in a tree two leaves exactly the same; you will not find two roses exactly the same. Existence never repeats. It always creates an original; it does not believe in carbon copies.

Ready-made answers don't function in the atmosphere of Zen.

So each time you can expect a Zen master to be fresh. He is always young and always fresh, and he responds to the situation. He is not concerned with his memory of past answers. He has nothing to do with them. He is always available to the present, just like a mirror.

Buson wrote:

I leave,
you stay –
two autumns.

What does he mean by this haiku? Autumn is very beautiful in Japan; hence it comes again and again in haikus. It is one of the most beautiful times of the year. Buson is a Zen master, awakened, enlightened. And when he says, "I leave. I am going—you stay," he is talking to the autumn. The autumn is going and it almost hurts that autumn is going. So he says to the autumn, "You stay. I will go. I am also another autumn; just as you are beautiful, glorious, so am I. Instead of you, I can go, you remain."

It shows tremendous compassion: "Why are you going when I am ready to go in your place? And people love you, they enjoy you. They dance when autumn comes. Don't disturb their joy. As far as going is concerned, I am ready to go."

I leave,
you stay –
two autumns.

"You are an autumn, I am also an autumn. You have blossomed, I have also blossomed. So there is no problem, I can take your place. You be here."

It is as if you are talking to a roseflower which is going to drop its leaves and disappear. You feel tremendous compassion for the rose and you say, "Don't go away. I can go away; you remain. People love you so much. They rejoice when you dance in the wind and in the rain and in the sun. Everybody loves you. And my time is over. I have blossomed, I have come to my ultimate peak. There is no further to go. I have come to the end of the road. I can go; you remain."

Only a Zen master can talk this kind of dialogue because he feels in tune with existence. Whether it is spring or autumn or summer or winter it doesn't matter. He feels himself in tune with the universe. And he would like whatever is beautiful to remain for other people to enjoy. He is ready to go, to disappear into this vast ocean of existence. It is a tremendously stunning haiku.

I leave,
you stay—
two autumns.

Just as you have a beautiful atmosphere, I am also just the same inside. My autumn has come. So I can leave. There is no need for you to go. People love you so much.

In his book, Daybreak, Friedrich Nietzsche wrote:
"In the midst of the ocean of becoming, we awake on a little island no bigger than a boat—we adventurers and birds of passage—and look around us for a few moments, as sharply and as inquisitively as possible, for how soon may a wind not blow us away or a wave not sweep across the little island, so that nothing more is left of us!
"We live a precarious minute of knowing and divining, amid joyful beating of wings and chirping with one another, and in spirit we venture out over the ocean, no less proud than the ocean itself."
Is not Nietzsche's trinity—cheerfulness, daring and love for life—of far greater worth than the trinity of the Hindu or Christian god? And is not Nietzsche's insanity more significant than the so-called sanity of the Christian who would die in defense of his fantasies?

Nietzsche is a great poet and a very unique poet. He writes poetry in prose—a very rare phenomenon. He never wrote poetry, but all his prose is sheer poetry. Every sentence is poetic, symbolic. Whatever he has said is so beautiful, although he never went beyond the mind.

I feel like saying to Nietzsche, as Sekito has said to the inquiring monk, "How sad! How sad!" This man deserved to be a buddha. But just because he was in the West, he could not find the way out of the mind.

You are right, the Christian trinity or the Hindu are not comparable to the trinity of Friedrich Nietzsche: cheerfulness, daring and love for life. That's what I have been teaching to you.

The Christian trinity is just a fiction. God, the Holy Ghost, and the only begotten son, Jesus Christ, all are fictions. Jesus Christ is ninety-nine percent fiction, one percent reality. Out of this whole trinity only Jesus Christ has one percent of reality as a human being. But all the miracles are invented. His walking on the water is nonsense; his raising the dead is absurd; his virgin birth, immaculate conception, is illogical, unscientific; his resurrection is a fake and a fraud. He never died on the cross, so there is no question of a resurrection. He simply escaped from the cave; it was a conspiracy between the Roman governor general, Pontius Pilate, and Jesus' followers. Pontius Pilate himself was feeling bad because crucifying Jesus was not his desire. But he was absolutely helpless.

The tradition was that at every Jewish festival, when criminals who had been sentenced to death were crucified, the Jewish rabbis, particularly the chief priest of the great Jewish temple of Jerusalem, had the right to ask one of the criminals to be released as an act of mercy.

Three persons were going to be crucified. Two were murderers. One was the worst kind of criminal, with seven murders and rapes and all kinds of crimes on his head, and he was a drunkard, though a very strong man, Barabbas. And the second man also was a criminal. Pontius Pilate was hoping that the Jews would ask for Jesus to be released. He was absolutely innocent; he had not committed any crime, he had not done anything illegal. He was absolutely innocent.

But the Jews were very angry because he was proclaiming himself to be the son of God. And the Jews don't believe that God has any family, because once you have a family, there is no end to it. You have brothers, and you have brothers-in-law, and you have sisters, and you have sisters-in-law, and it goes on and on. Then God will have a wife, then God will have a father and grandfather, and who knows where the line will end? God will become a joint family. Faraway cousins will also claim divinity. The Jews don't accept any trinity. God is alone; he has no son and no Holy Ghost. So the Jews were angry that this man was proclaiming himself to be the only begotten son of God.

Why "only"? What happened to God? Did he become impotent? Can't he create, just the way Hindus go on creating? One dozen children is normal in India. Two dozen seems to be a bit of an achievement. God had only one son, not even a daughter for the son to play with? It is absolutely against the Jewish mind; hence, they could not ask that he should be forgiven. Pontius Pilate was not a Jew, so he did not understand what the problem was. He was a Roman pagan and they did not believe in any God. So what was the problem? There is no God, and if this man is a little eccentric and thinks himself to be the son of God, there is no harm in it. The harmless declaration simply shows that he is a little bit out of his mind, eccentric, a banana! But you don't put bananas on the cross. You enjoy bananas, you don't put them on the cross. This fellow is a little foolish; enjoy him, but he is innocent. Laugh at him, but crucifixion does not seem to be just.

So Pontius Pilate was waiting, but the Jews did not ask; on the contrary they all shouted, all the rabbis—and there were two thousand rabbis in the temple. It was the great temple of the Jews which was destroyed. And the top priest of the temple was almost the king of the Jews—they all shouted in unison, "We want Barabbas to be released."

Barabbas could not believe it himself. He was also thinking that this young fellow, who was only thirty-three...and he had heard him, he was always talking around the place. He was moving around Jerusalem on his donkey, and whenever he could get an audience he would start talking. He was a street sermonizer—so once in a while Barabbas had heard him talk, and he liked him. The fellow was nice and he was saying beautiful things. He hoped, of course, that he would be released, but when he was told by the Jews, he could not believe it. He was shocked. When he was taken away from the cross he still could not believe that it was real. He looked back again and again, walking towards the pub. And within seven days he had killed another man.

So Pontius Pilate was very willing, and the cave in which Jesus was put was guarded by a Roman guard. The Jews could not do it because it was their Sabbath day, a day on which they cannot do anything. The crucifixion happened on Friday, it was an arrangement. The whole credit goes to Pontius Pilate, not to God and resurrection. It was arranged that on Friday—because Saturday is the Sabbath day of the Jews; they don't do anything, everything stops—on the Friday the crucifixion was delayed as long as possible, because until Pontius Pilate arrives the crucifixion cannot happen. He went as late as possible, so the crucifixion happened just after twelve o'clock in the middle of the day. And the Jewish cross is such that if a healthy man is on it, it will take forty-eight hours for him to die –it is a very slow process, a slow torture. Blood starts flowing out of the body from the hands and the legs. Only four nails are used: two in the hands, two in the legs.

So it takes forty-eight hours for a person to die on the Jewish cross because the blood goes on again and again drying; people have to remove the drid blood so that fresh blood starts coming again. It takes forty-eight hours, and Jesus was only six hours on the cross—from twelve to six. As the sun was setting he had to be taken off the cross, and locked up in a cave, because on Saturday nothing can continue. Everything stops; even crucifixion has to stop. In six hours a young man of thirty-three cannot die. This is a scientific fact. And no Jew would be ready to guard him, because that would be against his religion; he would be doing some duty, some work. So a Roman was on guard—that was perfect. The stone was removed from the opening of the cave, and Jesus' followers took his body. He was alive, just wounded—they took him out of Judea, which was a very small country, and kept him hidden for a few days till he was healed. Then they suggested that he should not go back to Judea: "They will crucify you next year, they won't leave you alone." So he came to India.

He had come to India before—that's why India was known to him—from thirteen years of age to thirty. The Bible has nothing to say about what happened to Jesus in those seventeen years, or where he was. He was in India studying, in Nalanda, in Takshsila, and he was in Ladakh and perhaps Tibet.

Buddha had died just five hundred years before; still his fragrance was around. Takshsila and Nalanda were two universities, the ancientmost universities in the world, which were mostly teaching meditation, because Buddha's whole message is meditation. So he was learning the Eastern approach. These seventeen years are missing, there is no record in the Christian Bible. But there were records in Ladakh, in a Buddhist monastery, of his second visit.

One Russian explorer, a hundred and fifty years ago, saw the records in the Ladakh monastery of Buddhists where Jesus was described exactly: that he visited the monastery, he remained there for three months, that he was a Jew, and he had come from Jerusalem, that he had been crucified but escaped after six hours…everything was there. And this Russian wrote a book, which is available, in which he describes the whole thing. But as Christians came to know this—and the country was under British rule—they destroyed those pages from the Ladakh monastery in which Jesus' description was given. Just those two pages are missing. And one can see that two pages are missing because all the pages are numbered. You can see in that Russian explorer's book that exactly those two pages are mentioned with their page numbers. It was the British Empire that destroyed those two pages to make sure that nobody claimed Jesus was in India and Ladakh, and perhaps Tibet.

But there is a grave in Kashmir, near Pahalgam…it is such a coincidence that there is Moses' grave, and just by the side of it Jesus' grave. Both came to India. Moses came in his old age in search of the lost tribe of the Jews, who had come to Kashmir and settled in Kashmir. He was too old then to go back to Jerusalem, and Kashmir really looked like God's land, it was so beautiful. There is nothing comparable to Kashmir in the whole world. He remained and died there. Jesus came and he remained long enough…he lived up to one hundred and twelve years of age. Everything is written on his grave. Those two graves are the only graves of Jews in India, because in India there are no Jews. And the inscription is in Hebrew. In India nobody knows Hebrew, and in India only Mohammedans make graves; Hindus burn the body. Mohammedans' graves have to be directed towards Kaaba; the head has to be towards Kaaba. Even when dying, the man cannot be allowed to have his feet towards Kaaba; that would be insulting. So in all Mohammedan graves the head is directed towards Kaaba. Only these two graves are not directed towards Kaaba because they are not Mohammedan graves. Out of all the graves in India—I have looked in so many cemeteries just to find one grave—only those two graves are not directed towards Kaaba because there were no Jews.

And all other Jews who had settled there have been forced to become Mohammedans. When Mohammedan rule came over India they turned all the Jews into Mohammedans. Only one Jewish family has been left to take care of those two graves, because Mohammedans respect both Moses and Jesus. So that family, traditionally, generation after generation, has been taking care.

The name of the nearest village is Pahalgam; in Kashmiri it means the village of the shepherd. Jesus used to call himself the shepherd, and used to call humanity sheep. So Pahalgam makes sense; it is the village of the shepherd. And just outside Pahalgam are those two graves.

Jesus never died on the cross and never was resurrected. All that is just fiction created by Christians. No contemporary literature of Jesus' time even mentions his name. You cannot believe it—if a person walks on water, cures people just by touching them; if blind people start seeing, the deaf start hearing, the dead come alive, do you think the whole country will not be talking about him? All the newspapers, all the literature will mention him. Such a man cannot be neglected. But no contemporary literature even mentions his name.

So only one percent seems to be real—the carpenter's son, Jesus Christ—out of the whole trinity. And the Hindu trinity is not even one percent real. It is absolute fiction. One man has three heads—it will be a constant problem! One wants to go this side, one wants to go that side, the third wants to go another way, and they cannot go anywhere unless all three agree. All three have wives…I am just puzzled, because the body is one, so the sexual mechanism is one, but three heads and three wives? How are they managing?

This is absolute mythology, an ugly mythology, obscene. And when I say such things then religious feelings are hurt—but what can I do? It is your own scriptures that are hurting your religious feelings. Just bring cases against your religious scriptures—they should be destroyed!

Nietzsche's trinity is certainly beautiful: cheerfulness, daring and love for life. These can be called the attributes of every seeker: cheerfulness, daring and love for life.

… After such serious discussion, a great laughter is absolutely necessary as an antidote.

Muffin Snuffler is suffering from what appears to be a case of shattered nerves. So after a long spell of heavy drinking and deep depression he finally decides to pay a visit to the psychiatrist.

The shrink asks Muffin a few questions and begins to get the picture.

"Mister Snuffler," declares the doctor, "you are in serious trouble. You are living with some terrible, evil thing—something that is possessing you from morning to night. You must find out what it is and destroy it!"

"Shhhhhh, doctor," whispers Muffin, nervously. "Not so loud—she is sitting out in the waiting room!"

Things are looking bad for the members of the Catholic Church. Their image is being damaged by stories of sex and perversion within the ranks of the priesthood. Their so-called celibacy is becoming a worldwide joke.

So Pope the Polack calls his press secretary, and orders him to create a cover-up campaign.

"Well, Your Holiness," says the secretary, "I have already given this a lot of thought. I am convinced that we need to change our style of dress. Right now, people look at us and all they see is a bunch of dirty habits!"

"Yes," says the pope, "perhaps you are right. So what should we do?"

"Simple!" replies the press secretary. "What I have in mind is a complete change of image. We will cover the city with posters of a nun in a bikini!"

"What?" cries the Polack pope. "A nun in a bikini? How is that going to promote celibacy in the world?"

"Well," explains the man, "the model for the photograph is going to look just like Mother Teresa!"

Now the meditation:

Be silent. Close your eyes and feel your body to be completely frozen.

This is the right moment to go inwards. Gather all your energy, your total consciousness, and rush towards your center of being—with an urgency as if this moment is going to be the last moment of your life. Unless such urgency is there, nobody gets to the center of his being.

Deeper and deeper… It all depends on your intensity. The distance is not great.

As you start coming closer to your center, a great silence descends over you, almost like soft rain falling. The coolness you can feel.

A little closer, and you start being surrounded by a great peace, what mystics have called the peace beyond understanding.

Just one step more, and you are at the center.

Suddenly you feel drunk with the divine. A great ecstasy arises in you; you become luminous, all darkness disappears. You are no more. You suddenly realize your original face.

In the East we have used Gautam Buddha's face as the original face of everyone. It is only symbolic. You are encountering Gautam Buddha, not from the outside but from his innermost source. You have become his very heart.

Just remember one thing, and that is witnessing. That constitutes Buddha's whole being. Call it awareness, call it total consciousness, call it what Buddha used to call *sammasati*, right remembering, but witnessing is the most important word out of all these.

Just be a witness that you are not the body. Be a witness that you are not the mind. And finally, be a witness that you are only a witness, nothing else.

At this moment you enter into the secretmost part of your center.

This is the beginning of a long pilgrimage, of disappearing into the cosmos. This is the door opening into the cosmos. We are one with the whole.

Just go on witnessing, and everything becomes deeper, deeper, deeper…

To make the witnessing more clear to you…

Relax. Let go. But go on being a witness.

As your witnessing becomes more and more clear, you start melting like ice in the ocean, melting into one consciousness, universal consciousness, eternal consciousness, immortal consciousness, consciousness beyond birth and death.

This is your authentic being.

What has disappeared was only a personality. Now, only the essential, existential, experiential has remained. And this existential consciousness is not only yours, it belongs to the cosmos. You are just dewdrops who have fallen from the lotus leaf into the ocean.

Rejoice in it.

You are the most fortunate people in the world. At this moment, when everybody is concerned with trivia, you are exploring the most majestic, the most splendorous experience; the most divine, sacred space you are entering in.

Collect all these experiences—this blissfulness, this witnessing, this silence…This is it. Get hold of it. And persuade the buddha to come with you.

He is your nature, he is your *dharma*, he is your ultimate secret.

Bring him with you.

These are the three steps of enlightenment: First, the buddha will come behind you as a presence. You will feel it, it will surround you, it is an energy field; it will change your whole behavior, it will give you a new sense of direction in life. It will give you a new morality, of your own, a spontaneity in existence. It will give you a love for life, a cheerfulness you have not known, and courage. The moment you know you are eternal, all weakness disappears, all inferiority disappears.

On the second step, the buddha comes in front of you—you become the shadow.

On the third step, your shadow withers away. You are no more, only the buddha remains. He is your eternity, he is your truth, he is your beauty, he is your godliness.

Now … Come back. But come back with the same grace, with the same silence, with the same peacefulness. And sit for a few seconds just to remember the path you have followed inwards. It is a golden path. The center that you have reached, it is not only your center, it is the center of the whole existence.

At the center we all meet. The birds, the trees, the rivers, the mountains, everyone at the center meets. We are different on the circumference but we are one at the center.

And to know this oneness is enlightenment.

For more information:

www.OSHO.com

A comprehensive multi-language website including a magazine, OSHO Books, OSHO TALKS in audio and video formats, the OSHO Library text archive in English and Hindi and extensive information about OSHO Meditations. You will also find the program schedule of the OSHO Multiversity and information about the OSHO International Meditation Resort.

To contact OSHO International Foundation visit: www.osho.com/oshointernational

About the Author

Osho's teachings defy categorization, covering everything from the individual quest for meaning to the most urgent social and political issues facing society today. His books are not written but are transcribed from audio and video recordings of extemporaneous talks given to international audiences over a period of 35 years. Osho has been described by the Sunday Times in London as one of the "1000 Makers of the 20th Century" and by American author Tom Robbins as "the most dangerous man since Jesus Christ."

About his own work Osho has said that he is helping to create the conditions for the birth of a new kind of human being. He has often characterized this new human being as "Zorba the Buddha" -- capable both of enjoying the earthy pleasures of a Zorba the Greek and the silent serenity of a Gautam Buddha. Running like a thread through all aspects of Osho's work is a vision that encompasses both the timeless wisdom of the East and the highest potential of Western science and technology.

Osho is also known for his revolutionary contribution to the science of inner transformation, with an approach to meditation that acknowledges the accelerated pace of contemporary life. His unique "Active Meditations" are designed to first release the accumulated stresses of body and mind, so that it is easier to experience the thought-free and relaxed state of meditation.

Two autobiographical works by the author are available:
Autobiography of a Spiritually Incorrect Mystic, by Osho,
St. Martin's Griffin (2001) ISBN: 978-0312280710
  Glimpses of a Golden Childhood, by Osho
The Rebel Publishing House ISBN: 8172610726

The OSHO International Meditation Resort

The OSHO International Meditation Resort is a great place for holidays and a place where people can have a direct personal experience of a new way of living with more alertness, relaxation, and fun. Located about 100 miles southeast of Mumbai in Pune, India, the resort offers a variety of programs to thousands of people who visit each year from more than 100 countries around the world. Originally developed as a summer retreat for Maharajas and wealthy British colonialists, Pune is now a thriving modern city that is home to a number of universities and high-tech industries. The Meditation Resort spreads over 28 acres in a tree-lined suburb known as Koregaon Park. The resort campus provides accommodation for a limited number of guests, in a new 'Guesthouse' and there is a plentiful variety of nearby hotels and private apartments available for stays of a few days up to several months.

Meditation Resort programs are all based in the Osho vision of a qualitatively new kind of human being who is able both to participate creatively in everyday life and to relax into silence and meditation. Most programs take place in modern, air-conditioned facilities and include a variety of individual sessions, courses and workshops covering everything from creative arts to holistic health treatments, personal transformation and therapy, esoteric sciences, the "Zen" approach to sports and recreation, relationship issues, and significant life transitions for men and women. Individual sessions and group workshops are offered throughout the year, alongside a full daily schedule of meditations. Outdoor cafes and restaurants within the resort grounds serve both traditional Indian fare and a choice of international dishes, all made with organically grown vegetables from the resort's own farm. The campus has its own private supply of safe, filtered water. www.osho.com/resort.